Crisis of Governance in Maya Guatemala

Crisis of Governance in Maya Guatemala

Indigenous Responses to a Failing State

Edited by John P. Hawkins, James H. McDonald, and Walter Randolph Adams

University of Oklahoma Press : Norman

Also by John P. Hawkins and Walter Randolph Adams

Roads to Change in Maya Guatemala: A Field School Approach to Understanding the K'iche' (Norman, Okla., 2005)

Health Care in Maya Guatemala: Confronting Medical Pluralism in a Developing Country (Norman, Okla., 2007)

Also by James H. McDonald

The Applied Anthropology Reader (Boston, 2002)

Library of Congress Cataloging-in-Publication Data

Crisis of governance in Maya Guatemala : indigenous responses to a failing state / edited by John P. Hawkins, James H. McDonald, and Walter Randolph Adams.
pages cm.
Includes bibliographical references and index.
ISBN 978-0-8061-4345-3 (pbk. : alk. paper)
1. Mayas—Guatemala—Government relations. 2. Mayas—Guatemala—Politics and government. 3. Mayas—Guatemala—Social conditions. 4. Guatemala—Politics and government—1985–. 5. Guatemala—Social conditions. 6. Guatemala—Race relations. I. Hawkins, John Palmer, 1946–, editor, author. II. McDonald, James H., editor, author. III. Adams, Walter Randolph, editor, author.
F1465.3.G6C75 2013
306.097281—dc23

2012044553

The paper in this book meets the guidelines for permanence and durability of the Committee on Production Guidelines for Book Longevity of the Council on Library Resources, Inc. ∞

Contents

ILLUSTRATIONS

MAPS

FIGURES

Tables

Preface and Acknowledgments

This is the third volume of student/faculty collaborative ethnography to emerge from the undergraduate field school of Brigham Young University's Department of Anthropology. Hawkins and Adams convened the field school in the municipalities of Nahualá and Santa Catarina Ixtahuacán, Department of Sololá, Guatemala, annually during twelve summers and three fall or winter semesters between 1995 and 2006, as well as during the summer of 2009. The 2006 field school focused on issues of governmentality and political resistance and resilience in these two dominantly Maya local units of social and territorial administration.

The student fieldwork that led to this book was conducted from May 15 to August 15, 2006. This book derives additional perspective from faculty fieldwork conducted in Mexico (McDonald) and Guatemala (Hawkins and Adams) at various times over the last forty-five years (Hawkins), twenty-seven years (McDonald), and thirty-five years (Adams), respectively. Two of the student authors, John Edvalson and Tristan Call, returned to the site several times each for an additional six or more months, in the conduct of fieldwork or language learning while still at BYU or while working toward graduate degrees at other universities. Becky Edvalson was pregnant throughout her field stay. The fact of pregnancy earned her social capital and brought her richer data and insight from the midwives and women of Nahualá, for they knew and shared with her the miseries and joys of carrying a child in a health-challenging environment. However, those same difficulties, including constant nausea—perhaps exacerbated by the 7,500-foot altitude—forced Becky to cut short her field stay by four weeks.

BRIEF NOTES ON COLLABORATIVE FIELDWORK AND WRITING

We emphasize that the process of developing this book and its individual chapters has been a decidedly collaborative effort. Hawkins anchored the recruitment and preparation of students for the field by meeting with them weekly to develop their project designs and theoretical framing in relation to four required preparatory courses (Ethnographic Field Methods, Politico-Economic Anthropology, Ethnography of Guatemala [taught by Hawkins], and Personal Preparation for Independent Off-Campus Projects). During this particular field stay, Hawkins and McDonald visited Guatemala briefly, conducting classes and visiting students at their field sites for three weeks each. Throughout the thirteen-week field school, Adams met with students weekly in a day-long class in which he reviewed the various methods advocated by H. Russell Bernard in his *Research Methods in Anthropology* (5th ed.), discussed field ethics, and analyzed how the students might profitably apply each method in their particular projects and situations. Students used the basic anthropological methods of participant observation, interviewing, card-centered elicitation techniques, focus groups, survey methods, indirect observation, and other techniques and lived with indigenous families, often local leaders, each in a different household. All traveled independently during a weeklong break halfway through the field school. All had access to K'iche'-Spanish translators and used them when needed. Each deployed his or her personality resources in that ineffable mix of field investigator/consultant interactions. All were functionally fluent Spanish speakers and had at least one intensive semester of K'iche' language preparation.

Upon returning to Brigham Young University, all students participated in a senior-thesis writing development seminar in the anthropology department and a semester-long advanced writing seminar in the English department. After graduation, student authors worked with McDonald and Adams on interactive critiques and rewrites. From 2010 to publication, Hawkins and McDonald anchored the final processes of restructuring, rewriting, polishing, and checking the ethnographic chapters while McDonald fleshed out the book's unifying theme of Foucauldian governmentality. We encourage those who desire more detail regarding the conduct of this field school and its follow-up publishing process to consult Hawkins and Adams (2005), Adams and Hawkins (2007), and two journal articles by Hawkins currently under review. In the latter two, Hawkins explains the logic of collaborative student/faculty authorship emerging from a field school setting, argues for the necessity of such coauthorship if ethnographic field school experience is to become widespread among undergraduate anthropology majors and lays out the post-field structures and procedures used to develop the analyses herein delivered.

ACKNOWLEDGMENTS

First, we thank those who made this work possible: the people of Nahualá and Santa Catarina Ixtahuacán who let us and our students into their lives and suffered our questions with such dignity and patience. We cannot begin to name them.

The National Science Foundation's program for Research Experience for Undergraduates (REU) directly and generously funded the students so they could travel to Guatemala, live with families in the two municipalities, and experience professional anthropology. NSF provided them a modest weekly stipend that circumvented the need to scrabble for summer jobs "flipping burgers." Without this support (NSF Grants SES 0139198 and SES 0354014), many students would have missed this opportunity. Brigham Young University's College of Family, Home, and Social Sciences and the Southern Utah University Provost's Faculty Development Fund generously funded a month of effort for Hawkins and McDonald's final edit of this volume. We found Antigua, Guatemala, congenial for work, thought, and decompression; the staff at the University of Texas at Austin's Mesoamerica Center in Antigua was helpful and collegial. In short, the center provided an excellent work setting. Coordinator of Operations Rene Ozaeta made us feel at home and offered support and help at every turn.

Dion Dennis, at Bridgewater State University in Massachusetts, read early drafts of the prologue, introduction, and conclusion and offered valuable feedback. Randle Hart and Michael Ostrowsky, both at Southern Utah University, and Don Kurtz, Professor Emeritus at the University of Wisconsin–Milwaukee, read and helpfully commented on the introduction.

We thank our students for their ethical and diligent behavior in the field. Even more important, we thank them for sticking through the longer, harder, and unpaid post-field write-up process. Without their continued efforts, long after the funded part of the project ended, these data would have disappeared into the oblivion of unpolished, unpublished first drafts.

Our families, too, deserve thanks. Spouses, children, grandchildren, parents, significant others—all had to make do (or celebrate!?) our absences while in the field or writing up.

Nothing is perfect, least of all this book. We are the authors of our own errors, of course. But in the give-and-take that is social science, we hope that any shortcomings of fact or interpretation you may find in our work will inspire you to do further fieldwork in Nahualá, Santa Catarina, or other Maya communities, fieldwork that will dig deeper into the fascinating issues we here open up.

John P. Hawkins, James H. McDonald, and Walter Randolph Adams
Antigua, Guatemala, July 2010

Crisis of Governance in Maya Guatemala

Prologue

James H. McDonald and John P. Hawkins

On July 11, 2010, we paid a visit to Tat Eliseo,[1] a shaman, elder, and Maya in Nahualá who was a longtime informant and friend of Hawkins. Tat Eliseo graciously hosted us in the room in his house compound where he practiced Maya rituals of veneration, protection for his clients, and renewal of the earth. Like other Maya altars, Eliseo's altar comprised three sectors (W. Scott, Hawkins, and Adams, in review). The highest table, running across the back wall of the receiving room, represented the upper vault of the cosmos and its principal deities. Separated by a two-foot aisle, another substantial table representing earthly matters and the Owners of the Earth, empty except for an array of representative candles, paralleled the high altar. A third altar—connected to ancestors and the underworld—constituted by planks with candles and figures, sat on the ground under the second. The fire basin in which copal, candles, sugar, and alcohol were laid out, lighted, and mixed until fully burned had been moved to a smaller, detached room so the smoke from its associated rituals would not blacken the room hosting the altars nor disturb those in the main house.

The elaborate back altar bears further description. Occupying the highest point on the altar, two figures, both wearing Ladino cowboy hats, represent the Heart of Christ or Sacred Heart. Between them stands a smaller figure—Santiago Matamoros (Saint James the Moor-Killer). The patron saint of Spain's seven-century war to reconquer the Muslim Moors became the patron saint of Spain's conquest of Guatemala and its Maya Indians. Occupying a similar height on the altar, the Archangel Saint Michael, the lead figure in the army of God against the forces of Satan, brandishes his sword. Next to these four, Santa Catarina (Saint Catherine), the patron saint of both Nahualá and Santa Catarina Ixtahuacán, observes from an honored place in a glass-fronted, protective wooden shadow box. Santa Catarina represents the virgin healer—something most needed in this highland community with so little access to health facilities.

Scattered most prominently across the altar, however, are multiple figures and representations of San Simón (Maximón), the rogue Ladino Judas-saint who can, with equal facility, reward with miracles and money or punish by a curse, just as do the modern-day Ladinos he symbolizes. Two masks of San Simón, separated by a wooden snake, peer out of another glassed shadow box; here the snake combines at least three symbolic attributes: as deceiver in the Garden of Eden, as a direct connection to the earth by its bodily movement in contrast to birds, and as a venomous threat. Elsewhere on the altar, Maximón appears as a small, seated figure dressed in black. A few inches away, he rides on horseback. Nearby, three votive candles bear his lithographed image. Finally, a life-sized image of Maximón wearing a Ladino felt fedora sits to the right of the high altar, structurally balanced by the chair on the altar's left (viewer's perspective), where Eliseo usually sits when conducting rituals and interrogating clients regarding their concerns (fig. P.1).

All the images of Maximón we have seen in Nahualá and Santa Catarina Ixtahuacán show him dressed in Ladino manifestations of authority: variously, a suit, dark glasses, a felted fedora or a military officer's brimmed and round hat, and a tie. In other communities, Indians likewise dress Maximón in symbols of Ladino authority and menace, though Maximón is also found dressed in indigenous garb or in a combination of the two clothing styles (Pieper 2002). In addition, Maximón may be also known in other communities as Nimalaj Mam, the chief ancestor, now divine (Mendelson 1965:62; Pieper 2002:4, 19). In the multiple personalities of this divinity we find the ambiguous complexity of indigenous life in the Western Highlands of Guatemala (Pieper 2002: 29–31). One's principal divinity may be helpful or hurtful and representative of the ancestral self or the often hated other. And why is this figure so dominantly Ladino in his attributes in Nahualá, Santa Catarina, and so many other communities?

A reasonable reading of Maximón/San Simón's multiple presence on this altar suggests that in K'iche' Nahualá, Indian submission and supplication beneath the gaze of a Spanish/Ladino deity and trickster appropriately represent the Indian's social order. Within that social

Fig. P.1. Shaman Tat Eliseo's high and middle altars, Nahualá. Photograph by James H. McDonald, 2010.

order, Indians confront a confusing mix of excruciating uncertainty and risk, as well as blessings. Both the risks and the blessings derive from the real-world relations of these K'iche' to a worldly society dominated by Ladinos and represented by this Ladino God-trickster. Hopefully, Indians can manipulate the mix of opportunity and risk to their advantage by making suitable offerings to Maximón. Indeed, uncertainty, risk, fear, and the search for occasional good luck suffuse a Maya's spiritual life, just as they dominate his or her earthly life.[2] Durkheim would have delighted in the accuracy with which these divinities reflect the structure of K'iche' society, risk, and reward.

As we leave, our generous host says goodbye and blesses our departure by rendering a simple but starkly ominous send-off. "There is much sickness," he declares without emotion. Eliseo is both warning us and urging us not to blunder into its grasp. Sickness is all around, amorphous but ever-present, like the clouds. He speaks not just of biomedical contagion, but also of misfortune caused by human aggression, mystical and otherwise, frequently unseen, but always expected. Thus, he incisively describes the environment of perpetual risk and threat that confronts Mayas as they navigate their world.

On a different day, a young K'iche' man, Maynor, told me (McDonald) that people in the greater Nahualá area were desperately poor and needed money. Three main ways existed to get money: First, you can migrate. Maynor, for example, goes to Costa Rica for six months each year, where he works as a carpenter making rustic furniture. Second, relatively few have extensive tracts of agricultural land and make a good living. Third, you can get involved with the narco-economy and make money illicitly. Maynor noted that he made just enough money in Costa Rica to make migration worthwhile.

We walked down the long gravel road to Antigua Santa Catarina Ixtahuacán, which, Maynor emphasizes, is far poorer and more marginal than Nahualá. In late 1998, Hurricane Mitch devastated the town center of Santa Catarina. In 2000, some 80 percent of its inhabitants relocated to a new site, carrying with them the offices of municipal government and the saints and bells of their old Catholic church. Those who stayed behind have faced myriad problems trying to get the state government to help them rebuild. Their efforts have been thwarted by the national government and its agencies and resisted by the leaders of the new, relocated town, who also succeeded in getting the original town site declared an unlivable hazard zone. The people who are still living there, however, vehemently disagree and continue to press their case.

In the original town center, now often called Antigua Ixtahuacán, I (McDonald) soon noticed that three of its residents began to follow us.[3] We stopped; they addressed Maynor in rapid-fire K'iche'. It boded ill. One of them, a young woman who spoke Spanish, was directed to come over and speak to me. She said people in Antigua Ixtahuacán were tired of outsiders coming to their hamlet only to tell them that they and their community did not exist. I told her I was taking photos to teach my students about the hamlet and its experiences. That seemed to satisfy her. In her view, outsiders take photos to document the physical dangers of living on an unstable alluvial fan, formed untold years ago, in order to force their removal or thwart their efforts to rebuild. Maynor noted that these Ixtahuaquenses felt betrayed by a corrupt government, where all officials are seen as untrustworthy. In their semiotic field of meaning, I am simply another of those outsiders—another bearded outsider in a fancy rain parka. To me, the conversation had ended amicably enough, so I continued down the street and prepared to take another picture. Forcefully, Maynor told me to put the camera away and that it was time to leave *now*. "This town is organized against outsiders," he said, ominously. Given the history of confrontations in towns and hamlets in the highlands, his urging seemed like prudent advice, indeed, and underscored the level of tension, fear, hostility, and desperation that embraces that locale.

The sense that Guatemala is characterized by uncertainty, risk, and danger is not just a Maya perception. In the Euro-Ladino city of Antigua, where we spent a month preparing the final manuscript of this book, we discovered a pleasant and inexpensive family-style *comedor* presided over by Doña Feliz, a humble Ladina entrepreneur. One Friday, we told Doña Feliz that we would not be in on Saturday or Sunday because we were going to Nahualá and Santa Catarina Ixtahuacán, a bus ride of about two and a half or three hours. In response to this simple description of our travel plans, Doña Feliz expounded on the physical beauty of Guatemala—its mountains, lush vegetation, birds, and beautiful waterfalls. She contrasted this with Guatemala's stark social reality. Doña Feliz admonished us that—"who knows?"—a two-hour trip might take five to seven if we were lucky; that we should not be on a bus at night; that three hundred bridges had been washed away a few weeks earlier by Tropical Storm Agatha. She gave us "chicken bus" travel tips: "Don't fall asleep; keep your bag in your lap and never put it in the luggage rack, let alone on the roof; don't take a camera out and shoot photos [or do so only in the most clandestine manner—she mimed holding the camera half-hidden by her blouse]." Above all, "take care of yourselves." Doña Feliz summed it up saying, with playful flippancy, that travel in Guatemala is "always an adventure" because, she added somewhat ruefully, "in my poor country, *nothing* works." She smiled and laughed, but her eyes told a story of weary, yet optimistic, resignation. Life, however it is constituted, must somehow go on.

Doña Feliz explained that she worked five jobs: she cooked and cleaned in her little restaurant; she catered lunchtimes at a local school; she helped with the bookkeeping for a friend's business; she sold products for a catalog operation; and she read tarot cards on Sundays for clients. It was normal, she said, for each of these jobs to have its ups and downs, but they had never been "all down at once," as they were now. Indeed, she had "never seen it this bad. Now, everything is dead." If the economy is stalled out in Antigua, Guatemala's premier foreign and domestic tourist destination, one can only imagine what is going on in the rest of the country.

Doña Feliz is not the only one in Guatemala concerned about personal security. On our arrival at the Guatemala City airport, we were immediately made aware that this is a country where personal security is a serious problem. After disgorging from the aircraft and walking down the Jetway, tunnels, and ramps that led toward passport control, we entered a long, wide hall with tourist advertisements from the Ministry of Culture interspersed with shops. Down the center, where one could not miss them, stood three plastic advertising kiosks covered with seven-foot tall, greater than life-sized, backlit posters. The first advertised a private security service offering armored cars and machine-gun toting bodyguards. Thus, one's first intellectual encounter in the country promulgates the message of pervasive danger and the need to take extraordinary measures to secure oneself from violent threat (fig. P.2).

Within a few minutes of departure by taxi, our driver, Alfonso, noted that *maras* (gangs) control the poor, working-class neighborhoods. They demand "security taxes" from households and small businesses and kill or maim those who refuse to pay. "People have fled, leaving their houses abandoned. That has never happened before, people leaving their houses empty, just like that." As a taxi driver, he said, he was constantly exposed to threats of extortion and robbery. In short, Alfonso lived in a state of perpetual mistrust and fear as he went about the business of trying to make a living.

Whatever the ultimate, empirical veracity of these perceptions from different vantage points in the Guatemalan scene, they underscore a pervasive feeling of a permanent state of emergency. The comedor owner, Doña Feliz, noted that if one's life is not battered by some disastrous natural event (earthquakes, hurricanes, volcanic eruptions, landslides, floods), then it is challenged by a lack of personal security or by economic meltdown. In short, the only certainty is uncertainty.

In an official admission of this endemic state of danger, Guatemalan president Álvaro Colom stated in his weekly radio address to the nation that a recent series of "'extraordinary' savage acts will continue, but that his attention is permanently focused on the reinforcement of [Guatemala's] institutions of national security" (*Prensa Libre* 2010b). Those "extraordinary" acts included a horrific bus bombing in San Juan Sacatepéquez, five dead in Guatemala City's gritty Zone 18 (ironically

Fig. P.2. A security company advertisement sends a disconcerting greeting in the airport on the way to immigration control, Guatemala City. Photograph by James H. McDonald, 2010.

dubbed locally as "Paradise"), and four murdered bodies recovered in Zacapa. Colom noted that these recent incidents "sought to terrorize the population" and were "reactions to the discipline and order that the government is seeking to impose" (*Prensa Libre* 2010b).

Colom thus admitted that there is no end in sight to the widespread lethal violence that terrorizes Guatemala's citizenry. On the one hand, there is a permanent state of terror. Yet Colom also noted that these events are "extraordinary" and constitute "reactions" to an asserted government crackdown on organized crime that the government is still "seeking to impose." So, on the other hand, the outbreak of "extraordinary violence" signals government failure in controlling violence.[4] Interior Minister Carlos Menocal, moreover, characterized the latest Guatemala City bus bombings and attacks as acts of defiance against the government: "It is a clear provocation" (Lara, Valdez, and Contreras 2010). President Colom has now labeled these and other like events as "terrorist acts" (Lara, Orantes, Valdez, and Bonillo 2010). One could debate the levels of perverse irony here. What cannot be debated is this: violence and the threat of it are regnant facts of life in the minds of contemporary Guatemalans, both Indian and Ladino, from peasant field-laborers to the president of the country.

This volume explores some of the myriad forces undergirding the risk, threat, and fear that pervade contemporary life in postwar Guatemala. We examine how such fears operate dynamically within Maya political and legal structures in two indigenous communities in the Western Highlands: Nahualá and Santa Catarina Ixtahuacán. Each of the volume's chapters explores one or more dimensions of political conflict and negotiation over power, control, and authority, both within these small communities and between Maya villages and the political-economic institutions of the nation and the world.

The primary strength of these chapters lies in their ethnographic detail. They provide windows on how Mayas struggle to mesh their lives and their local circumstances with political nationalization and economic globalization. Indeed, nationalization and globalization rush into their homes and villages like an unexpected tsunami. Yet, at the same time, the villagers deliberately try to access nation and globe as a solution to some of their problems and a fulfillment of some of their desires. The rich descriptions of each chapter are much the weightier matter; theorization in them is secondary.

Our authors engage often-overlooked struggles experienced by Mayas in their communities, including structural contradictions in politics, resource management and competition, intergenerational conflict, and health care marginalization. Through fine-grained ethnographic analyses, our authors unpack the complexities of these struggles and detail how Mayas seek to cope with and understand a rapidly changing world. Today, old cultural norms, old forms of social organization, and old behavioral patterns no longer apply—at least not readily or comfortably. The Mayas in these communities have little option but to forge on as they, for better or worse, try to cobble together a road map to the future. This book describes and seeks to explain that hardscrabble Maya effort and its ironies and pains.

Notes

1. A pseudonym, as are all other names of our informants in this prologue and throughout the book.

2. The Maximón/San Simón/Judas manifestations of this important divinity in Nahualá and Santa Catarina bear a striking resemblance in name and attributes to June Nash's (1968) description of the multifaceted and ambiguous deity-character in Sololá's neighboring departments of Quetzaltenango and Totonicapán, down to the felt fedora. Nahualá's Maximón/Judas operates similarly to the earlier described Maximón in Santiago Atitlán (Hart 2008: 175–92; Mendelson 1965; Pieper 2002; Tarn and Prechtel 1997) but is conceived of as more Ladino. When Hawkins visited Santiago Atitlán's principal shrine to Maximón in the early 2000s, the saint wore a mix of Indian and military-Ladino clothing. In other towns he was, strikingly, a senior military officer in full-dress uniform and aviator sunglasses. As Goldín notes, the Earth Lord is also Ladino, capable of treachery or blessing, and can consult with and use Maximón as an emissary. But they are quite distinct. Maximón brings divinity into worldly relationships of patronage; the Earth Lord is more distant, but always gets his due when contracts with him have blessed the Indian with sudden wealth (Goldín 1999, J. Nash 1968).

The notion that an individual representing a deity can have such distinct attributes as Maximón—bearing, indeed, three or more names—should not perplex us, but remind us of both the triune character of the Christian God, the various names and talents of the Virgin Mary, and the multifaceted nature-manifestations of the pre-Columbian Maya gods, who, likewise, can both bless the earth and its crops and destroy them at will in their manifestations as thunder, lightning, rain, cold, and earthquakes.

3. In the following chapters, first person singular—I, me, my, mine—refers to a chapter's first author.

4. This contradictory construction in Guatemala's official discourse is highly reminiscent of Mexican president Felipe Calderón's remarks on Mexico's unbridled violence. In Mexico, cartels engage in open warfare against the government and among themselves, with declarations of over 60,000 reported deaths since January 2007, according to the newly elected Mexican president, Enrique Peña Nieto, who will serve from 2012 to 2018. No doubt we can assume numerous additional unreported deaths, and no one predicts an end to such violence in either country.

Introduction

Crisis of Governance and Consequences of Indeterminancy in Postwar Maya Guatemala

James H. McDonald and John P. Hawkins

> Indeterminacy of threat, the intensely problematic holding together of what actually cannot come together, is unbearable.
>
> Brian Massumi (2009)

Massumi aptly characterizes the human condition in the current neoliberal, globalized era in Guatemala's largely Indian Western Highlands. In this new era, however, old economic relations persist. Mayas and Guatemalans thus experience a double exploitation: one under the powerful residuals of their colonial heritage, one under the new intrusions of supposedly free-choice global capitalism. Old forms of social constraint blend into the new fields of power ushered in by neoliberal policies and economics. These intertwined projects of maintaining the old and fostering the new inexorably shape and transform the Maya world.

This volume explores the political and legal dynamics of Maya communities as they confront intense forces of change—forces in complex internal and external dialectic—that carry Maya people into an ambiguous, indeterminate future. How the state fails its Maya citizens is a central theme of the volume. It fails through multiple modalities including corruption, judicial weakness, and lack of state service penetration. When they do penetrate, the state's services often displace or destroy local institutions rather than cooperate with and support them. Our authors confront sensitive topics such as lynching, gangs, struggles over communal and individualized property, the place of women in community health work, and acceptance or rejection of a cultural heritage. They situate these topics as local processes affected by the interplay of larger external forces. In doing so, they contribute to an understanding of internal political-legal dynamics in the kinds of poor, marginal communities that shape the reality of the vast majority of rural Mayas and, we might add, that shape the reality of indigenous peoples on all continents.

Our authors describe a K'iche' world turned upside down, a world that emerged out of Guatemala's tragic thirty-six-year civil war (1960–96). In the postwar era, advocates of neoliberal economics exposed the country to a harsh global economy that eroded the forms of power, authority, and legitimacy that once guided Maya communities. This process has been under way since the beginnings of the nineteenth century. Hale (2002:499–500) argues, for example, that throughout Central America and Mexico, elites embraced a liberal modernism that sought to establish: (1) citizens as civilized subjects; (2) individual rights to and within citizenship; (3) capitalism and a market economy as the core drivers of economic growth and development; and (4) a commitment to the creation of a homogeneous national culture. Out of the final tenet grows the ethos of *mestizaje*—a culturally and biologically hybrid nation-state. As Hale (2002:501) notes, being Indian is not vilified in this construction. But neither do Indians find themselves with recognized citizenship or a place in the system of governance.

In Guatemala, however, without a policy that values mestizaje, Ladinos (light-skinned, culturally Euro-Guatemalans) became privileged and segregated from the Mayas, whom they saw as "inferior"—a form of "separate and unequal" (Hale 2002:502). Coffee and other agrarian industries initially spurred the move toward global markets. Ladino-controlled plantations and their profitability found support in laws that reduced indigenous communal landholdings and drove indigenous labor into the market. Finally, laws encapsulating Indian communities were abolished, thus permitting Ladinos to move into, and quickly dominate, local systems of governance (McAllister 2005:3–4). McCreery (1994) confirms these processes in detail.

The post–World War II "revolutionary" regimes of Juan José Arévalo (1944–50) and Jacobo Árbenz (1951–54) challenged the entrenched Maya-Ladino divide. These governments enacted a series of liberal reforms that brought some basic protections and resources to Maya communities, to include health care, education, and labor and land reforms (Hale 2002:502–503; McAllister 2005:4). Árbenz also enacted reforms that provided the Mayas with more democratic participation in and control of municipal politics, which anticipated the 1985 Constitution and 1996 Peace Accords (discussed in more detail below). Under Árbenz, political parties were introduced and political participation was opened up significantly among the Mayas. Traditional forms of office-holding and authority that combined civil and religious functions were challenged by a more secular political system. Additionally, new forms of politically oriented community organizations emerged (Annis 1987:62; Handy 1990: 163–64; Montejo 2005:115).[1] At the same time, global expansion provided a new and fertile environment for opening the Guatemalan economy to the global market. The colliding interests generated an inherent tension between liberal reforms benefiting Maya communities and the desire of plantation owners to further harness Maya land and labor to take advantage of global market demand for their agrarian products.

The fall of the Árbenz government in the wake of a CIA-backed Ladino coup brought back much of the pre-Arévalo ethnic and economic status quo. Reforms were dialed back, expropriated lands were restored, and new infrastructure, designed to benefit commercial production, was initiated (the Pan-American Highway being the most prominent). All of these set the stage for political tensions and indigenous unrest, framed as Cold War conflict, that started in 1960 and terminated officially in 1996 (McAllister 2005:5; Perera 1995).

In the 1980s, in spite of overall economic decline due to the civil war, Guatemala experienced another wave of neoliberal opening in the Guatemalan economy, in part expressed through the establishment of *maquiladoras* (foreign-owned, offshore manufacturing and assembly plants). Some of their production remained in Guatemala and undercut local products, especially apparel (Benson, Fisher, and Thomas 2008; Goldín 1999). During this period, state government also actively and intentionally fomented some policies to articulate with the Maya communities. Take, for example, the 1985 Constitution, which included provisions for a more open electoral process. At the local level in Maya communities, however, the new electoral process accelerated the breakdown of gerontocratic institutions that had maintained order, respect, and generational succession, as Brintnall (1979) and Watanabe (1992) have documented.

In other instances, social problems evolved from complex and dynamic forces that derived only indirectly from the civil war or constitutional change. For example, the state has challenged robust local traditions such as indigenous midwifery, subjecting such practices to state government regulation and accountability, thereby making midwifery a conflicted occupation. In other cases, a faltering economy, poverty, and erosion of the political-religious hierarchies of authority have resulted in intergenerational conflict, rising levels of alcoholism, and interpersonal violence. Taken as a whole, our fieldwork suggests a country still racked by turmoil ten years after the formal end of hostilities, and nothing that has happened since suggests an end to the tensions. Quite the contrary. In short, the Maya live in a world in which a thin veneer of civil society hides a dysfunctional governmental-judicial system, a precarious economy, and uncertain physical and social safety.

In this context of faltering state systems and a turbulent economy, the 1996 Peace Accords provide the only resource—the only foundation—for Indian communities to escape the state's often dysfunctional and destructive reach. The accords' provisions for protecting and respecting indigenous culture allow Mayas to create and re-create "traditional" mechanisms of self-governance and admonish Ladinos to respect such indigenous institutions. Now Ladinos and the state must legally recognize the Mayas' right to govern themselves, as they managed to do with somewhat greater success, in spite of exploitation, prior to 1944. Since then, Mayas have tried to govern themselves, often surreptitiously and, unfortunately, with great conflict and much cultural erosion.[2] The ultimate irony is that the internationally imposed Peace Accords, designed to bring peace and internationally accepted human rights to Indians through democratic government, actually serve as a mechanism to buffer Indians against the ills of the failing state. In an environment of rampant postwar crime and endemic personal and social insecurity, the accords have, thus, allowed Indians to re-impose their own notion of human rights deeply rooted in cultural concepts of *respeto* (respect).

The Peace Accords were designed to demilitarize, reconstruct, and democratize Guatemala, including Maya Guatemala, and to redefine the state as officially multicultural, ethnically plural, and multilingual (Warren 2003). When put up for public referendum in 1999, however, the Peace Accords failed to win a majority vote by an overall margin of 53 percent "against" to 47 percent "for." Warren (2003) notes numerous intertwined reasons for the referendum's failure. First, the election process suffered from high absenteeism; relatively few voted in this nonpresidential election year (81 percent chose to abstain). Guatemalans could only cast ballots in municipal seats, greatly disadvantaging the votes of the overwhelming majority of Mayas, who live at some distance from the municipal administrative centers. This clearly skewed the election against indigenous interests. Moreover, a poorly organized grassroots effort to get out the vote in the majority-Maya areas of the country led to minimal indigenous participation. Finally, a media-based advertising campaign for the referendum was slanted toward an urban and Ladino audience.

Warren (2003) does note that the first question on the referendum, concerning indigenous issues, won a plurality in Maya-dominant departments (but nationally, it was defeated). Carey (2004:90) also finds the election results to be complex, and observes that the Kaqchikel Mayas with whom he worked saw the defeat as "a continuation of the natural cycle of events" (such as ongoing racism, exploitation, injustice). He does note, however, that some Kaqchikels voted against the referendum on the principled grounds that the referendum would extend the reach of the government in perhaps unwanted ways, did not include far-enough reaching reforms, and was undergirded by a woefully inadequate electoral process. The referendum—intended by pro-Maya advocacy groups to demonstrate popular support for the official creation of a multicultural state—thus failed.

Hale (2002) sheds some light on the referendum's failure in his incisive analysis of "neoliberal multiculturalism" in Guatemala. He notes the limited and contradictory nature of cultural rights reforms—cultural and linguistic recognition coupled with economic marginalization and no suggestion of redressing past injustices. Both the 1985 Constitution and the 1996 Peace Accords had expressed this reconciliation, which the 1999 referendum was meant to further legitimize. Thus, Hale (2002:485–87) highlights the uneasy juxtaposition of globalized neoliberal policies, which care little about ethnic rights, and international efforts to protect indigenous cultures. Some Mayas did not see the reforms as going nearly far enough, while some Ladinos saw them as menacing—a mix of Maya ascendency coupled with a withdrawal of the protection of the state. The failure of the 1999 referendum suggests that the process of multiculturalism remains barely nascent in Guatemala compared with other parts of Latin America.

Evidence of a Crisis in Governmentality

Michel Foucault (1991) developed the concept of governmentality as an alternative to "state" and "government," which are typically framed as having an essentialized, consistent, well-controlled monopoly on the production and deployment of power. Foucault counters that our focus should be on "governmentality"—"the art of governance"—as played out through potentially competing, hierarchically arranged state and non-state agents and their relationships, practices, and discourses. What we call the state or government is thus epiphenomenal of a complex mix of people, practices, and ideological rationales, and official government institutions are not the only sites where power is produced. Rather, Foucault contends, institutions outside the standard domain of the state (for example, hospitals, schools, and corporations) are equally sites of governmentality. Thus, Foucault, like Gramsci, rejects the binary notion of state versus civil society in favor of an approach that suggests their constant interpenetration, with power and influence flowing in both directions (see also McDonald 1999:275). What Foucault has given us is a theory of both power and its operation, as well as a method for tracing its geneology.

To examine the Foucauldian nature of Guatemala's crisis of governmentality, we begin with the proposition that Guatemala suffers from rapid cultural change, radical structural adjustment, and a chronically weak system of state governance resulting in compromised civil liberties. Four recent sociopolitical incidents portray the country's fragility and the threats that challenge its democratic governance, social sovereignty, and civil society. While these cases exemplify the crisis in governmentality in Guatemala, they also demonstrate that the Foucauldian notion of governmentality can be expanded beyond a national focus and understood also as a transnational phenomenon. Thus, Guatemala's faltering judicial, political, and economic (both legal and illegal) systems are shaped in complex ways by transnational neoliberal networks within which the country is enmeshed.

> **Incident 1:** On May 10, 2009, a well-known lawyer and conservative, Rodrigo Rosenberg, was murdered in downtown Guatemala City; so-called "security" cameras conveniently recorded the event. Rosenberg left a self-produced video, made four days before his death, in which he accused left-leaning president Álvaro Colom (2008–12) and two of the president's colleagues (Gustavo Alejos, the president's personal secretary; and Gregorio Valdez, a businessman) of his murder. In the video, Rosenberg tells a believable tale—if you live in Guatemala—of unbridled corruption in Banrural, the government-run development bank, which, he claimed, Colom and his close friends had used to enrich themselves. Because the government

> had historically been so closely associated with corruption and graft, the charges sounded plausible. Rosenberg's death and his selfless message from beyond the grave galvanized conservatives. The government was implicated in his murder, for the video testimony Rosenberg had made for release in the event of his death alleged government efforts to eliminate him. Pressure on the government mounted as thousands of upper-class protestors rallied against President Colom, crime, and corruption.

Why might these upper-class, anti-government protestors find Rosenberg's death such an open opportunity to attack a recently installed president? First, we note that Guatemala is among the countries with the greatest inequality in wealth distribution in Latin America, yet its GDP stands the highest in Central America (CIA World Factbook 2010; Hammill 2007; Little 2009; United Nations Development Programme 2008; United Nations Development Report 2009; U.S. Department of State 2010; World Bank 2004). According to the United Nations Development Progamme (2008) for the year 2000, Guatemala's richest 20 percent—the Euro-Guatemalan Ladino elite—control 64 percent of the country's total income.[3] Guatemala has a Gini coefficient of 58.3, making it the second most unequal country in Latin America. It also has the third lowest human development ranking in Latin America and the Caribbean, with only Nicaragua and Haiti scoring lower, and it ranks at 122 of 182 countries worldwide (United Nations Human Development Report 2009).[4] Sixty-three percent of Guatemala's population is crowded into the bottom 15 percent of the country's wealth distribution; moreover, the ratio of Guatemala's top 10 percent to its bottom 10 percent is 58.6 (World Bank 2004).[5]

Despite a broad economic recovery in Latin America in the 2000s, Guatemala has seen little in the way of an economic rebound (Hammill 2007), and that has pinched the well-to-do, who were benefiting from tourism and were hoping for profits from consumerism. Of course, a stagnant economy hit the poor much harder. As evidence of economic developmental malaise, Guatemala's population remains largely rural (over 50 percent) and illiterate (65 percent), with the greatest levels of poverty concentrated in its Maya communities (Hammill 2007; World Bank 2004). The rich, in sum, are highly advantaged in the Guatemalan economic system, and they seek to maintain their position of power and authority at the expense of the poor.[6]

Self-interest among the rich, thus, provides reason to protest. President Colom—an industrial engineer, entrepreneur, moderate socialist, and social reformer who had directed the National Peace Fund (FONAPAZ, which helped resettle displaced refugees after the civil war)—was elected on a modest platform of social reform. Those reforms included taxing businesses and providing the country's Maya majority with greater inclusion in civil society.[7] These proposals curried little favor with an elite determined not to give up any of its power, wealth, or privilege.

Their present position, as has been abundantly noted, is deeply rooted in Guatemala's colonial and post-colonial past and reproduced in the present (Carmack 2009; Hawkins 1984:54–134; Little 2009; T. Smith and Offit 2010; Stoll 2009). In much the same vein as the Árbenz government, Colom attempted to make inroads into Guatemala's entrenched dynamic of "separate and unequal" and was met with vigorous resistance from the country's Ladino elite, who have little to gain from a more empowered Maya majority. Increased public expenditure on education, health, and rural infrastructure would require a more substantial tax base funded by commercial agriculture and industry. Furthermore, greater equality would challenge control of the land and labor central to the dominant position of the country's small, wealthy elite. And as Hale (2002:489) notes, Ladinos express deep anxiety about increased Maya participation in political and civil society while acknowledging that the Ladino-Maya ethnic power balance must change "as long as it does not go too far" (Hale 2002:490).

Guatemala's entrenched elites could not throw the 2007 election in favor of hard-liner General Otto Pérez Molina of the conservative Patriot Party, whose evocative campaign symbol was a clenched fist—the *mano dura*—a code phrase for their intent to reinstate harsh, civil-war period responses to crime and increase class controls. Instead, and perhaps in consequence, they seized upon such opportunities as Rosenberg's revelations to discredit and delegitimize the Colom government.[8]

Colom's government was imperiled by the Rosenberg murder and corruption allegations; the accusation triggered substantial pressure on Colom to step down from the presidency. Again, Guatemala's governmentality seemed forced to a brink by internal class strife. Only the initiation of a United Nations investigation, led by Carlos Castresana, director of the United Nations International Commission against Impunity in Guatemala (CICIG), eased tensions.[9] Castresana, a well-respected judge and legal expert from Spain, became the inaugural head of CICIG in September 2007. In an unexpected and ironic twist, Castresana shocked Guatemalans by discovering and revealing that the Rosenberg murder was in fact plotted by Rosenberg himself as a ploy to topple the Colom government (Franklin 2010). It was a page right out of the darkly tragic Russian comedy *A Friend of the Deceased* (Krishtofovich 1997). In this film, Anatoli, a depressed, despondent professor, lives in a lawless, corrupt post-Soviet Russia. Unwilling to live in such a society, yet unable to muster the will to commit suicide, he anonymously contracts with a criminal organization to have himself murdered. As the contracted ex-military hit man closes in, the professor gets cold feet and kills his would-be killer. Rosenberg, however, had no such reversal of intent. We liken the Rosenberg case to this sinister piece of fiction because, as so often in Latin America, fiction pales in comparison to real life.[10]

Had the UN commission not been present to conduct a thorough and impartial investigation into the Rosenberg affair, replete with its outlandish accusations, the Colom government might well have collapsed. In the end, Rosenberg emerges as a tragic lost soul, a desperately lonely person mired in a failed marriage and middling law practice (Franklin 2010). In the vacuum of an unfulfilled life, he fabricated an elaborate scheme where he would—through the loss of his own life—uncover massive government corruption and become a hero figure for the conservative elite. Carlos Fuentes and Gabriel García Márquez, among many others, have had yet another great plot line stolen away by real-life events in Guatemala.

The Rosenberg case, though dramatic and fascinating in its own right, underscores several larger and important points. First, Guatemala has a remarkably weak civilian central government. It is vulnerable to threat and intimidation, even if by utterly fantastic accusations, when the country's elite and their interests are challenged. In short, governance or governmentality in Guatemala is not located securely in the supposedly governing institutions but is in fact distributed within the networks of Guatemala's social and ethnic elites. Second, the case reveals a failed, ineffective security system; a compromised, dependent legal system; and a weak civilian political system, each of which is riddled by corruption. On its own, the state's criminal justice system would probably have been incapable of making the discoveries that vindicated Guatemala's president. The legal system needed international intervention to function effectively. In sum, Guatemala's governmentality is complexly dependent on international and transnational institutions, ideologies, and processes. Third, in an environment of rampant bribery and fraud, it is not surprising that Rosenberg's tall tale resonated with elites and commoners alike, because it confirmed people's deeply entrenched cultural themes and day-to-day experiences regarding government corruption. Finally, for a suicidal and despondent fellow of such minor elite status to be able to organize such a complex assisted suicide suggests tightly interwoven elites with enormous anger and resistance arrayed against any adjustments to state and therefore class structure.

Incident 2: A similar example underscores the degree to which corruption has penetrated the political system to its top. Again through the efforts of the CICIG, former Guatemalan president Alfonso Portillo (2000–2004) was arrested in Guatemala on embezzlement and money-laundering charges in his home country and for money laundering in the United States. Portillo stands accused of embezzling tens of millions of dollars from the state and then laundering that money in the United States (Al Jazeera 2010b; Glovin and Harris 2010). As one attorney for the U.S. government put it, "Portillo is charged with converting the Office of the Guatemalan presidency into his personal ATM" (Glovin and Harris 2010). Here again, the state's capacity to step in the direction of ethical governmentality hinged on international buttresses that supported changes in national processes. Governmentality is not simply a local or even a national project.

Incident 3: Our third social drama regarding governmentality picks up on the plot line started in incident 1, above: the CICIG director, Carlos Castresana, and his efforts to reform the judiciary and bring government corruption under control (Turner 1972[1957]:xvii, 91–94). By March 2010, Castresana's group had built a case that led to the detention of Guatemala's civil police chief, Baltazar Gómez, and the country's anti-drug czar, Nelly Bonilla. The two were accused of being linked to a criminal network within the national police. The catalyst for CICIG's investigation was an April 2009 shootout between rival gangs over stolen cocaine that left five national police officers dead. One of those gangs was actually made up of national police who had stolen 1,500 pounds of cocaine from other traffickers. Investigators noted that anti-drug police had blocked federal prosecutors from reaching the crime scene and that the national police had failed to open an investigation into the deaths of their officers (MSNBC 2010). They reported that the national police had stolen the cocaine shipment from Mexico's infamous Zeta cartel.

The case reflects why Guatemala holds a number of attractions for foreign drug cartels (Replogle 2008, 2009). First, Guatemala's geography logically makes it a major transshipment zone between Colombia and Mexico in the pipeline to the United States. Second, Guatemala's weak and corruptible state government makes it a haven for cartels feeling pressured by strong anti-narcotics campaigns being waged in Colombia and Mexico. Third, Guatemala's endemic rural poverty makes for fertile recruiting conditions as the cartels, especially from Mexico, seek new foot soldiers for their efforts to gain control and eliminate competitors in drug operations in their home countries (*The Economist* 2010; Hawley 2010; MSNBC 2010). Indeed, drug cartels from both Mexico and Colombia operate with impunity in the north and east of Guatemala and have those areas largely under their control.

The spread of Mexican cartels into Guatemala has led the U.S. State Department to declare that Guatemala is "the epicenter of the drug threat" in Central America (Malkin 2010). Furthermore, Anthony Placido, the chief of intelligence for the U.S. Drug Enforcement Administration, stated on record that "violent traffickers are relocating [to places like Guatemala] to take advantage of permissive environments and [are] importing their own brand of justice" (MSNBC 2010).

Given that a group of national police officers, in league with high-level officials, has set itself up as a criminal operation, one might reasonably conclude that elements of the state government are themselves emerging as a form of cartel in their own right. As Rodgers (2006:326) underscores, while state government may be charged with creating and enforcing the law, nothing forces the state's agents to live within the law—they are not encapsulated by it.[11] That the Guatemalan government's actions blur from legal to illegal underscores the weakness of that institution. From a governmentality perspective (Foucault 1991), Guatemala exemplifies the ambiguous interplay between state government and external "constituencies," in this case in the form of organized crime groups. Guatemala's condition calls into question key issues about whether and which elements of state government unambiguously represent the rule of law, and to whom that law extends.

Incident 4: The final incident continues to follow Castresana and his UN commission's efforts to find ways to re-engineer Guatemala's byzantine and faltering legal and security system. As so clearly outlined above, the inability to effectively confront organized crime and deal with the corruption that pervades all levels of Guatemalan governance and security is a key threat to social sovereignty and the maintenance of a civil society. Indeed, as a measure of the depth of judicial dysfunction, the CICIG estimates that 98 percent of all crimes committed are not successfully prosecuted because of Guatemala's weak and corrupt judiciary (BBC News 2010). Castresana resigned in June 2010, stating bluntly, "Nothing that was promised is being done. On a personal level, I feel I cannot do anything more for Guatemala" (BBC News 2010). Though there is undoubtedly a complex backdrop of broken promises and betrayals behind his comments, a key event seems to have brought his decision to a head. The event was President Colom's appointment of Conrad Reyes as Guatemala's attorney general, even though Reyes was rumored to have ties to organized crime. The appointment led Castresana to resign (BBC News 2010). In the wake of Castresana's departure, President Colom succumbed to the pressure and removed Reyes from office. In summarizing the reasons he resigned, Castresana said, "The problem is that in Guatemala, criminal organizations had never been confronted. . . . Let's say it: we are looking the monster in the face, we are holding its gaze, and it is reacting. The question is: Where were Guatemalans at the most critical moments of this Commission? We are not making the effort in the interest of the United Nations or the people that make up CICIG. We are working for Guatemalans, but if you [do not support our efforts] and do not take charge of your destiny, after a while nothing will be left" (Schieber 2010b; brackets in original). In response to Castresana's probing, Guatemala's elite "occult powers" perversely began a smear campaign against Castresana.[12] He was subjected to rumormongering about his personal life as a way to undermine the work of the anti-impunity commission (Schieber 2010a).

The Challenge of Exploring Governmentality in the Postwar Maya World

Overall, government responses in these four cases suggest a weak, faltering state apparatus that is compromised by "occult powers" of the elite who operate both legally and illegally. As Rodgers (2009:950) points out for Central America, the political violence of the 1980s has been transformed into the broader social violence of the 1990s–2010s. This shift in violence is both caused by and the result of a crisis of governance fueled by economic liberalization, globalization, and corruption further liberated by the cultural ethos of Ladinos and leaders being above the law. Unfortunately, Central American countries stand in a highly disadvantaged position relative to economic liberalization, and this position is exacerbated by each country's incomplete democratization. In Guatemala, endemic social violence, economic liberalization, globalization, state corruption, an inequitable and inaccessible political system, and extraordinary maldistribution of wealth—all intertwined causes and consequences of the civil war—still persist. They provide the powerful backdrop and context for the chapters in this volume, which treat the position and activities of Indians in their interaction with the Guatemalan state, the country's Ladino ethnicity, and the twin global forces of neoliberal economic globalization and the non-governmental organizations (NGOs) that monitor national conditions.

The civil war has also affected academic scholarship on Guatemala. As Little (2009), Stoll (2009), and others observe, the imprint of the legacy of the thirty-six-year civil war on scholarship has resulted in entrenched, reductionist, Manichean binaries: Mayas versus the army; Mayas versus an interventionist state; Mayas versus Ladinos in an ethnic or class struggle. We ourselves come close to falling in this trap, above, as we set out to develop the complexities behind the oppositions. As Stoll (2009) notes, the legacy of war has, not surprisingly, led scholars into a moralist paradigm to find and assign blame for the tragedy that has befallen the Mayas. Stoll goes on to argue that the moralist paradigm also served as a kind of intellectual trap that has led analyses away from exploring the complexity of Maya communities' internal dynamics and the quite varied engagement both within and between communities and with external political and economic forces. The on-the-ground reality has always been far more complex than that portrayed in a reductionist, Manichean model. As Little (2009:8) contends, postwar Mayas exist in a dynamic matrix that includes "internal community conflict over economic and political resources, changing labor conditions in a global economy, and problems concerning basic services, such as education." All of these complex processes—including inter-ethnic conflict, difficulties with state penetration, and internal contradictions and disputes within the Maya community—display themselves in the chapters that follow.

LOCAL POLITICAL AND LEGAL ETHNOGRAPHY IN POST-CONFLICT GUATEMALA

One powerful dimension of this volume is that the peoples, cultures, and political economies of the Guatemalan highlands are seen through the eyes of undergraduate students who are not wedded to these preconstructed scholarly visions of Guatemalan social relations. We do not mean to suggest that these student ethnographers are somehow more objective than others. They also lack depth in their cultural and linguistic experience, as well as theoretical immersion. These limitations, however, also have some advantages—the students are not particularly shaped by theoretical preconceptions nor awed by ideologically motivated or biased ethnographic analysis (Tedlock 1993; Watanabe 1995). On the other hand, Tedlock (1993) further cautions us about the unconscious hazard of smuggling Western concepts into our analyses—a problem for seasoned researcher and novice alike. Simply put, their job was to immerse themselves in the highland Guatemalan scene as open-minded participant-observers, describe that scene as carefully and thoroughly as possible, and generate a thematically oriented, descriptive ethnography that sheds new light on ever-changing ethnographic detail and understanding. As noted above, much of contemporary ethnography is structured and influenced by a political stance toward the civil war that has resulted in constructions—such as Maya versus the state—that do not capture current complexities and dynamics, especially those internal to Maya communities (Little 2009; Watanabe 1995). In conformity with both Watanabe's (1995) and Little's (2009) call for more attention to village dynamics and Maya micro-politics, the focus of these chapters is almost exclusively on the internal processes that exemplify the everyday world of the vast majority of Mayas who live in small, marginal communities.

There is a drawback to this lack of historical embeddedness, of course. Highland communities have been shaped by that war and its many forms of violence, though the war impacted some communities far more than it did Nahualá and Santa Catarina Ixtahuacán. On the one hand, to lack sensitivity to those historical and experiential connections brings a certain analytical cost of not seeing and understanding the often subtle ways that civil war experience indirectly influences contemporary society (cf. Carmack 1988; Green 1999). On the other hand, without the weighty baggage of what Little (2009:7) calls "the dark legacy of war and violence that permeates the literature," these chapters offer a refreshingly different focus on the internal dynamics of these poor, marginalized places, a focus that does not fall into the traps of the moral paradigm or Manichean constructions. Indeed, these chapters are locally oriented and largely descriptive; their engagement with social theory is relatively light.

Many of the analyses in this volume posit the central importance of the 1996 Peace Accords, a historical signpost of the postwar era. In spite of the nullification by referendum, international NGOs and multilateral United Nations organizations take the accords as representing legitimate human rights and continue to build their funding policies around their provisions, forcing the government to comply. Little (2009:2; see also Carmack 2009:181) suggests that the Peace Accords have had a major impact on local political representation. Though the ability to elect Indians rather than Ladinos began much earlier (Brintnall 1979), the 1985 Constitution and the 1996 Peace Accords accelerated Indian representation of Indians. Where Ladino mayors once presided, we often now find Mayas in their place.[13] Political access for rank-and-file Mayas, at least locally, has increased. Nevertheless, Little sees almost no actions that would bring any wealth and prosperity to the Mayas, and levels of crime and violence are rapidly increasing. Stoll (2009:167) further highlights the importance of the Peace Accords' demilitarization of the highlands. But, like Little, Stoll sees new forms of largely nonpolitical violence erupting not because of state actions but because of state weakness.

Several of the chapters in this volume bring a nuanced analysis to this broad postwar outline sketched by Stoll and Little. Our chapters show, for example, that while the Peace Accords may have provided the Indians new political access, they foster an environment in which Indians feel a "right" to express their frustrations over mayoral decisions. This has led to an erosion of respect for local political leadership and may have increased intra-village conflict.[14] On the other hand, the Peace Accords have protected indigenous culture; its provisions call for cultural respect, which has enabled local leaders in these towns to restrain the outbreak of heightened violence and lynchings that had resulted from the state's failure to deal with rising crime in Maya communities.[15] The chapters by Dracoulis and Bybee, for example, show that political rank formerly came from an age-graded order of elders who had proven themselves through Catholic *cofradía* service to the community.[16] The 1985 constitutional reforms, however, opened political office to anyone with the financial resources and external party backing to run for office, thus precipitating a legitimacy crisis in the indigenous mayoralty, because election winners lacked the appropriate moral-spiritual authority once vested in community office. Increasing crime and violence are set against a backdrop of a nearly invisible state government presence in these small, marginal Maya communities beset by a nearly bewildering variety of external global influences. We find virtually no viable national security force or reliable national judiciary in these places. These communities stand very much "on their own" and must deal with their problems, for better or worse, through forms of popular, indigenous justice.

Given this context, we see multiple ironies. First, this vacuum of national institutions forces indigenous justice to draw upon traditional practice and authority at a time when traditional practice and authority have been eroded or attacked by the very practices of the state. Second, we have seen multiple instances wherein the state has punished the vigilantes and has let the objects of indigenous justice—the locally defined criminals—go free. In effect, the state fails to provide credible justice and public security and yet punishes the communities—rather than the criminals—for stepping into the vacuum. No surprise that Mayas distrust the state.

Moreover, Mayas must not only deal with other Mayas as agents in their own communities, they now face a confusing plethora of new agents who perpetrate often seemingly random acts of violence. For the Mayas and others in Guatemala, levels of violence are escalating precipitously (Orantes and López 2010). In recent Maya history, sources of potential trouble were mainly associated with political institutions—the army, police, paramilitaries, or civil patrols—that could usually be identified and perhaps avoided.[17] Now, however, crime and violence are

Fig. I.1. Private security guard stands watch, Los Encuentros, Department of Sololá. Photograph by James H. McDonald, 2010.

multisourced and more random, more unpredictable, and therefore, in many ways, more frightening (cf. McDonald 2009:18, and see fig. I.1).

Furthermore, organized crime has penetrated state government and the judiciary, though it is not clear if it has done so yet in these small, marginal communities. There is random carjacking, all manner of thuggery, and myriad forms of trafficking (in drugs, children, arms, women), all backed by threat of violence. The unpredictability of these criminal acts imposes a heavy psychological burden on ordinary people (McDonald 1997a). Many of the volume's essays delineate the K'iche' struggle to control, through imperfect local means, this unpredictable and sometimes chaotic social and cultural reality.

Ethnographic Studies on the Maya Margins

The chapters in this volume report ethnographic research by students (as lead chapter authors) and faculty (as coauthors and volume editors) in three town centers and several hamlets of Santa Catarina Ixtahuacán and Nahualá (see maps 1 and 2). These two municipalities stand on the western rim of Sololá, a department in the center of the Western Highlands of Guatemala. While the majority of people in Sololá are Kaqchikel Mayas, Santa Catarina and Nahualá are decidedly K'iche'-speaking towns on the boundary between K'iche'-, Kaqchikel-, and Tzutujil-speaking zones. It is worth remembering that in the Western Highlands, dialects and identities are tightly compacted in space, and notions of community and dialect-based identity remain strong. These intertwined identities, tied so closely to the land, exacerbate the conflicts that arise over ill-defined or contested physical, symbolic, and social resources implicated in municipal boundaries, especially when an impotent and untrusted state system tries to re-define land tenure that has been held and managed by customary tenure for generations.

Work by Timothy Smith (2009), which lays out the recent historical-political context in Sololá, is highly relevant to the chapters in this volume. He outlines changes in the political structure and operation of the municipal government of Sololá that accompanied 1985 constitutional changes, the end of the civil war, and the implementation of the Peace Accords. In Sololá, what had been a unicameral civil-religious municipal government was split into a bicameral system: a civil council and a religious council. The split was designed to create a stronger secular government. As we shall see in this volume (in chapters by Dracoulis, Bybee, J. Edvalson, and Call), such a decoupling accelerated the ongoing erosion of traditional forms of authority and respect while also opening up political space for greater democratic participation.

Articles in this volume by Dracoulis, Dabb, and Bybee analyze this new political dynamic as it is manifested in the hinterland communities that surround Sololá. Recent work, for example by Burrell (2009:102; see also Burrell 2010), parallels Dracoulis's attribution of the demise of respectfulness to the breakdown of civil-religious hierarchy. Thus, Burrell observes: "Traditional civil-religious hierarchies have broken down in many places, contributing to fuzziness in terms of age or grade and what one ought to do at a particular point in life, roles that were formerly sharply defined." This reconfirms earlier work on the generational split induced by religious change and party politics described by Brintnall (1979), Warren (1978), and Watanabe (1992). It also helps us understand the undefined and therefore dangerous position of youth in these communities, à la Mary Douglas's notion that categories need to be

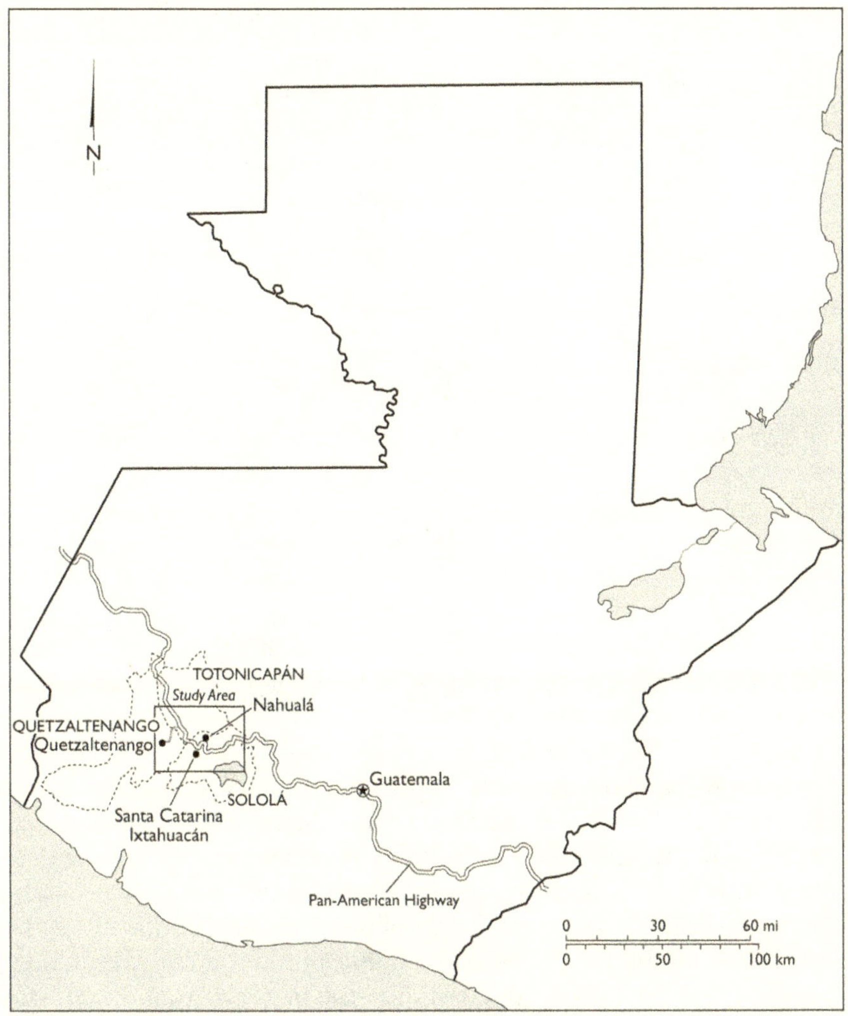

Map 1. Overview of Guatemala. Based on a map by Kellee Koenig in *Health Care in Maya Guatemala*. ©2007, University of Oklahoma Press.

pure and in place and that the objects that go in them need to be clearly placeable. Otherwise, the objects themselves, in this case the youth, become "matter out of place," dangerous and impure (Douglas 1966). Thus, youths symbolizing their desire for more connections outside the village become labeled as "gangs" of murderers and kidnappers, as J. Edvalson and Call, both in this volume, so clearly show.

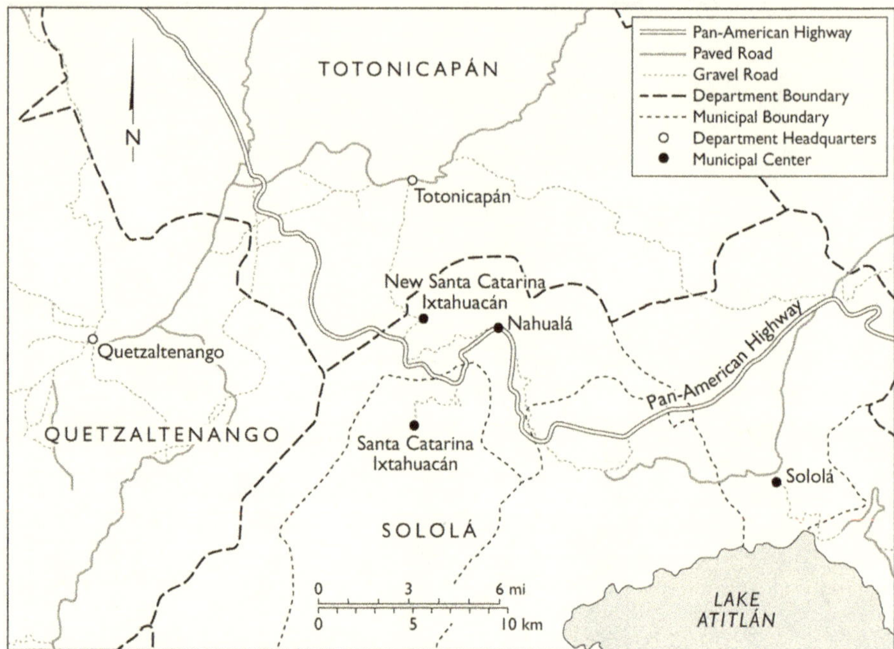

Map 2. The study sites. Based on a map by Kellee Koenig in *Health Care in Maya Guatemala*. ©2007, University of Oklahoma Press.

Donald Dracoulis (chapter 1) provides a nuanced analysis of the ambivalent, conflicted, and sometimes contradictory relationship between state government and local communities. He pursues in detail how state intervention in the position of mayor in Nueva Santa Catarina Ixtahuacán produced a legitimacy crisis in local politics. Dracoulis outlines how the new 1985 Constitution instituted a more pluralistic and democratic form of selecting a mayor that removed the position from the control of the age-graded hierarchy of elders. It also took away the mayor's ability to punish crime, even minor crimes, passing that function to a nationally appointed justice of the peace. Yet, the community's citizens maintain the expectation of local control and adjudication of crime in protection of the municipality. Moreover, their experience of the national judicial apparatus is abysmal.

The notion that the mayor should keep internal order, by internal community means, lies at the heart of Maya notions of identity and safety in and through community (Watanabe 1992). In this context, mayors have implemented "traditional Maya punishment" under the cover and instigation of the Peace Accords' provisions to protect indigenous rights. Thus, an internationally inspired document designed to protect and bolster indigenous culture has allowed the mayoralty to reclaim judicial functions ripped away by state government, and to some extent, to fulfill local cultural expectations—in spite of the state's attempt to centralize judicial functions. The decidedly transnational has allied itself with the eminently local against the national. The state in this case failed in its attempt to revamp governmentality. We find here a political analog of kinship's alliance of alternate generations (Radcliffe-Brown 1967[1950]:28–29).

However, mayors now find themselves tethered to the state through political parties. And because of the link to the state, mayors now possess new forms of power resulting from larger budgets that they manage and spend without transparency. Even on the Maya margins, a generally higher level of education among townsfolk makes these Mayas more critical political participants and followers. The Peace Accords have thus empowered the Mayas to engage in sometimes strident local political critique. Because the position of mayor is now less embedded in kinship, sentiment, and traditional values, followers are shifting from attachments that are moral and respectful to those that are transactional, reward-based, and frequently discordant (cf. Bailey 1988, 2001).

In F. G. Bailey's (1969) vernacular, *moral* teams of followers attach to leaders though enduring cultural ties that are animated through mutually held values that leaders reflect back to their followers. Leaders under these circumstances operate in a highly conservative, change-averse political world where leaders stand as exemplars and embodiments of cultural values and serve to protect those values. By contrast, *transactional* teams of followers connect to leaders because they get some immediate benefit—most often a material benefit—from the relationship. Leaders of transactional teams have to work hard to keep their followers and, in an ongoing fashion, must be able to secure resources for them. Transactional followers are far more fickle than their moral counterparts. When a leader fails to provide transactional followers with benefits, their patience quickly wears thin and they seek a more productive leader. Thus, in the Western Highlands, the nature of political leadership has changed—quite quickly—from one anchored to moral forms of authority to one that is transactional, far more fragile, and open to contestation.[18]

Curtis Dabb (chapter 3) analyzes the increasingly conflicted communal land tenure system wherein villagers seek to record their families' long-term usufruct by registering with the municipal property office. Such claims, once registered, can secure the registrant much benefit wherever the state's Ladino administrators intervene with their own notions of private property tenure. The fight over community boundaries, communal land, and pressure by the state to privatize formerly communal landholdings has led to violence between the residents of Santa Catarina Ixtahuacán and neighboring Nahualá.

Pressures to privatize landholdings in Guatemala compare to the 1992 revision of Article 27 of the Mexican Constitution. This revision ended land reform and paved the way for the privatization of *ejidos*. Ejido land had been held in trust by the state (rather than by the *municipios*, as in Guatemala) with use rights going to farmers who worked the land. Any land that lay fallow for too long was subject to reallocation, as in these Guatemalan municipios. The rules of reversion, however, were simply the idealized and formal set of rules and practices established by the state government. The reality was far more complex, as McDonald experienced through fieldwork in the west-central state of Michoacán (cf. DeWalt, Rees, and Murphy 1994). Especially in ejidos with good, arable land, there was and is often a thriving land rental market and even land "sales" (that is, long-term unregistered arrangements), most often to other *ejidatario* community members. None of this is, of course, a matter of official record, since it is illegal under Mexican law. With the 1992 opening for ejido land privatization, the stakes ratcheted up significantly. Much like in the Guatemalan situation, advantage went to those individuals currently using and improving land rather than to the individuals or families who had originally been given the use right, perhaps many years prior, and had rented out or "sold" their use rights. Needless to say, this was a point of potentially significant conflict between those with formal use right and those actually working the land. Indeed, ejidatarios recognized that the conferral of private title would not only affect family survival, but would indelibly recast the class structure of those communities. And those were matters worth fighting over.

Much like the Mexican ejido case, in the Guatemalan highlands, large families eke out livings on a small, fixed land base where land is increasingly fragmented by the pressures of inheritance by an expanding population. The resulting economic stress reduces a household's ability to purchase fertilizers and other inputs that would increase maize yields. Under a subsistence farming strategy, declines of even 5 or 10 percent in a family's income might lead to economic disaster for that household (cf. McDonald 1994, 1997b), culminating in land sales, the need for illegal labor migration to the United States, migration to the city, or children being removed from school so they can seek out work. Such options make household and municipal access to and control of land a flashpoint, especially where state government has little ability or will to mediate such conflicts.

Mexico's Chiapas Rebellion (1994–present) provides an excellent example of the dynamics of wealth, power, and state policy that is highly relevant to the Guatemalan case (G. Collier and Quaratiello 1994). Like Guatemala, Mexico's highland Maya population is highly marginalized and under extreme demographic and land pressure. Moreover, much indigenous land falls within the ejido system, making it theoretically impartible. Nevertheless, Tabasco's Chiapanecan oilfield workers, displaced by the global economic crisis in the early 1980s, brought their hard-earned pesos back to the Chiapas highlands. There, they "purchased" ejido land and installed technologies that enabled them to out-compete their poorer neighbors, often resulting in more land entering a fluid market, leading to even greater inequalities. Local forms of authority were also turned on their head as these younger, wealthier, former oilfield workers came to dominate politics, displacing a kin-based, age-graded system of authority. Those displaced completely from their home communities often flowed into the eastern lowlands known as the Lacandón jungle, where many joined with the Zapatista Army of National Liberation (EZLN).

The end of land reform in 1992 effectively shut off any further possibility of access to land for the poor and the marginal. The imposition of the North American Free Trade Agreement (NAFTA) in 1994 proved the final element provoking the indigenous uprising that continues as a low-intensity war to this day (G. Collier and Quaratiello 1994). Though neoliberal reform had long been underway in Mexico (see McDonald 1994), NAFTA institutionalized transnational structures of inequality and ensured that Mexican maize farmers, such as those in Chiapas, would be increasingly uncompetitive when exposed to the global market. In sum, outside forces doomed their way of life and livelihood. What happened in the 1980s in Chiapas demonstrates how the system worked in practice, and how quickly political and economic dynamics in those highland communities could be transformed.

Eric Bybee (chapter 2) engages the sensitive and complex issue in which the members of a Maya community collectively effervesce into a lynch mob directed against other community members or, more commonly, against outsiders. This phenomenon increased precipitously in the postwar era (cf. Fernández García 2004:1). Bybee does not link lynching to the legacy of civil war as directly as Fernández García. Rather, Bybee makes an argument that first ties lynching to the erosion of traditional age-graded hierarchies. Next, he explores the state-sponsored warping of traditional Maya popular, indigenous justice. This indigenous justice emphasized reform and redress rather than the state's construction of regimes of brutal punishment (or, with bribes, none at all). Finally, he notes the lack of any state judicial protection and due process for alleged perpetrators of offenses when indigenous justice is being prosecuted.

However, the "witch hunt" that Bybee describes—wherein the parents of lynched boys threaten to accuse dozens of families and take bribes to have the threat removed—reproduces the vindictive accusations of being a "subversive" that was experienced during the civil war. During the war, likewise, people leveled such accusations against neighbors if they had experienced any reversal at all in their relationships. Thus, Bybee notes that one person was accused and extorted through the vengeance of a spurned mistress, and another as reprisal by a fired employee. Such acts precisely reproduce in the succeeding generation the accusatory violence of the war years, wherein behavior that offended someone became the basis for retribution by accusation. In the war years, a mere accusation led to death or required immediate flight. In the present, an accusation leads to extortion or prison. In either period, the gambit thrived on the known willingness of the state to impose violence on the Indian community without regard for evidence and in the context of a failed, inept, powerless judicial system.

In a sad irony, the lynching that responded to a failed judicial system generated a litany of extortions and wrongful imprisonments that also succeeded because of the failed judicial system. The whole lynching conundrum—the motivations for lynching, the reasons for not lynching, and the excruciating consequences that result from either choice—derives from a state government that has insistently penetrated the indigenous community and imposed an abortive and feckless judicial institution that has undermined a working indigenous judicial process. We see this theme reprised in other analyses in this volume, albeit with different ethnographic examples, to include Brown's analysis of forestry and R. Edvalson's account of midwifery.

Other chapters in this volume probe internal community conflicts that also center on the erosion of once robust age-graded hierarchies of power, authority, and legitimacy. John Edvalson (chapter 6), for example, unpacks the elders' reaction to threats on age-graded hierarchies, which results in their labeling nonconformist youths as gang members (*maras*) in Nahualá. His work corroborates Burrell (2009, 2010), who finds manipulation of the fear of gangs to be a pernicious labeling game used by elders to stanch the challenging advances of youth from largely prosperous families who have the time and money to affect the gang style. This labeling aligns closely with Vigil (1988), who finds similar stereotyping among gangs in Los Angeles. As Edvalson describes it, however, Nahualense gangs do not yet provide the micro-regimes of order and collective identity needed in a sea of insecurity, exclusion, and chaos that Rodgers (2009:964) attributes to gangs in urban Nicaragua.

Tristan Call (chapter 7) also addresses intergenerational conflict and the contestation of power, place, and culture in society. In contrast to John Edvalson, Call argues for an ultimately egalitarian society. The pain embedded in his paper derives from a realization that cultural transmission—the intergenerational war for the world—cannot be an egalitarian enterprise. Hierarchical intergenerational dynamics require one generation to serve as trusted custodian of the material and informational apparatus of a cultural system. Cultural transmission cannot be random, nor can it be allowed to fail. Hence, it cannot be egalitarian, perfectly agreed upon between generations, or conflict-free. Moreover, outside pressures and intrusions do not bear down identically on elder and junior generations, further complicating matters and exacerbating the potential for conflict. The challenge concerns cultural transmission across the generations and how much adaptive input each new generation is allowed to, or demands to, contribute. The everyday tension in a relatively stable society becomes excruciating conflict when external forces impose change so rapidly that survival requires decreased heritage transmission and increased adaptive opportunism. Such is clearly the case in K'iche' Guatemala today.

In another example of state-local conflict, Jason Brown (chapter 4) examines natural resources that were once under the control of town governments. Today, however, natural resources, in this case forest reserves and their contents, are now being contested, stolen, or privately appropriated because both local and national governments fail to respond adequately. Brown argues convincingly that state government efforts to decentralize the National Forestry Institute through the creation of municipal offices has actually done little to incorporate local people or local knowledge about common property into forest management efforts. One might think this a case of new wine in old bottles. Actually, it is new (centralized) wine in new (state) bottles with antiqued "newspeak" labels that praise decentralization in word but not deed. In spite of the verbal ethic, major decisions and actions still remain highly centralized because *técnicos* (agro-forestry extension agents) report to and take their orders from centralized superiors and because they perceive community members as backward and lacking useful ideas and strategies (cf. Arce and Long 1993; McDonald 2003).[19] In the process, state government actions have dismantled or thwarted effective local institutions, yet the state has proven itself weak and ineffective in providing the services formerly delivered by respected and community-supported local procedures.

Following Foucault, Massumi (2009:155) suggests that neoliberalism coupled with governmentality results in "environmentality." That is, governments act upon environments and modify them. These interventions result in crisis rather than sustainability, because the environment is an autonomous, complex system that defies prediction and risk assessment. Brown, on his part, outlines a clash of paradigmatic approaches to natural resources that erodes local autonomy, further marginalizes local people, and results in environmental degradation. This contrasts with Arun Agrawal's contention that co-governance is possible, so that state, market, and community can operate in mutually beneficial and sustainable ways (see Lemos and Agrawal 2006). In Brown's Ixtahuacán case, unfortunately, such synergy in governance does not emerge as an outcome of state-local relations.

Finally, chapter 5 in this volume analyzes another unexpected consequence of state intrusion. In this case, Rebecca Edvalson looks at the conflicted role of traditional midwives. On the one hand, government provides midwives with birthing education because it lowers the death rates for mothers and their infants. On the other hand, midwives find their place in the childbirth process challenged and undermined by the state's threat of prosecution if a mother or child dies on their watch. This risk injects fear and reluctance to help into what was previously a familial and communal volunteer project. Focusing on the relationship between midwives and the Guatemalan medical establishment, Servando Hinojosa (2004) finds that a similar form of displacement is occurring. In his case, Guatemalan health authorities seek to reshape midwifery along the lines of the Western medical model, thus devaluing traditional knowledge. Edvalson, along with Hinojosa (2004), highlights the basic dynamics of race and class as they operate in various ways to the detriment of rural Mayas.

CONCLUSION

Each chapter in this volume analyzes a tragic contradiction. Hale (2002:492) poignantly captures this contradiction when he asks, "How can the state turn over clusters of rights to cultural groups without relinquishing its central responsibility to protect the individual rights of each and every member of society?" Cumulatively, these contradictions force the Mayas to try to cope with problems largely not of their making and out of their control. These analyses do not hinge on the stereotypic figures and binary oppositions so often found in recent ethnographic work on Guatemala that blames problems on the aftermath of war. Indeed, the mainstay characters of post–civil war ethnography—former guerrillas, civil patrol members, activists, refugees, dissident protestors either exiled or dead—are nowhere to be found in these chapters. Rather, the people in these studies are simply poor, marginalized Mayas living in the hinterland of the highlands—that is to say, in apparent isolation, though not sufficient isolation, from their perspective. These communities seem to have been largely forgotten by the state government and, indeed, the rest of the world, except where the state seeks to capture some or another of their resources, be it timber, votes, or international public health kudos. In this context, these K'iche' try to make as much of a living as possible from subsistence corn farming cobbled together with other economic activities. Perhaps family members contribute meager wages through a job in a larger, more urban community or through petty craft production. Parents compare their *cuerdas* of land with the family headcount and conclude that most of their children have little future in pursuing a farming way of life.[20] This has led to massive labor migration, mostly to the United States. But what awaits them when they return home to Nahualá and Santa Catarina?

Fig. I.2. Nahualá: rural house built with international labor remittance funds. Photograph by James H. McDonald, 2010.

Migrants often build houses upon their return—nice brick and block affairs, as one can see comparing figures I.2 and I.3. They invest in consumption but not enough in production. There is no land to buy, and it is not clear that they would want to return to a farming lifestyle even if there were. To underscore the irony of their situation, many of these houses have a living space above with storefronts below. Unfortunately, many of the storefronts remain shuttered and empty. Given where they are built, often in rural hamlets, what would they sell that is any different from the small sales stand that can be put in the front doorway of any home? The postwar Maya world, in sum, is one with relatively limited economic potential and opportunity in a country shaped by aggressively neoliberal policies.

This disjuncture between neoliberal and local practices, however, is not unique to Guatemala. Similar incongruity exists elsewhere in Latin America, such as in rural Mexico (McDonald 1999). In the Mexican version, the formerly committed welfare state shifted the burden of risk from the state to the individual. At the core of Mexican neoliberal thought was a hypothetical "economic man" within whom the economic and social seamlessly interpenetrated. The position, however, was based on the assumption that economic man is a rational decision-maker who also is appropriately educated with full-blown skills to make rational choices among diverse, understood options. The assumption bears little resemblance to the conditions experienced by university professors, let alone Mexican small-scale farmers. Thus, farmers were suddenly subject to the notion of "individual as enterprise" (Gordon 1991:44). The state exhorted farmers, though utterly unprepared, to organize in the name of the neoliberal ideals of quality and efficiency. A double manipulation occurred. On the material level, the state reduced tariff barriers, withdrew price supports, and restricted access to credit as it downsized itself by selling off para-state assets to its politically connected crony class. On the symbolic level, the state prescribed quality and efficiency standards virtually impossible for small farmers to achieve. Thus, rational choice was valorized in neoliberal discourse, but farmers were not equipped to assume the role of rational actor. Neoliberal ideals and on-the-ground reality differed vastly.

Guatemala never experienced Mexico's Revolution of 1910 that led to the demise of the landed aristocracy. Out of the revolutionary ashes arose Mexico's new business-industrial plutocracy and mestizo-based welfare state (see Nutini and Isaac 2009). But the social safety net

Fig. I.3. Nahualá: typical rural house built without remittance funds. Photograph by Winston Scott, 2003.

has never been stretched beneath Guatemala's poor majority. The end of the civil war smoothed the path to further trade liberalization and foreign investment culminating in the Central American Free Trade Agreement (CAFTA) in 2006. While the opening of the Guatemalan economy has bolstered its gross domestic product, it has not created jobs or alleviated poverty. Furthermore, well-intentioned neoliberal NGO development models that proved seductive to many Mayas have also largely failed. Two prime examples—fair-trade coffee and ecotourism—offer no safety net. When world coffee prices crash, peasant coffee growers, enticed by NGO projects to cash crop, also crash. Likewise, when news of systemic violence crushes mass tourism, NGO-advocated, boutique ecotourism also dies and takes down peasants who went into debt to upgrade their facilities (Fridell 2007; Miller 2004). Poverty remains endemic. So, like their Mexican counterparts, Guatemala's poor, marginal majority has little chance of participating successfully in this new neoliberal world other than as displaced labor migrants.

Guatemala also never had the large government apparatus of Mexico that could be downsized in keeping with the neoliberal zeitgeist. In the wake of the civil war, the Guatemalan state did, however, shrink the military by half (Little 2009). With the massive reduction of thc military, the reach of state institutions was greatly diminished, and the central government has not been able to expand to meet basic needs (even if it were capable of doing so, given current levels of corruption).

How long Guatemala's fragile civilian government and antiquated justice system can maintain themselves remains unclear. As we shall see in this volume, state failures have meant that local communities must govern themselves, for better or worse, under conditions of eroding systems of power, authority, and legitimacy. Swiftly shifting global economic pressures, combined with rapidly changing local culture, challenge community survival as well as individual and family adaptability. The attractiveness of sense-deadening alcohol, the edgy flashpoints of mob lynchings, the surging risks of rampant crime, the real worries of economic and personal insecurity, and the stressful intensity of Pentecostal Protestant and Charismatic Catholic religion—all conditions sweeping the country—suggest that Mayas still do confront the threat of social, material, and cultural dispossession. As Massumi suggests, "the indeterminacy of threat," for them, "is unbearable."

This book's ethnographic data force us to rethink certain issues in Foucault's theory of governmentality. In the Guatemalan context that is at once so uncertain and so unbearable, Foucault's concept of governmentality provides an especially useful idea and method through which to explore the fluid relationship of highland Maya communities in the neoliberal Guatemalan state. Foucault treated modern forms of power and their operation, albeit from a Western perspective. He sought to understand the shift from the *liberal* state (based on a foundation of social welfare that intervenes on behalf of its citizens so they can be "free") to the *neoliberal* state (that rejects direct government intervention and privileges the individual as an active, accountable, and ethical seat of governance). In an idealized neoliberal state, the individual on whom the burden of governance rests is a well-prepared, well-educated, flexible, and adaptable rational actor who makes well-reasoned choices. The impersonal market operates in support of those actors and the process promotes the larger social good.

Anthropologists have embraced the governmentality concept, in part as an entry point into the critique of the neoliberal project and in part because it suggests a method for tracing out power and its operation in contemporary governmental systems. Inda (2005) provides what is arguably the best current synthesis of work on governmentality. He underscores the broad applications of the concept: the construction of lived space; medicine and the medicalized self; poverty, unemployment, and insecurity; insurance and actuarial science as it relates to vectors of risk; control and regulation of human reproduction and sexuality; crime, punishment, and discipline; self-help programs; globalization; and colonialism. What all these areas have in common is a concern for how constellations of people, practices, and ideas shape the conduct of individuals and collectives in order to affect their welfare (Inda 2005).

This impressive scope of work can be placed within four categories with associated exemplars: the effects of colonialism (e.g., D. Scott 1999); the use of techno-scientific authority as a form of population management (e.g., Rouse 1995); the use of biopower/biopolitics as a form of control and governance (e.g., Rabinow 1992); the global operation of neoliberal politics (e.g., Ferguson and Gupta 2002).[21] The final category is the most immediately relevant to this volume, for these studies explore the unstable and precarious political-legal relationship between Guatemala's central government, non-governmental institutions and practices, and the highland Mayas in this period of contradiction when neoliberal policy and state centralization both permeate Maya communities.

McDonald (1999) has summarized the Foucauldian view of the state and the operation of "governmentality." Foucault notes that it is an intellectual error to conceptualize the state as an essentialized object in which power is concentrated and from which power flows. Rather, states are composed of a hierarchical web of agents, their practices, and accompanying legitimizing discourses. He further notes that it is equally erroneous to assume that those state agents operate consistently and collaboratively. The state, thus, merely reflects those agents' collective actions and practices. Indeed, the state is fluid, dynamic, and often conflicted and contradictory as its agents pursue their various ends. A key concern for Foucault was how a state's agents manage intended and unintended outcomes beyond their direct reach. In the idealized neoliberal scenario, the art of governance is internalized in the individuals and realized through a reinvigorated civil society in collaboration with a wide variety of non-state institutions—NGOs, religious entities, business enterprises, schools, prisons, civic organizations, or communities themselves. As Hale (2002:496) notes, "the neoliberal state unloads onto its neoliberal citizen-subjects the responsibility to resolve the problems—whether daily or epochal—in which they are immersed."

Our chapters address the precarious balance between the neoliberal diffusion of governance and the state's mandate to protect individual rights and, we would add, well-being. Each chapter contextualizes and explores the diverse effects of neoliberalism as they operate in impoverished and marginalized indigenous communities within a weak and failing state. Collectively, the chapters show that what happens on the ground in Guatemala is not neoliberal. Indeed, Guatemala's socioeconomic conditions make it virtually impossible for a neoliberal order to take hold. Thus, these chapters document the struggle of highland Maya people to make sense and order out of a world of endemic risk, uncertainty, and fear, a world where duplicitous Maximón still sits comfortably beside every diviner's altar, a world made nearly "unbearable" by its "indeterminacy of threat."

Notes

1. In some instances, Ladinos took advantage of these new openings to solidify their political control (Carmack 1995:225–26).

2. Wagley (1944, 1949) observed Mayan elders informally intercepting problems and dealing with them before they could be raised to the level of

Ladino authorities who ruled their communities. The Peace Accords now make this a Maya right rather than a clandestine activity.

3. As another proxy for the concentration of poverty in Guatemala, it is estimated that 51 percent of the population lives on between US$1 to $2 per day and another 15 percent lives on less than US$1 per day (U.S. Department of State 2010).

4. Human development rankings are based on indicators including infant mortality, literacy rates, chronic child malnutrition, and the like.

5. By comparison, Uruguay has Latin America's most favorable wealth disparity index, at 15.8. This puts all of Latin America below Europe's poorest and least equal country, Italy, whose index stands at 11.2.

6. Kristof (2011) outlines the cost of a radical neoliberal state that has "minimal taxes, high levels of inequality, free-wheeling business and high military expenditures." Rather than investing in infrastructure and social support, such as health care, education, and security, the radical neoliberal state shifts the burden to the individual. Not surprisingly, the rich take care of themselves, while the poor are left vulnerable.

7. The World Bank (2004) reports that Guatemala's tax revenue constitutes only 8 percent of GDP. By way of comparison, for the United States, tax revenue equals just over 28 percent of GDP.

8. Pérez Molina was indeed elected president in the 2011 presidential campaign and will serve 2012–16.

9. Hudson and Taylor (2010) provide a detailed discussion of the structure and function of this UN commission, the CICIG. In its Guatemalan incarnation, "CICIG is tasked to support, strengthen and assist Guatemalan institutions in identifying, investigating, prosecuting, and ultimately dismantling domestic illegal security apparatuses and clandestine security organizations. CICIG was granted the authority: (1) to investigate any person, official, or private entity; (2) to present criminal charges to Guatemala's Public Prosecutor and join criminal proceedings as a private prosecutor; (3) to name civil servants who commit administrative offenses and to participate as a third party in resulting disciplinary proceedings as a private prosecutor; (4) to recommend public policies and legal and institutional reforms; and (5) to request statements, documents, and cooperation from any government officials or entity" (Hudson and Taylor 2010:54). CICIG, however, has no means to *enforce* the prosecution of its activities independently and must therefore operate through and with the cooperation of the Guatemalan government's legal system. Despite possible barriers to successful prosecution, the CICIG has been quite successful. Its efforts to identify and root out corruption have been instrumental

in removing two thousand police (about 15 percent of the total force), ten federal prosecutors, and a small group of judges. One hundred and thirty have been jailed, including two national police chiefs, former ministers, and a variety of businessmen and politicians (Feiser 2010). Perhaps the most spectacular arrest was of former president Portillo, who is being extradited to the United States on money laundering charges (Al Jazeera 2010a).

10. The Rosenberg case ended up being far more fantastic than its Russian movie counterpart, whose plot is straightforward in comparison. CICIG investigators analyzed a hundred thousand cell phone calls and videotape from four security cameras. They determined that five vehicles were used in the crime, seventy-eight witnesses testified, at least thirteen individuals participated in the crime, and nine were sentenced to prison terms, with the four major participants receiving between thirty-eight and forty-eight years each in prison. The assassin group had ties to no less than twenty national police officers, from whom they obtained high-powered weapons and who served as lookouts during the crime. The size of the Rosenberg conspiracy group, level of communication, and complexity of the operation undoubtedly made it far easier for authorities to piece together the crime and its perpetrators than would have been the case had they followed the simpler model of our Russian professor (Acuña 2010).

11. Hawkins (1984:112) has argued that the Guatemalan state and Ladino ethnicity are systematically and ideologically "above the law," in contrast with Indians, who are ideologically subject to the law because the law's purpose, since Spanish colonization, was primarily to constrain, control, and exploit the Indians by extraction. Political anthropologist F. G. Bailey (1988, 2001) would undoubtedly concur. He argues that political leaders, by virtue of their office, must appear as if they always follow the rules and promote cultural values. The reality of the situation, he argues, is that they often transgress their rules and values. Leaders do this most commonly to promote cultural change that is patently in the interest of themselves and their followers. If caught, however, they must either try to explain away the transgression or admit to it and offer an acceptable justification. That is, it is either "all just a big misunderstanding and the transgression did not happen," or "the transgression did occur but was crucial to promoting the common good and therefore permissible in this instance." Gómez and Bonilla were forced to take the former path. Gómez denied he tried to cover up the involvement of the five dead officers in drug theft and trafficking: "When that happened, I informed my superiors. These things happen in our country." Bonilla goes well beyond Gómez's diffuse denial when she states, "I have enemies and I was in their

way." On the one hand, there was a simple procedural snafu (the Gómez defense), and on the other, Bonilla invokes the defense of law along with her role as martyr (Al Jazeera 2010a).

12. See Little (2009). Spanish *oculto* refers to that which is hidden, obscured, or removed from view. The phrase appears with some frequency in Guatemalan newspapers to refer to the power elite manipulating the civilian government from behind the scenes.

13. Timothy Smith (2009) likewise notes the shift from Ladino to Maya mayors starting in the early 1980s in Sololá, so that Mayas now control both the position of mayor and the indigenous municipal government.

14. Benson (2004) provides a dramatic example of mayoral frustration in Tecpán municipio, wherein issues of class and corruption resulted in a protest that culminated in the burning of the mayor's house and his lucrative mattress-and-bedding business.

15. See Goldstein (2004) for a comparison with urban Bolivia, where lynchings have also reached epidemic proportions.

16. Waldemar Smith (1977) caught the end of the hegemonic civil-religious hierarchy, where the linkage between local economics, religion, and politics was still intimately intertwined, and participation was the only status game in town. Annis (1987), Brintnall (1979), and Watanabe (1992) document the erosion of this system as demographic pressure led to increasing economic stress among many Maya households, thus creating the inducement to opt out of the old system of status and power. Our papers demonstrate its continued erosion and replacement with new forms of politics, power, and control.

17. The obvious exception to the predominant political sources of violence, of course, is domestic violence against women and children.

18. Mayors clearly sense their precarious position and have sought realignment with the religious council of elders. Thus, to some extent, some mayors may seek to shore up their weakened position with a source of traditional legitimation (J. Edvalson, personal communication, July 11, 2010). However, their bid for legitimacy is incomplete, at best, since a good part of their constituency no longer participates in the traditional Catholic religious system (Hawkins and Adams, forthcoming).

19. Perera (1991, 1995) argues that not all government agencies should be treated equally, citing the National Council of Protected Areas (CONAP) as an exemplar of stewardship in balancing legitimate usage with environmental protection against damaging activity such as logging and ranching. However, he characterizes the Guatemalan Forestry Institute as thoroughly corrupt and

uninterested in stewarding natural resources. Brown merely suggests a cultural and structural conflict but does not impugn intention to do good in either ethnic sector.

20. In Nahualá and Santa Catarina, a *cuerda* is a unit of land area 25 *varas* by 25 *varas* square. A *vara* is approximately 84 centimeters or 33 inches.

21. Inda (2005) would add a fifth category, "necropolitical projects," which we see as fitting more broadly within the category of biopower/biopolitics.

CHAPTER 1

"The System Changed to Voting"

Respect, Electoral Democracy, and the Public's Anger toward Mayors in Santa Catarina Ixtahuacán

Donald Y. Dracoulis, John P. Hawkins, James H. McDonald, and Walter Randolph Adams

> In the past, all who participated as *alcalde* were chosen more democratically. They were chosen by consensus, by the *principales*. And they were always older men who were well respected in the community. Now, the only people who can be alcaldes and win are people with money, because it takes money to win an election. And why do they want to be alcalde? To control money in town. Before, the alcalde was seen as a volunteer position without monetary benefit. A poor, simple man could be alcalde and the people respected that. Now, only the rich, who want to use their position for their own ends, want to be in charge. The control over money has made the people respect the alcalde less.
>
> An Ixtahuaquense resident

The residents of Nueva Santa Catarina Ixtahuacán acknowledge that they have become increasingly aggressive and hostile in their interactions with the leaders of the municipality during the last twenty years, according the leaders less respect. Residents note that the trend toward openly expressing anger, hostility, and disrespect toward the mayor (alcalde) and municipal officials has increased both in frequency and fury in the last decade. Previous to two decades ago (roughly 1986), Ixtahuaquenses maintain, the public showed great deference to and respect for the civil government post of mayor and his council. Even when people did not agree with the mayor's decisions, residents say they treated him personally with respect, never reproach.[1]

Ixtahuaquenses sense that the public's descent into disrespect for their local officials began in the late 1980s and has continued to this day.

I argue that the expression of contempt toward the mayor and municipal council results from a perception that mayors have lost legitimacy in their communities. This loss of legitimacy, I suggest, derives from four key changes in the recent evolution of Guatemalan society that bear upon respect for authority:

- The *cofradía* system fell into disuse. Its demise reflects a long-term decline in the religious legitimation of traditional community politics. More recently, it reflects the constitutionally imposed separation of religion from politics in the process of electing mayors.
- Recent constitutional changes have altered mayoral responsibilities and the form of selecting mayors. Mayors and other leaders are oriented toward the national political system rather than toward the municipal population that formerly recruited them.
- The level of education among youths, and especially among elected municipal leaders, has increased relative to that of the average municipal citizen, thereby subtly distancing leaders from the peasant agricultural base.
- The 1996 Peace Accords and attendant international monitoring have oriented municipal leaders toward global processes and human rights protections, further distancing them from a formerly inward municipal view and from a commonality with their fellow citizens.

Each of these factors has driven a wedge of difference between the ordinary indigenous peasant villagers and their elected municipal leaders, a wedge that lessens the respect and trust Maya municipal citizens have for their local leaders. The demise of the cofradía, for example, unties the mayor from a web of moral obligations once vouchsafed in religious covenant. Changes to the constitution and movements in political parties have Ladino outsiders, rather than vetted local elders, ultimately picking candidates for mayor. Above-average education makes mayors stand out, for education is a Ladino and nationally oriented institution. Finally, the Peace Accords tie mayors to international as well as national government interaction, and to that degree, breach notions of community autonomy and isolation and separate the mayor from his constituency.

These processes interact synergistically. Moreover, they enmesh and transform the Indian leader in directions that are symbolically Ladino, making mayors partake of feared and exploitative ethnic otherness. The mayor, operating under these stresses and within these networks, increasingly dresses like and interacts with Ladinos. As mayor, he has risen in the institutional ranks of education, wealth, travel, power, and connections as compared with ordinary Indians in the community (Hawkins 1984:173–212). Thus, one mayor of Nahualá, forced by national circumstance to interact with Ladinos and appease Santa Catarina Ixtahuacán, became so alienated from his own citizens that he fled the community in fear of his life.[2] In a culture that prizes equality, similarity, and balance, the status differences introduced by national electoral and educational processes have undermined the systems of respect formerly allocated to those chosen and rotated through the office of mayor. Over the past twenty years, ordinary villagers have perceived mayors to be less like themselves, less connected to them, less representative and understanding of them, and therefore less legitimate than the leaders they honored in the more distant past. While all of these attributes have a class aspect, in the Maya mind they are ethnic transformers, making the acquirer of class mobility also an agent of ethnic transformation, a *nahual* (one's animal alter-spirit) of sorts in their midst.

RESPECT IN THE MAYA COMMUNITY, PAST AND PRESENT

Ethnographies of the Maya people have long reported a deeply held culture of respect for elders, which has privileged the male elder in the local political system. La Farge (1947:42, 45, 72, 186) acknowledges the importance of respect in Santa Eulalia. Although Vogt does not use the word "respect," he documents the extraordinary place of age-based and seniority-based ranking and details the wide variety of behavior by which juniors (in age or duration in office) show expected deference (Vogt 1969:238–45). These matters of rank and deference suffuse the social and cultural system—affecting gender and generation, kinship and *compadrazgo*, ritual and civil offices—through a variety of channels of authority (Vogt 1969:289). Brintnall (1979:83–104) portrays the importance of respect and authority in Aguacatán and shows how these lines of respect are rooted in dependence on the land and on the inheritance mechanism that ties younger men to their parents well into mid-life. Warren highlights the core value of respect—for authority, age, ancestors, and the replication of *costumbre* (traditional religion) through intergenerational submission—in San Andrés Semetabaj (1978:56–59, 68–70).

Even a few hours in the colonial archives provide ample evidence that the attitude of respect toward elders and particularly toward municipal authorities, whether autochthonous or imposed by the colonial regime, has been in place since the 1600s. Today, indigenous scholars reaffirm the concepts. Both Wuqub' Iq' (1997:253) and Otzoy (1997:267), for example, highlight the central place of respect in current indigenous theology and culture, whether traditionalist, Catholic, or Protestant. Likewise, Nayap-Pot (1997:107–108) declares that "respect for the old by the young is a law."

Ethnographies also document the premises of isolation, autonomy, and relative indigenous equality as manifested at the level of the *municipio* (municipality). Indians are "the poor" and "the uneducated" vis-à-vis Ladino elites and external systems. Tax (1937) early noted the municipio as the unit of conceptual and social orientation and its isolation from other municipios. Richard Wilson (1997:122) reaffirms the idea, citing Carol Smith's (1990:18) assertion that "Indian identity is rooted in the community (rather than in a general sense of 'Indian-ncss.'" Warren (1978:60–64) likewise highlights the notions of autonomy and separatism idealized in San Andrés, though it was squeezed and compromised by population growth and land shortage. This municipalization presumably incorporated residuals of the Maya city-state but more directly applied the Spanish colonial policy of setting apart "pueblos de yndios" to thereby allocate and facilitate *encomienda/repartimiento* extraction (Hawkins 1984:54–80). These sources alone establish the depth of the cultural traditions of respect, relative equality, and comparative isolation vis-à-vis the outside world and help us appreciate the consequences of their erosion. Few early sources for Santa Catarina Ixtahuacán exist in the published literature, but accounts such as Von Tempsky (1858) still document the deep tradition of these cultural premises.

Before the structural changes of the last two decades, residents of Santa Catarina Ixtahuacán considered the civil government position of mayor to be invested with secular responsibilities but also religious charisma. The mayor was a middle-aged man chosen to serve by the council of *principales*—the respected ritual and secular leaders who had completed careers in the civil-religious hierarchy. He had not chosen to be mayor; respected community elders chose him.[3] No one aspired to the mayorality as a position of privilege; rather, it was viewed as a venerated cargo or burden.[4] One could not gain money from the position, though one did gain status.

In Santa Catarina, the idea of insulting the mayor because he did not please a constituent was unheard of. People did have disagreements with the mayor in the past, but residents handled discord in a respectful way. One informant shared this experience of his father's measured reaction to an unfavorable ruling:

> When I was about twenty years old, my father and I went to the mayor to complain about some issue of other people entering our land. . . . It was a long time ago. What I do remember is that we entered [the room] very respectfully and took off our hats when we entered, and we patiently waited our turn to speak with the mayor. In the end, he did not give us what we wanted. We tried to convince him for a few minutes to do so. He would not budge. I remember that my father was not happy, but he accepted the decision, thanked the mayor for his time, and we left. We did not insult the mayor or accuse him of corruption or favoritism. Afterward, my father did not even insult the mayor in private. He did not like the decision, but he accepted it.

Not only did people treat the mayor with respect, the mayor treated people with respect. Many informants noted that the mayor did not try to appease a particular interest group in the community; he tried to do what was right for all. An individual understood that if the mayor did not decide in one's favor, it was not out of vindictiveness.

While the above quote might over-romanticize the past, it shows that Ixtahuaquenses believe that much more respect and fairness existed between mayor and public in the past than nowadays. Ixtahuaquenses today passionately affirm that the mayors of the past deserved and received respect. One former member of the mayoral council put the matter thus: "This business of yelling and insulting the mayor and council is new. It has only begun in the last ten years. Before, the *pueblo* [people or town] used to consider the office of the *alcaldía* [mayoralty] as a sacred position.[5] They treated the men called to serve with respect and dignity. They solicited help. Now, they pressure you. It is very different from the old days." In past times, Ixtahuaquenses had little reason to treat mayors with anger or disrespect. If serious problems between the mayor and the public existed before, none of the older members of the community can remember them, and the middle-aged generation cannot recall stories where the community acted out in anger against the mayor.

Things have changed. Today, Ixtahuaquenses see the mayor's office as a self-serving position where the incumbent has much to gain. As before, people address the mayor when problems persist. Today, however, they go before the mayor with an adversarial attitude. A twenty-five-year-old male member of the community's development committee asserted:

> The most extreme way that the townspeople (pueblo) deal with alcaldes who refuse to meet their demands on an important subject or fail to live up to essential promises they made, is to try to force their resignation. After holding a *manifestación pasiva* (peaceful demonstration) and getting the alcalde to promise certain things, if he fails to do them, they [the townspeople] all force him to meet with them, lock the doors, and shout at him until he resigns. They will not let him leave until he writes and signs his resignation. . . . The people are willing to shout down any leader in whom they perceive failures. . . . Sometimes it can get violent. Sometimes the police are needed to protect the political leaders.

In the past, mayors judged a petition or a dispute and decided one way or the other based on gerontocratic counsel. The outcome stood in doubt until decided. Today, citizens assume that the mayor will always deny the petition. As a result, almost all members of the community have a poor opinion of local political leaders.

To solve problems, individuals or small groups come to the mayoral office from the various rural hamlets or cantons of the municipality. They wait their turn to seek an audience in the generally crowded anteroom to the mayoral office and council chamber. The mayor and council meet daily during the week, unless a *comisión*—a required trip or obligation—takes the mayor away on a journey of local inspection or national business, in which case the "second mayor" stands in his place.

The problems people bring to the mayor's attention and request him and his council to solve include land disputes, lack of water, and other issues. One day I witnessed a small group of people arriving at the municipal office to ask the mayor to adjudicate a land dispute. One young man claimed as rightfully his a piece of land that an older man also claimed. The older man explained he had been working it for years and had the right to sell it to a third young man, also present.[6] In the end, the mayor and council decided that the older man was right because he had brought along an elder as a witness. The first young man reacted angrily. He insulted the mayor and council in K'iche' and stormed off. He did not want to accept the decision and he made his negative opinion of the mayor known.

When individuals or groups do not receive what they feel is their due, they vociferously manifest their poor opinion of the mayor. When just one person does not get what he wants, he might berate or mock municipal leaders, but it ends there.[7] When the entire community gets upset, however, the situation becomes much more intense.

One informant related how the community reacted in 2005. As background, the bulk of Santa Catarina residents, and all of its offices and leadership, had moved in 2000 from the old site, prone to flooding and ground subsidence, to a new location: Nueva Santa Catarina Ixtahuacán. In the process of the move and the land disputes it generated with Nahualá, Nueva Santa Catarina residents received a negotiated block of milpa land that Santa Catarina claimed and Nahualá's squatter-tenants were willing to give up for a price. The government exercised eminent domain over the relatively unproductive land, paid the Nahualense squatters a healthy price, and gave it to Santa Catarina leaders to distribute to, and thereby placate, the residents of Nueva Santa Catarina's town center. The mayor of Santa Catarina, however, delayed and did not facilitate the final land divisions or arrange the distribution of plots from the new land acquisition. Moreover, the mayor was not from the old town center. Rather, he was from a coastal hamlet that had grown and become dominant in the southern tip of the municipality. As such, he had not been in favor of the town center's relocation.[8] The residents of Nueva Santa Catarina Ixtahuacán town center reacted with anger:

> A number of years ago, the land was supposed to be finally divided. The commission in charge of the transfer had been working on it for years. The commission had divided the land by neighborhood. The commission could not actually make any decisions by law without the presence of the mayor and his final approval of everything. The commission tried to get him to attend the meetings and sign off on things, but he was busy and did not get around to it. Eventually, the public got upset

> with the commission last year. They accused it [the commission] of not doing its job. The commission said, "It's not our fault, talk to the mayor." So the people all got together to talk to the mayor. The meeting started out pleasant enough, but it soon turned abusive. Some men started insulting him. They took advantage of the situation to call him corrupt. They said he never did anything for the community. They mocked him and swore at him. This riled up the crowd, who now began to shout for his resignation. The people even shut the doors on him in an attempt to prohibit him from leaving until he resigned. Somehow, he got them to calm down and he promised to complete the task soon. He is still the mayor, but this is an example of the anger and disrespect that the people show the mayor now.

This account demonstrates the contrast between how people react toward the mayor now as compared with the past. Communal public displays of anger are uncommon, however, happening once or twice a year at most. But such displays of anger never happened some two decades ago. Now, communal expressions of anger occur regularly, if infrequently, and individual expressions of anger are commonplace.

Santa Catarina Ixtahuacán is not alone in its lack of respect for mayors; such expressions of anger and disrespect occur in other municipios, too. Benson (2004:447–49, 456) and Benson, Fischer, and Thomas (2008:43, 45) detail an outburst of anger and disrespect aimed toward Tecpán's mayor, though they do not investigate the historical transformation in the way mayors have been treated or the frequency of such outbursts. Clearly, the issues of respect and its absence relate to the status of authority and legitimacy in the indigenous community, a status altered by the intrusion of government, the penetration of the global economy, and the population-driven necessity to look outside the agricultural community for subsistence.

Authority and Legitimacy as Sources of Respect

The manifestations of disrespect for local political authorities appear to reflect a reduction of their legitimacy in the eyes of the people. What defines legitimate authority? According to Uphoff (1989):

> Authority derives from the existence, exercise, and maintenance of certain roles whose incumbents claim a right to have people's obedience, whereas legitimacy derives from the beliefs and judgments of persons who are subject to those roles. Legitimacy is produced when members of the public accept such roles, their incumbents, and the resulting decisions or commands as right and proper, regardless of the basis on which acceptance rests. Legitimacy is not so much traded for other resources as it is granted or accorded in keeping with the beliefs people have about what is right and proper, when procedures or outcomes meet normative expectations. (Uphoff 1989:310)

Legitimacy, therefore, is accorded not by those with authority, but by those subject to it.

Max Weber, of course, theorized extensively about the processes by which authority gains legitimacy. According to Weber, authority can be made legitimate if it is invested with culturally perceived traditional, charismatic, or rational attributes (Weber 1958).

- Authority is legitimized through *tradition* when the public believes that the tradition must be respected for its own sake and that authority is acting in a traditional way. As long as power has passed down through traditional means, it is legitimate. Traditional forms of authority are inherently conservative and change-averse; authority is conferred in a context whereby a leader reflects shared cultural ideals and values back to his or her constituency. Authority can also be legitimized if the leader is *charismatic*. A charismatic individual is perceived to have special attributes of personality, style, creativity, or program that attract allegiance. Less tethered to tradition, effective charismatic leaders are able to push agendas of culture change by instilling confidence that their vision is viable, if untested.
- Regarding the *rational* category for legitimization of authority, Weber stipulates that the public views authority as rationally legitimate if it accomplishes the intended tasks in a manner culturally judged to be functional, efficient, and technically appropriate to the task's goals. In much of the West, legislative and bureaucratic governance is believed to be rational and is

> often expressed as "authority by the consent of the governed" (Matheson 1987:206–10).

In Santa Catarina Ixtahuacán, the legitimacy of the mayor and other community leaders draws from all three of Weber's sources. Ixtahuaquenses perceive the office of mayor to be rooted in tradition, to be charismatic in the sense that the mayor can be inventive if the inventions appear to be traditional vis-à-vis Ladino cultural models, and to be rational—that is, technically appropriate to the tasks at hand.

Factors that Affect Authority, Legitimacy, and Respect

Over time, a number of factors have eroded the authority, legitimacy, and respect for the office of mayor in this Maya community. We focus on just four: the demise of the cofradía (roughly 1950–1990), the impact of constitutional change (1985–present), the rise of education in the community (roughly 1990–present), and the implementation of the Peace Accords (1996–present). The first, demise of the cofradía, has been the subject of major discussion in the academic literature regarding its impact on respect, and consequently, we shall not treat it extensively here. Of the other three factors, we concentrate on the key impact of the changes embodied in the 1985 constitutional reform.

The Demise of the Cofradía

The demise of the cofradía system caused the office of mayor to lose the sacredness once associated with the position, eroding one of its traditional bases of legitimacy (Brintnall 1979; C. Larson, in review). The *cofradía* is a social group of village officials who perform rituals on behalf of their community. All men, as Catholics, traditionally were expected to participate, if asked, in one of several cofradía groups and to alternate "back and forth between civil and religious posts" (Chance and Taylor 1985:1). DeWalt (1975:90) and others before him call it the "cargo system," a system in which men perform most civil and religious services without remuneration and on a rotating basis.[9] In this section, we refer to the demise of the cofradía in Santa Catarina Ixtahuacán, similar to that which occurred in other Guatemalan communities.[10]

The cofradía system ran parallel to and connected with the political system in this community. Young men began to build up social respect in the municipio by helping out in some official position in the cofradía, usually helping in religious processions by holding up the saints or fulfilling other functions. As a young man aged, he was placed in positions of increasingly greater responsibility in the cofradía and in community administration. His positions often alternated between the cofradía one year and a civic position, such as a member of a commission, the next. This alternation continued throughout the life of a male until he was asked to fund the cofradía as its chief officer. Men considered it an honor to incur debt to do so, and shameful if they refused. After a man had funded a cofradía's ritual cycle, the town elders might ask him to serve as mayor. Nearly all men who became mayor had funded a cofradía cycle. The mayor's status was therefore associated with the religious symbolism, respect, and traditional legitimacy of the cofradía. Religious respect for cofradía elders suffused, sustained, and undergirded politics.

Therefore, in past times, criticizing the mayor entailed something akin to criticizing the local priest or denying the known cosmos. The mayor, because he had sustained the cofradía, was a proven man of God and servant of the people. Everyone knew he had shown himself willing to sacrifice and take on heavy debts to serve the church and the community. People respected him because they believed he had the support of God. And if God supported the mayor, the people did not have the right to rebuke him.

The cofradía system, under pressure across much of Guatemala in the second quarter of the twentieth century, fell into relative disuse in one community after another during the latter half of the twentieth century. In Santa Catarina, it lasted with some vigor into the 1980s. Nevertheless, throughout the last decades of the twentieth century, more and more men declined to participate in Santa Catarina's cofradía. This community celebrated its last cofradía event in 1996.[11]

Today, the men running for mayor continue to profess their faith in Christianity to the people, but they no longer must show that faith through costly prior religious service. With a lack of past religious service, the office of mayor now lacks the symbolic status of respect associated with traditional religious leaders. As one Ixtahuaquense, a university student, put it, "The cofradía system had made it so that the alcalde was almost a religious as well as a political position. When the cofradía system stopped, the alcalde may have lost that sacred position he had before, thus making it [the office of mayor] more open to criticism." The mayor's office lost all symbolic religious prestige. In doing so, it lost the respect embodied in Weber's category of "tradition" and it lost the devotion inherent in having religious charisma attached to political office. While the core processions were conducted according to tradition and with dignity, the surrounding celebratory events—dances, alcohol distribution, music, drunkenness, sociality—all had charismatic notes of rituals of rebellion and, by Maya standards, bacchanalia. In effect, these ancillary activities were also charismatic (in the Weberian sense, not in the recent Catholic sense of charismatic renewal). The disconnection of traditional religious activities from the processes that validated the mayor's office hurt mayoral respect.

Thus, Ixtahuaquenses feel free to criticize the mayor because he is no longer a proven man of God and servant of the people. Before, the mayor automatically gained charisma because of his connection with priestly service, with the shaman-priests among the *pasado* elders,[12] with the Roman Catholic village priest, and with God. Town elders in the mayoral corporation similarly have lost much of the respect they once commanded because they had all participated in the cofradía and walked in the institutional path toward mayorality. Lack of religious participation permits people to feel freer to criticize, insult, and disregard the decisions of the mayor. He is just a normal person. There is no reason to believe that God supports him any more than any other man. Because he does not have the specific favor of God, he is open to criticism. Without the cofradía, the mayor and his council lost their religious status among the community, and thus, the foundation of the esteem in which they were held.

Clay Larson (in review) summarizes scholarly discussions of the reasons cofradía practices fell into disuse and details the history of their demise in Santa Catarina Ixtahuacán. One reason is people's rejection of the costs entailed in sustaining cofradía ritual when new job opportunities, new agricultural possibilities for cash cropping, and new ways to invest in social status outside the community overwhelm the inward focus (Brintnall 1979; Warren 1978; Watanabe 1992). These scholars also note the increasing popularity of Evangelical and Pentecostal Protestantism and their use as justifications to refuse further investment in cofradía ritual. To this, we must now add Charismatic Catholicism, which firmly rejects participation in the fiesta activities now associated with non-cofradía Roman Catholic processions.

An additional reason the cofradía fell into disuse derives from Guatemala's constitutional changes of 1985. The constitution and its follow-up laws and practices removed the power of the elders to choose a man who had served the community in both political and religious positions. Under the constitution, an individual could now run for election without the approval of the elders and therefore had little to gain by participating in a cofradía. It would be more effective to spend his money on campaign costs than on sustaining the cofradía. Thus, the community no longer needed to force men to sustain the costs of a religious system in order to validate the political order, because that order had been exogenously changed by electoral imposition. Though already in decline long before 1985, the remaining vestiges of cofradía activity and organization in many communities became cultural sideshows, if they were held at all. In part, this occurred under the impact of constitutional change; in part, under the impact of war-induced cultural disorganization and militarized reorganization of many communities (Manz 2004; Stoll 1993); and in part, because of neoliberal economic and religious alternatives. We turn now to examine how the constitutional changes, implemented in 1985 and thereafter, further and more directly precipitated a loss of respect toward mayors.

The Impact of Changes to the Constitution

At various intervals during the twentieth century, Guatemala has implemented political changes in an effort to bring greater political participation to its citizens.[13] The first of these electoral changes took place after 1944 with the Arévalo-Árbenz democratization and transformation. Local mayors were supposed to have been chosen directly by the people after 1944; in fact, Ixtahuacán's elders continued to choose its mayors long after, in defiance of constitutional law. Token elections were held to appease the national government, but only the man chosen by the elders ran for mayor. Ixtahuaquenses simply ignored the political parties.

The municipalities were fairly autonomous in how they chose their leaders. For example, until 1994, Guatemala's electoral law called for mayoral elections of large cities on a five-year election cycle and smaller "second-class municipios" on a two-and-a-half-year cycle.[14] Thus, in Santa Catarina, the town elders gathered every two and a half years to pick a new mayor. The only conditions the elders placed on themselves were that their choice should be unanimous, the candidate must have participated in the cofradía, and the candidate must have served as a *síndico* (councilor) on the municipality's mayoral council. The choice required unanimity of the members of a group who had proven their capacity to work hard and honorably in the community, specifically, those who had become principales by successfully completing the graduated stages of the civil-religious hierarchy. The person selected as candidate for mayor also had to have passed through that system. As a result, the man chosen typically had a reputation as honest and hardworking. The principales would never choose a drunk or someone perceived to have taken advantage of others. Moreover, the election generated no campaigning because it entailed only one candidate.

The 1985 Constitution was thus the first national edict to effectively force direct elections in the municipalities. We may speculate why this change occurred post-1985 and not post-1944, when the national government first mandated direct election of mayors in this and other communities. For one thing, by 1985, the cofradía was under severe stress from the kinds of economic intrusions and integrating forces detailed by Brintnall for Aguacatán (1979) and Watanabe for Santiago Chimaltenango (1992), although Santa Catarina's path in this regard is unique. Another factor leading to acquiescence to the new electoral system is that, by 1985, Santa Catarina (and the nation) had experienced the full fury of internal warfare and dissension. The civil war had shattered any illusion of political or cultural autonomy. Thus, from 1985 to the present, the national government has much more thoroughly and aggressively imposed itself in indigenous village affairs.

As a result, national political parties began to choose the local mayoral candidate even in such holdout communities as Nahualá and Santa Catarina. The political party with the highest percentage of votes got to place its candidate as mayor. One man explained, "One does not vote for a specific candidate, one votes for a political party. That decides the mayor. In reality, everyone knows who the candidate of the party is, so it is just like voting for a specific man, even if his name is not on the ballot." Because the party with the highest vote wins by a plurality, mayors typically have had much less than majority support, let alone the former condition of complete consensus. Table 1 documents the issue as found in nearby Nahualá. While these figures are higher than those reported by Dracoulis's Santa Catarina Ixtahuacán informants, they confirm that the problem of mayoral election

Table 1
MAYORAL VOTING IN NAHULÁ, 1985–1995

Election date	Number of coalitions on ballot or receiving votes	Total votes cast	Votes for winning (mayoral) party	Mayoral party's % of votes cast	Mayoral party's % of estimated eligible voters*
Nov. 3, 1985	8	4,956	1,917	39	(Not available)
April 24, 1988	5	3,141	1,234	39	(Not Available)
Nov. 11, 1990	12	4,813	1,304	27	(Not available)
May 9, 1993	7	4,080	1,393	34	7
Nov. 12, 1995	18	5,169	1,234	24	6

*Based on assumption that the population age 18 and above (voting age) constitutes 50% of total population.
Source: FUNCEDE 1995:14–18; Instituto Nacional de Estadística 1994; X Censo de Población.

by plurality, rather than majority or consensus, extends beyond Santa Catarina. This substitution of less-than-majority-vote for consensus seems a key factor in the reduction of respect granted to mayors. Furthermore, since Guatemala uses a proportional representation system for their legislature, a number of national political parties have evolved. That trickles down to the municipal level in the form of multiple candidates for mayor. Thus, five political parties or more typically put up candidates in the municipal election, which reduces the plurality who voted for a seated mayor to a tiny percentage of the electorate and an insubstantial percentage of those who voted.

The 1985 Constitution also substantially changed the procedures for funding the municipalities. Before, many municipalities such as this one received few or no funds from the national government. Now, the constitution mandates the central government distribute funds to all municipalities based on population, setting the stage for actual and perceived corruption. The mayor controls these funds with the help of his council but has little other managerial oversight.

At the same time, the mayor's office lost its judicial functions, transferred to the now separated *juzgado de paz* (justice of the peace) office run by the National Ministry of Justice.[15] Whereas before, the mayor could punish lesser crimes (Asociación CODEIN 2008:49, 93), from 1985 to the present, the mayor has had no administrative authority to try or punish anyone. Barrios (2001:219) confirms the import of both the 8 percent of national funds that began to flow to the municipios and the loss of the mayor's judicial functions.

The people responded to these changes with shifts in attitude and expectation, specifically a reduced sense of the need for consensus, an increased perception of corruption, and an expanded notion of what services might be expected from the office of the mayor. Each of these changes helped foster the anger and public lack of respect now extant between the municipal public and the mayor and has contributed to the corrosion of the legitimacy that mayors previously possessed. We examine each factor.

Lack of Consensus

The 1985 Constitution requires all municipalities to hold mayoral and council elections; installation by the consensus of respected elders no longer exists. The switch to elections foments occasionally intense competition between community members. One informant described the resulting friction: "When people run for office, they seem to change. People who are neighbors (*vecinos*) now treat us as enemies if we do not support the same candidate that they do. The candidates themselves become very abusive to those who do not support them, when before and after the election they were and are friends. I do not understand it, but politics seems to divide our tiny town every four years." Such competition often leaves people upset when their candidate loses and leads to disrespect when they must communicate with a mayor whom they did not favor.

In the Guatemalan electoral system, people must choose between the candidates of some five political parties. As a result, the winning party usually only receives some twenty-five to thirty-five percent of the vote, with no requirement for a runoff election at the municipal level to establish a majority. Thus, in most cases, a considerable majority, often amounting to 65 to 75 percent of those voting in the municipality, did not vote for the eventual winner.

This constitutionally based resort to a simple plurality with no runoff at the mayoral level results in widespread disaffection among those motivated to vote. Before, when culturally accepted consensus selection by the respected elders was the norm, some individuals here might not have liked specific mayoral decisions, but they showed respect because they knew the mayor had the support of the community. A mayor was not accused of favoritism, because he had nobody to reward for support. By contrast, the divisiveness of current campaigning and the lack of general support for one leader considerably threaten the legitimacy of the mayor's office. Those who unsuccessfully petition the mayor find his decisions suspect and believe that he inappropriately favors those who supported him.

In sum, the constitutional change that has moved the town from a respected consensus government to a simple plurality vote system has resulted in a loss of legitimacy in two ways. First, with the new electoral system, the mayor lacks the authority and the sacred aura of participating in recurring religious tradition and the annual festival. As time passes, the new system will acquire routinized elective authority and may even become traditional. For the present, however, many Ixtahuaquenses aged thirty and above, of both genders, regardless of education, yearn for the old days. Second, the electoral reforms initiated in 1944—reaffirmed in the constitutions of 1945, 1956, and 1985, and finally imposed after 1985—brought unmediated direct voting to Maya individuals. This was supposed to provide stronger rational legitimacy than the indirect voting system represented by the consensus of the town elders. Yet, by relying on a weak plurality in a multiparty free-for-all rather than a stronger majority vote between two candidates or a consensus of the most respected elders of the community, postwar elections have in fact undermined mayoral legitimacy. As Watanabe (1992) has shown, national party politics has injected divisive partisanship into the Maya community, breaching consensus, empowering relative youths and Spanish speakers, and undercutting the aged *pasados*. Many Ixtahuaquenses feel that the old system represented the will of the people more effectively than the new one. As one man observed, "The new system feels less democratic." In consequence, Ixtahuaquenses sense that the mayor elected under the new system is less legitimate than the old appointed and vetted one, and that belief impacts their relations with him.

Corruption

The widely held belief that mayors are corrupt further erodes the legitimacy of Ixtahuaquense mayors. Does corruption in fact exist in Ixtahuacán? That is hard to establish factually. Nearly all informants, however, think corruption runs rampant at the municipal level. When asked about corruption in the past, they assert that if there was any, it was minor. Regardless of the factual status of municipal corruption, the important questions are: what has produced the perception of increased corruption, and what are the consequences of this perception?

In a country where the national government is widely proven to be corrupt and culturally expected to be corrupt, the constitutional mandate that the central government give the mayor access to funds proportional to a municipio's population has injected the perception of endemic corruption and probably has created an increase in actual corruption—though the latter is impossible to prove.

Nobody expected the mayors of the past to be corrupt. Corruption may have existed because there was always some money to be managed, but if so, it was on a much smaller scale. No one aspired to or campaigned for the position of mayor with the prospect of corruption in mind, because little could be gained economically. The Ixtahuaquense who provided the epigraph for this chapter has two years of college course work and works in a government agency in Nueva Ixtahuacán as an outreach educator. He summed up the principal issues leading to dissatisfaction with the mayor as "self-interest" (*interés)* and "corruption."

Today, excessively expensive campaigns, in tandem with offers of money and favors to voters, have created the perception that a person has much to gain by winning mayoral officc. Thus, informants have wondered, "Where else will he get the money to pay for the promises he makes?" According to Ixtahuaquenses, people become angry when they do not get the construction or development projects they think they were promised. These citizens feel that the mayors just use up the considerable money available on themselves, rendering themselves unable to support legitimate requests or fulfill campaign promises. In short, any association with elected office implies corruption. As one man explained, "I would never run for office because everyone thinks you are corrupt, even if you are not, so it is not worth it."

Some feel they have proof of corruption. Once, when I gently mentioned the problem of "perceived corruption," an informant corrected me: "It is not 'perceived' but *real, open* corruption. The people see a normal, poor Maya become alcalde and suddenly he has new improvements on his home, a new car, finer clothing, and the most modern cellular phone. What distinguishes Guatemalan governmental corruption from other corrupt states is that the corruption is so blatant and out in the open."

Ixtahuaquenses say such changes cannot come from a mayor's salary of less than two thousand quetzales a month. An informant explained that he heard from various engineers that almost all construction projects cost too much because local leaders tell the construction companies to bill in excess of expenses so both can skim off the top, calling it "administrative costs." In a public meeting on the importance of volunteer efforts in the community, one of Ixtahuacán's volunteer firemen, backed up by the head volunteer firefighter of the department, openly discussed corruption:

> For everyone to succeed, we all need to know our place in our groups and what I need to do in the group. All action is thus community based. The community [members] need to trust each other and not worry about anything else. Two of the biggest problems facing disaster relief are politics and dishonesty. Disasters always bring out politicos posturing to show the public the things that they are doing for them in order to win reelection, and those who want to be politicos point the finger and blame the politicians in charge. This takes away from the crisis at hand. Volunteers need to ignore the politicos and focus on their jobs, and if possible, get the politicos out of the way. Dishonesty is a problem because lots of money comes in from the national government and from abroad. It is very easy to skim some off the top. We must always remember that God is watching and judging us.

Thus, politicos, even those from the town, partake of the outsider status of the proverbially thieving Ladinos. Politicos, even local politicos, succumb to self-interest and obstruct the community work that needs to be done—in this case, disaster reconstruction after five-sixths of the community moved to Chwipatán in early 2000 as a result of flooding caused by Hurricane Mitch in late 1998, land subsidence over the years, and an increasing interest in "progress" and "development" in Antigua Ixtahuacán.[16] Moreover, the only restraint to rampant corruption comes from the firm belief in watchful and punishing gods. But the belief that traditional divinities watch over cultural conformity and punish disrespect has diminished substantially. Secular-political Guatemala has no mechanism to track or restrain graft and corruption, while fear of the gods has been pushed aside. Corruption, consequently, runs unabated.

Corruption—or the perception of corruption—angers Ixtahuaquenses. They resent local leaders telling them that there is not enough money to fund projects, given that they believe local leaders divert money to their personal accounts that should be available for public expenditure. While the members of the community are happy to have more funds allocated to their town, they feel that there is no proper mechanism to ensure wise use of these funds and prevent their going into the mayor's pocket. Due to this lack of transparency and accountability, the mayor loses legitimacy.

New Expectations Unmet, Old Expectations Thwarted

It is ironic that because the mayor controls state money, many citizens have come to expect more than the funds will allow. They believe he has enough money to improve the living conditions of the hamlets and cantons throughout the municipality. People from all the hamlets and urban barrios see an opportunity to improve their local conditions. In Ixtahuacán center, they want regular water, stable electricity, better roads, and a host of other benefits, things the villagers never expected before the mayor started receiving state money. Local leaders compete with each other to request that funds be earmarked for their hamlet or canton project. Unfortunately, the funds are never enough. When a mayor thwarts a perceived opportunity by saying, "it is not possible," the citizens become angry. The availability of money has thus altered people's expectations of the mayor and the way they relate to him when their new expectations remain unmet.

One might wonder if the residents know the actual quantity of funds allocated and their inherent limits. But the Guatemalan government does not operate here with transparency. Most citizens do not know the amount allocated to the municipalities. Moreover, they do not know the amounts derived from the many NGOs engaged in state or municipal projects in the municipio. Finally, the culture of corruption, widespread in Guatemala—indeed screaming from the headlines almost daily—does not lend credence to any figures published. After all, contact with the government symbolically Ladinoizes the mayors and their cohorts, and Ladinos, by dictionary definition and as taught in school and in the home, are "astute, sagacious," and corrupt tricksters. Mayors, as proto-Ladinos who are Indians and brokers between the two ethnic cultures, become the very embodiment of the two-faced Judas/San Simón trickster seated prominently at traditionalist religious altars and dressed most often in Ladino, or a mix of Ladino and Indian, clothing.

In one important regard, Ixtahuaquense expectations under the old and new systems have remained the same. Residents still expect the mayor to keep the community safe from crime and to punish delinquents. However, the mayor no longer has the ability to meet those expectations because the new constitution terminated the mayor's responsibility to judge local crimes and delicts and vested it in the outside-appointed justice of the peace. So, while the expectation remains for the mayor to protect the town, he has no legal authority to act and no material basis to do so. The national police in the town do not answer to the mayor, nor do the lawyers or the justice of the peace. From 1985 through 1996 (the date of the Peace Accords), the mayor had no legal basis to meet the judicial and safety functions his citizens expect of him, because the constitution stripped him of direct judicial power and left him with only the power of persuasion.[17] From 1996 to the present, as Bybee, J. Edvalson, and Call (this volume) show, Mayas in these villages have contested with Ladinos and the national government for the right to punish under the not-yet legally clear right encoded in the Peace Accords to maintain indigenous tradition.

In sum, past mayors did not have many expectations imposed on them. No one expected development projects, because they knew no money existed to fund them. The only substantial expectation people had of the mayor was to punish those who disturbed the peace. Since this community was relatively crime-free in the past, he did not have to do much to keep the people pleased. Today, however, people expect the mayor to deal with local crime when he no longer has the institutional tools to do so. In addition, Ixtahuaquenses expect much more now of a mayor concerning construction and public projects because they know he controls more money. With these key expectations unmet, anger and disrespect boil up when dealing with the mayor. Two additional changes—increased educational access and the continuing influence of the 1996 Peace Accords—further undermine mayoral respect.

The Impact of Education

The education system has improved over the last few decades throughout Guatemala and in Ixtahuacán. Over time, the average level of formal education completed has steadily increased. Tables 2 and 3 give some indication of the rising importance of education. Primary school is now required for all children. To be sure, many people remain illiterate

Table 2
CHANGE IN LEVEL OF EDUCATION, POPULATION AGE SEVEN AND ABOVE

Census date		Total	Number and (% of total) completing indicated primary school grade	
			1, 2, or 3	4, 5, 6
Santa Catarina Ixtahuacán	1964	9,717	482 (5.0)	29 (0.3)
	2002	31,459	6,800 (21.6)	8,635 (27.4)
Nahualá	1964	17,060	590 (3.5)	93 (0.5)
	2002	40,419	9,229 (22.8)	12,182 (30.1)

Source: Dirección General de Estadística 1964:765, 811; Instituto Nacional de Estadística 2002:93

and with little education, but many, especially men and younger women, have attended at least six years of primary school in the community. Men and women aged fifty and above report little or no schooling. Most individuals under fifty report some schooling, and many say they have over six years. Today, quite a few have completed high school and a handful have acquired some university experience.

These advances in education have contributed to an increased awareness of national issues among members of the community. That increased knowledge, however, has also had the effect of facilitating their anger and contempt toward local political leaders when Ixtahuaquenses feel they do not receive their due. Education contributes to an awareness of Santa Catarina's relative deprivation compared with other largely Indian communities, including Nahualá. Given the ideal of equality in the Indian community, such perception of inequality offends cultural expectations.

In the past, education was unavailable or rejected by most in the community. For example, one man related how his father did not permit him to go to school, even as a boy of about nine. The school director would go around to each house in the community, asking about the children. The man's father would hide him from the director because the father felt school was a waste of time and that he needed his son's help working the fields. One day, the director saw the boy playing in the street. The director grabbed him by the ear, dragged him to his father, and told him, "If you do not put this boy in school, I will call the police and they will put you in jail for ignoring the law." From that

Table 3
LITERACY RATE IN POPULATION AGE SEVEN AND ABOVE

		% of males who are literate	% of females who are literate
Santa Catarina Ixtahuacán	1964	10.7	3.4
	2002	56.7	43.5
Nahualá	1964	8.8	1.2
	2002	61.7	45.3

Source: Dirección General de Estadística 1964:496, 765, 811; Instituto Nacional de Estadística 2002:93

day on, the boy went to school. Now he is a teacher and wants to continue his studies.

Today, many parents aspire to send their children to good schools, and if possible, to a university, reflecting a changed understanding of what education can do for a person. Most of the wealthiest in the community completed *diversificado*, the equivalent of high school in the United States. Villagers notice the connection between relative wealth and education. Several high school graduates now teach the community's children, and everyone in the village knows that teachers receive regular, and by local community standards, handsome monthly incomes. Only the few who have immigrated to the United States and returned with *remesas*—their cash savings from illegal immigrant labor—or who have children in the United States sending them regular remesas, have more money than the teachers and educated government employees.[18]

A shortage of land further fuels the Ixtahuaquense urge for greater education. Over time, as people have reproduced and then subdivided their land in inheritance, they have less land to farm than their forebears. Consequently, they need other vocations to pay for their needs. Education is now seen as a doorway to survival in the face of land shortage. Not only does education offer a way out of dependence on land, but ironically it also enables those with education to earn steady incomes that enable them to buy more land. The result is the concentration of land in the hands of the educated.

As the school system improved and the state obligated parents to send their children to school, education suffused greater knowledge of law and government into the community. One community member remarked: "Before, when everyone had less education and knew less about what the possibilities were, they demanded little and rarely complained. Now, they always demand [*exigen*] the things they want. Now, they want better roads, potable water, electricity, and more education."

Increased literacy also gave a few interested Ixtahuaquenses direct access to information from the outside world, largely through newspapers, as well as an increased interest in receiving information from other sources such as radio and TV. Many began to perceive that their local political system was not meeting their expectations of correct government, leading to frustration aimed at local leaders. Whereas, in the past, most were ignorant of their rights, with education, Ixtahuaquenses began to feel they had rights and deserved to exercise them.

Increased education has also fostered the perception of universal corruption. Nearly everyone in the community believes that corruption exists today at the municipal level. While Ixtahuaquenses may not know exactly how much a mayor receives from the state government or from NGOs, education has led them to understand that substantial funds do come from such sources. Absent transparency, many people in the community now try to calculate how much the community development projects should cost and estimate how much the mayor receives. When they perceive a difference, they accuse the mayor of stealing. In addition, increased education and literacy have enabled community members to read about frequent corruption in other parts of the nation. Moreover, schools now present some information about the history of endemic corruption in Guatemala and the rest of Latin America. Thus, the expectation of corruption has entered the local cultural milieu. Students in the schools learn about corruption through their teachers, as well as through the ubiquitous reporting in the media. From taxi drivers to newspaper columnists, everyone in Guatemala talks about the existence of—and the need to end—corruption. Ixtahuaquenses learn of this corruption, come to expect it, and want to fix it, in part as a byproduct of the increased literacy and access education affords. If corruption exists among all politicians in Guatemala, it must exist in this municipality, goes the logic. Access to the nation's pulse, through education and the media, undermines unconditional respect for local political leaders now connected to the nation. While these are perceptions and expectations, many in the village interpret any anomaly they see as evidence of corruption, thereby confirming their belief.

In sum, improved local education has influenced Ixtahuaquenses to claim their right to, and voice their opinions about, good governance. Although education does not create disrespect or anger, it has facilitated the expression of anger. Increased knowledge has made people aware of things in their local system that they dislike, vis-à-vis their expectations, which in turn produces anger. The current political system has lost legitimacy because the people now know that something better could or should exist.

The Influence of the Peace Accords

The signing of the Peace Accords in 1996 reaffirmed the rights of the indigenous people in Guatemala. Its provisions call for increased attention to and protection of Indian people and their cultural heritage as a political right. It is true that a 1999 referendum held in an off-year (non-presidential) election voted down the provisions in the accords that guaranteed indigenous cultural protection. But Indians and academics see this vote to nullify as a largely Ladino reaction to the special protections afforded the Indians (Carey 2004; Warren 2003). These sources note, moreover, that the polling stations for the 1999 referendum were located only in municipal seats. Thus, polling stations were readily accessible to most Ladinos but incredibly inconvenient to most Indians. So, even if formally vetoed by a supposedly national referendum, the cultural protections clauses of the accords have altered the structure of national funding, national procedure, and local political culture.

One informant suggested that the Peace Accords did not give the indigenous people any new rights; it merely reaffirmed existing rights. It is true that provisions of cultural protection in the accords closely follow parts of the 1985 Constitution. Nevertheless, the Peace Accords represented a turning point for many in the indigenous community, including Ixtahuacán. Thus, one heard variations of the following local sentiment: "The people now feel a right to express themselves and organize as they wish." During the 1980s—the decade of the most brutal government attacks on Indians and Indian communities, indigenous people feared to voice their opinions and criticize what they felt was wrong. The signing of the Peace Accords granted protected space to those who wished to express their dissatisfaction with the failings they saw in local and national government. From 1996 to the present, many Ixtahuaquenses have felt they have new freedoms rooted in the internationally backed, actively monitored, and humanistically universal provisions of the Peace Accords, regardless of its post-referendum legal status in Guatemala.

Some Ixtahuaquenses believe this perception of freedom has been carried to excess. One municipal council member of Ixtahuacán noted that this new sense of freedom is transforming into a feeling of licentiousness: "Improvements in education have shown the people the rights that they should have. And now that the army is gone, they do not feel they have anything to fear. . . . This is good, but the people are confusing *libertad* [liberty] with *libertinaje* [unrestrained license].[19] The people go to excess in their demands and demand things they cannot have because the money is not there. Further, they think they now have the right to act so disrespectfully."

While increased education has given Ixtahuaquenses expanded knowledge of their rights and civic inclusion, the Peace Accords have served as a tool to express and protect those rights. Though not everyone is literate, the college-educated, teachers, and community leaders all avidly read and impart to students and community members the content of the accords in public meetings and over the radio. The knowledge of protected cultural rights has fostered the notion that Ixtahuaquenses do not have to accept what local political leaders do unless they, as a pueblo and indigenous culture, approve.

Moreover, Ixtahuaquenses chafe at a system imposed on them by Ladinos. They want a system that will respect their traditions per the protections voiced in the constitution and the accords. The current system's lack of a connection to the Maya past—and Ladino lack of interest in it—deprives these Mayas of the legitimacy they crave. Thus, to the degree that mayors, for whatever reason, collude with external Ladino political connections, and to the degree that indigenous mayors symbolically become more "Ladino" to accommodate to or benefit from the external system, they distance themselves from their legitimate cultural roots and draw anger upon themselves.

Evaluating the Structural Causes of Anger

We have argued that loss of respect for and anger expressed toward Indian mayors in Ixtahuacán is related to structural changes systemwide. We have suggested such factors as new economic pressures and opportunities, globalization, cofradía collapse, constitutional change, educational and electoral penetration into the community, and a changing legal landscape brought on by the globalization of human rights monitoring. By implication, such processes would apply to most indigenous mayors of largely indigenous communities in Guatemala.

Some might argue, by contrast, that anger with mayors is a phenomenon unique to Santa Catarina Ixtahuacán and Nahualá, occasioned by their land dispute over a botched set of measurements made after the bulk of Ixtahuacán center's residents relocated. We treat this matter in detail in Hawkins and Adams (in preparation) and Dabb (this volume, chapter 3). Briefly stated: inadequate land surveys and failed procedures for paying off the Nahualense squatters created a no-win situation for the mayors of both towns. The unique events guaranteed the loss of respect and anger Dracoulis and others witnessed.

There is some merit to this proposition. While the relocation of Santa Catarina Ixtahuacán's municipal headquarters was largely successful, certain aspects were indeed accomplished poorly, leading undeniably to increased conflict, anger at the mayors, and loss of respect. We maintain, however, that the botched aspects of the relocation are merely a local condition that amplifies the underlying widespread, systemic reasons generating anger. We adduce three reasons for this position.

First, the escalating expressions of anger and diminishing respect for Santa Catarina's mayors were a process well underway before Hurricane Mitch (October–November 1998), the relocation (January 2000), and the repercussions from the botched measurements (approximately 2003–present). Without doubt, the mishandling of parts of the *traslado* inflamed the underlying process. But these unique events in Nahualá-Ixtahuacán relations do not account for the fact that the process was already under way. The mishandling of the relocation does, however, help us understand the increased amplitude and stridency of anger expressed in these towns from 2000 to 2006.

Second, arguing local conditions unique to Santa Catarina or Nahualá does not account for the widespread occurrence of the phenomenon of increased anger and loss of respect toward mayors. The ethnographic literature alludes to the issue in other towns. For example, we cite Fischer and Benson's (2006:100–102, 107, 133, 135) description of the attack on the mayor of Tecpán in which informants alleged corruption, inequality, and the mayor's (and his bodyguards') distinctive dress in "polished boots, sombreros, crisp Hilfiger jeans, and denim or plaid shirts." Their description confirms our assertion that this anger is new, for, as an informant remarked, Tecpán's mayor was "the first with bodyguards and the first with a burned-out house." One sees new levels of violence and disrespect seething in indigenous mayoral politics in Sololá (T. Smith 2009:24, 26), likewise inflamed by recent injections of money, party politics, and the expectation of corruption.

Third, local land disputes from 1998 to 2006 in one pair of municipios cannot account for the rise in anger against mayors. Land disputes have been a perennial problem in Guatemala for four hundred years, yet, until recently, indigenous communities maintained the integrity of respect for mayoral authority. We must look, then, beyond local historical idiosyncrasies and beyond long-standing national problems to try to get at what has occasioned the breakdown in mayoral respect across Guatemala in the last twenty years.

Prospects for a Return to Respect

With near unanimity, Ixtahuaquenses suggest that less respect exists between the public and the mayor now than two decades ago. While most people think recent local politicians have not earned respect, some feel Ixtahuaquense citizens should still accord the mayor respect because of the office. "The office of mayor was treated as sacred in the past, and it should be treated that way again," one informant suggested. But how might respect for the position of mayor be regained?

> Should Ixtahuaquenses return to consensus decision-making through a council of town elders?
> Should the community stop accepting government money?
> Should the mayor's office be reconnected with cofradía religion?
> Should the level of education be reduced?

Everyone that I asked these questions said no to each.

While consensus is a good goal, direct voting is not bad, if it were not so contentious, they reasoned. Furthermore, many do not trust town elders to lead the town without input from the rest of the community. Those times are past. Ixtahuaquenses did not suggest any changes in the way the mayor should be chosen. We, however, offer some suggestions that might help and might be possible. For example, a runoff election for the top two mayoral candidates—if no one received an absolute majority—might generate more support for the eventual winner. That would, of course, require a second campaign and second election in a patchwork of municipios throughout the country and might be deemed logistically or financially infeasible. It would be an improvement, however, in the sense that a majority of votes more closely approximates consensus than does a plurality of votes.

One might also reduce levels of disrespect and anger directed at the mayor by establishing checks on his power. Right now, the town council is divided by party, with the mayor's party automatically getting most of the council seats. If, by contrast, members of the town council were chosen directly by the people, independent of party, these representatives would feel more beholden to municipal citizens rather than to the political parties or the mayor. Under such a scenario, the mayor would not be able to act without the independently elected council's approval. Thus, the caudillo-like power of the local mayor would weaken, and people might not feel the need to direct anger against the mayor specifically. They would expect less of him and know more about his mayoral activities and therefore might not become so angry. An independent town council with access to records of financial input and outgo might also lessen both real and perceived corruption.

Regarding money, not one person wants to stop the influx of government funds. They do, however, want an end to rampant corruption. Ixtahuaquenses think that decreasing corruption would restore respect between citizens and the mayor. Ixtahuaquense suggestions on how to limit or end corruption include greater transparency, greater oversight, harsher punishment, and simply choosing leaders who are more honest. Since nobody wants to limit the money coming into the municipio, either the people have to be able to monitor the spending of funds or they have to pick leaders who will not abuse the position. The human record provides little basis for optimism regarding the latter option, so improved monitoring seems the order of the day. One man suggested that public committees or commissions could be formed with the sole purpose of monitoring all expenditures on public projects. Furthermore, all of the meetings of oversight committees should be public. This would allow individuals in the community to personally oversee the process whenever they wanted. By increasing transparency, people would have more confidence in local leaders. In the minds of these Ixtahuaquenses, community participation and full transparency would, they hoped, reduce corruption and lessen or end public displays of disrespect.

A few would not mind a reconnection with Catholic religion, but the evangelicals strongly object. According to the evangelicals, it is not *justo* (fair) that the Catholics continue to dominate when they are steadily losing their majority position in town. In turn, the Catholics do not want the office of mayor to have an evangelical connection.

Despite the opinion of many that increased education has led to greater disrespect, nobody proposes limiting education; indeed, most favor increased educational opportunities.

In the end, many different paths might work to reduce the disrespect that emerges from the mayoral legitimacy crisis. Clearly, however, Ixtahuaquenses regard fixing corruption as their top priority. They feel that if corruption disappears, respect for this and future mayors might be restored. That being the case, the community must strive to pick leaders with a record of honesty, and they must create some way to monitor leaders and achieve transparency and accountability so their trust, so easily betrayed, is restored. In a culture that distrusts everyone, honesty without transparency counts for little.

Conclusion

The opening epigraph alludes to a pronounced shift in ideology and practice concerning access to money, authority, and leadership, a shift that erodes respect for the status of mayor. It manifests the change from government by a respected, consensus-oriented council of elders to a more distant elected slate; it alludes to the simultaneous monetization and party factionalization of the community; it attends to corruption, class interest, unleashed individualism, a new caudillismo (wanting "to be in charge"), and lack of respect. Although there are, no doubt, more factors, we have identified and focused on four aspects of social life and structural change that contribute to the rising disrespect expressed toward mayors.

First, the waning of the cofradía has altered the local political structure. The mayor was originally a religious figure in addition to a political one. While the mayor retains the status of community leader, he has lost the status of a leader of the sacred system and of selfless economic service to the traditional Maya-Catholic community. While a *político* today merely has the favor of men, leaders under the old system had the favor of both men and God. By not participating in the cofradía, current mayors have lost the charisma of contact with godly things and thus have lost a fundamental source of respect.

Second, the constitution implemented in 1985 has changed the political attitude of this community. The mayor was previously chosen by consensus of its religiously vetted respected elders; today, the constitution mandates that in elections for mayor, the highest vote-getter wins, with or without a majority. This typically has meant that a candidate with 25 to 35 percent of the vote wins. The implication of that fact, however, is that most in the community actually voted for someone else; this in a culture that prizes unanimity and community cohesion. Before 1985, the mayor did not receive or control any money from the national government; after 1985, the national government gave the mayor of every municipality an allotment of funds to manage, based on the municipio's population. This control over money has led many in the community to believe that most mayors are corrupt and that those who desire to be mayor are only in it for the money. The mayor's office has also acquired additional responsibilities, which has added to the community's expectations. Before the 1985 changes, the mayor did not control significant money and people did not expect much out of him concerning public projects. His real authority pre-1985 was as a justice of the peace. To keep his co-villagers satisfied, he only needed to punish local delinquents, which the whole community supported. Now, the public expects the mayor to carry out many public projects. Hamlets and barrios petition for more projects than the mayor has funds for, although residents think otherwise. Moreover, while the mayor is no longer a justice of the peace, many still expect him to carry out those functions and take care of delinquents, which, legally, he can no longer do. As Bybee (chapter 2) shows, the matter of punishment is in considerable flux. Mayors and their communities are making up new traditions to enable the mayor to exercise the functions of a justice of the peace in a newly emerging domain of indigenous cultural law. Yet according to the supposedly binding 1999 referendum, such Peace Accords–justified law does not exist. This ambiguity and anomaly has caused some to question the purpose of the mayor.

Third, rising levels of education have also altered people's political attitudes. More aware of their rights, they demand more of local leaders. In addition, they can see that other communities with greater access to education—such as Nahualá—prosper relatively more than they do. This has led to frustration and anger.

Finally, the Peace Accords have given the people a newfound feeling of freedom and a sense of rights, which also leads to greater criticism against local leaders. The public now feels they have the right to complain.

One cannot say that any one of these items—the demise of the cofradía, changes in the constitution, improvements in education, the Peace Accords—accounts for the new atmosphere of disrespect. These and other factors intertwine in an assault on the culture of respect generally and on respect toward the mayor specifically. One middle-aged man expressed the linkage of these multiple facets in the genesis of disrespect: "It is the youth who took over in the past. That started this path of anger and disrespect. Before, only the principales were in control of the alcaldía. But now it is the young guys of thirty or forty [years of age] or so. They decided that because they were better educated than their fathers, they should lead the people. And since the system changed to voting—instead of by consensus of the principales—the younger men have led."

I (Dracoulis) asked why the younger generation, which is not really even that young, would show greater disrespect toward the alcaldía now. "One reason is that they are talking with their peers instead of their elders. Another reason is because of greater education, which is good. But it [greater education] has caused a little extreme behavior. Before, people were scared to criticize. Now, because of greater awareness of their rights, they feel they have the right to criticize. And this has now become an extreme form of great criticism. They have just taken it too far."

Formerly, the residents of Santa Catarina Ixtahuacán had little experience with Ladino politics; today, however, extensive ties to Ladino national parties and electoral politics have induced Ixtahuaquenses to consider their local leaders more as Ladino politicians than co-village kin. For example, I asked one young mother why the Mayas seem to pressure their leaders during open meetings. She responded:

> The people are so disillusioned by the políticos that now they just want to demand things. Corrupt leaders promise and promise and never deliver. Maya leaders now are not real Maya leaders—they are only leaders that are Mayan. They are part

> of the Ladino system now. . . . Ladinos began to permit local leaders more power in the last decade. These [local] leaders had never had the power and the money that they have now. Granted, this is still not much money, but it is still more than before. They became part of the Ladino system. The connections with the Ladino system, which is entirely corrupt, corrupted these leaders. This frustrates the people so much, they have lost respect for the same positions that before, had lots of respect.

I asked her why that happened. "Because power corrupts," she responded. "The leaders have more money now, so they are corrupt with it." This Indian woman conflates power, money, and graft, as do most Guatemalans. And if their mayor is just like a Ladino, how can Ixtahuaquenses trust him to look after their indigenous interests? This new system seems much more individualistic and Ladino than the community-oriented standards the elders remember. The candidates try to win for themselves; no consensus exists. Corruption serves to better oneself, not the community. The public's anger expresses a reaction against what they see as illegitimacy and rampant corruption induced by democratic change.

Assuredly, other influences exist as well. Media influence and globalization, among other things, have impacted Guatemala's constitution and its electoral and financial entailments, improved its education system, contributed to the demise of the cofradía, and fostered international pressure to impose the Peace Accords. But the virtual disappearance of cofradía, changes in the constitution, improvements in education, and the opening created by the Peace Accords that nurtured an environment of indigenous rights free of fear have also anchored the processes that drive the new levels of disrespect and anger unleashed at the office of the mayor, processes that evidence radical, subversive cultural transformation that these Mayas could not have predicted and might not have wanted.

We conclude with an observation on governmentality. Foucault's approach to governmentality notes the force and brutality needed to coerce cooperation in feudal and post-feudal emergent European state systems. The question is, how does the modern Western system manage to acquire compliance with minimal state effort? The answer seems to be that democratic voting, perception of rights, and access to market wealth and products creates a multifaceted system of institutions that induce and train up that compliance. In this regard, Foucault's approach is an updated rendering of Gramsci's notion that the cultural institutions of civil society lead to a hegemony that induces compliance.

The case at hand, however, would suggest that Foucault's approach is theoretically culture-bound. In the first place, Guatemala's formerly feudal, and from the 1910s through the 1960s, largely peasant society operated with substantially dispersed governmentality under the cofradía system. Contrary to Foucault's expectation, the addition of democracy, constitutional protection, and market access have *decreased* the level of governmentality rather than increased it. Both internally in the villages and externally with Indian-Ladino relations, Mayas appear to be less peaceful or at ease with the internalization of their self-governing than before. They have lost internalized respect and exhibit much more anger and violence in their relations with authority. Moreover, as we shall see in the next chapter, Mayas are inventing "traditional" institutions of local self-government and bodily inscribed punishment and discipline precisely because state democratic and neoliberal market processes have failed in the task of generating govern-mentalité. The Maya case would lead us to question any simple application of Foucault's notion of the co-evolution of democracy and governmentality. These Guatemalan Mayas have experienced the addition of many institutional layers, institutional regimes that supposedly inscribe upon them and discipline them into the inclination to govern themselves in compliance. Clearly, the process of increasing governmentality does not work in the way Foucault might have predicted, largely because the Maya are culturally and experientially quite different and have chosen to reemphasize a different govern-mentalité, one more compatible with K'iche' culture.

Notes

Fieldwork: 2006

1. Indigenous mayors have served Ixtahuacán for the past thirty years. Prior to that, the record is not clear. Because only males have participated as mayor and other official positions in this community, I use the masculine version of pronouns and other words referring to these positions. For anonymity, I forgo using any names and, on occasion, resort to descriptions that are more general or obscure than the data in my field notes.

2. Speaking from his experience in Santa Eulalia, La Farge (1947) records how the indigenous "Principal del Pueblo"—the prestigious town leader—tends

to be Ladinoized: "In almost every village these individuals are extremely prosperous, fluent in Spanish, and tend to wear the Ladino costume, as a result of which we failed to perceive their importance during our study of Jacaltenango and the neighboring villages. The Principal of Jacaltenango is a mixed-blood who appears more Spanish than Indian, and we did not recognize his Maya character in the important part which he and his house played in the Fiesta. In view of the union of civil and religious power, at the head of which stands the Principal, it is not surprising that these individuals are rich. They may be formally selected, but I received the impression that they obtained their position by a process of common consent, in which force of character, intelligence, pure political ability, and the wealth necessary for maintaining a large and comfortable house and taking an important part in the outlay for dances and other functions are all factors. Such individuals at the present time in Guatemala will show a tendency to Ladinoize themselves in externals. They will wear European clothing, their sons are likely to be literate, while their daughters will be reared rather strictly as Indians" (La Farge 1947:137–38).

3. Such collective action to choose a leader, including the mayor, is well attested in the literature. For example, Oakes conducted fieldwork in Santa Eulalia from 1945 through 1947. She reports that following the 1944 transformation whereby mayors were to be elected, instead of Ladino *intendentes* appointed by the central government, as occurred under Ubico, "All civil officials (other than those appointed) are elected for a year. The *principales*, the Chimán Nan [chief ritual officer] and the Alcalde Rezador—all religious dignitaries—decide who is to be put up for election except for the posts of *secretario* and *tesorero*" (Oakes 1951:35; brackets added). This system continues into the present as a means for choosing leaders for a wide variety of civic duties.4. The notion of fleeing the burden of office, and of capturing officeholders both in the ritual hierarchy and in civic government positions is well documented (Cancian 1965; Wagley 1949). The Spanish word *cargo* implies a heavy load, as does the root K'iche' word that refers to an office held: *eqa'n* (*carga*, burden); *-eqele'n* (*oficio*, municipal office).

5. *Pueblo* refers to a town but also, with equal force, the people of a particular town, and generically, people. Ixtahuaquenses clearly use the term in the sense of "the people of Ixtahuacán." To refer to the "people of Ixtahuacán" as the Ixtahuaquenses do, I use the following terms interchangeably: *pueblo*, "the people," "the public," "the townspeople," and "Ixtahuaquenses."

6. That is, to sell its use rights. For practical purposes, such a transaction between two members of the community constitutes a sale.

7. I did not record any instances of women insulting the mayor. However, I suspect more attention needs to be paid to this issue of gender in the mayor's office. In the cases I observed, men represented the family's issues and hence did the talking and the insulting, if any.

8. For a fuller record of the fission and resettlement of Santa Catarina Ixtahuacán, see Hawkins and Adams (in preparation).

9. Chance and Taylor (1985) note that the cofradía must be understood in an ever-shifting historical context shaped by larger political-economic forces. Thus, the "cargo system," as characterized by DeWalt (1975) and many others, is not a timeless institution traceable to pre-conquest times, but rather a form of the cofradía system created under conditions of aggressively implemented liberal reforms, most notably the expropriation of Indian lands.

10. See Clay Larson (in review) for details on the operation and demise of the cofradía system in pre-resettlement Santa Catarina Ixtahuacán.

11. In 1996, Hawkins witnessed what we think was the last indigenous performance of the last remaining *cofradía* (of five). That celebration took place because it had funding from a government agency that fostered indigenous culture under the emerging terms of the Peace Accords. By 1996, the cofradía system in Ixtahuacán was effectively moribund.

12. *Pasados* were those elders who had completed a cargo career culminating in either funding a cofradía or serving in a high administrative office.

13. Information in this section obtained from *Diario de Centro América* 1985, Constitución Política de la República de Guatemala.

14. Not until 1994 did Guatemalans reconcile the presidential election with the two-and-a-half- or five-year cycle of the municipalities so that both presidential and municipal elections occurred on the same date in a four-year cycle (Seminario Permanente sobre el Rol de los Partidos Políticos [21st] 2005:42).

15. Mendelson (1965:44) notes explicitly the mayor's justice of the peace functions in Santiago Atitlán of 1952.

16. For a fuller record of Hurricane Mitch and its aftermath in Santa Catarina Ixtahuacán and Nahualá, see Hawkins and Adams, in preparation.

17. In the decade from 1996 to the present, mayors and citizens have struggled mightily—or groped anxiously—to find ways to reconstruct the mayor's legal basis of judicial authority and appropriate methods for implementing it.

18. Since 2006, migration patterns may have changed due to increased dangers in transit and decreased economic opportunity in the United States.

19. The dissipation of army presence was a consequence of the Peace Accords, international pressure, and international monitoring called for in the Peace Accords.

CHAPTER 2

"Saved from Being Lynched"

Reinvention of Customary Law in Nahualá

Eric Ruiz Bybee, John P. Hawkins, James H. McDonald, and Walter Randolph Adams

January 9, 1997, began like any other Thursday in Nahualá, with thousands of people from surrounding highland communities filling its streets to buy and sell at the town's biweekly market. Though not as large as the Sunday market, Thursday's market contains all of the local colors, smells, and sounds that one would expect from a typical Maya market: women in colorful hand-brocaded *trajes* milling about to resupply the family larder and men mostly in plain-colored, store-bought pants and shirts; the odors of dried fish mingling with those of fresh fruit for sale and vegetable rinds rotting in the sun; and vendors of goods, medicines, and religion shouting to advertise their wares over the evangelical and pop music blasting from sales stands.

Near the end of the day, a series of memorable events occurred. Two women from nearby Totonicapán, on their way home from market, were robbed and wounded by two Nahualense youths with a history of violence. An angry mob soon formed, located the youths, and beat them to death in the town plaza.

Almost ten years later, on Wednesday, June 14, 2006, a similar event took place. A few days prior, three youths who also had a history of delinquency had robbed a street vendor and badly wounded him. As before, members of the community located them and brought them to the plaza to be judged before the community. By the time the youths were delivered to the mayor at midday, perhaps a thousand Nahualenses, many of whom were present at the deaths of the first two, filled the plaza. Given such similar circumstances, one might expect a crowd that included some of the same members and of similar ethnic composition to act the same as the previous crowd, but it did not. Instead, the three delinquents were made to kneel for an hour and a half on rocks spread out on the tiled floor of the balcony-corridor that fronts the municipal offices and overlooks the town plaza, fully visible to anyone standing in it. Municipal leaders gave each youth being punished a lighted candle to hold while they knelt on the rocks. Once they confessed their gang affiliation and showed sufficient remorse, they were released.

These two occurrences illustrate the central question I (Bybee) explored during my study in Nahualá: how do two events that occurred under such similar circumstances result in such drastically different courses of action? Answering that question necessitated exploring the connections between two related phenomena: one, the practice of "traditional" punishment in the community; and two, the communal vengeance that often results in lynching. Ethnographic data reveal that the primary causes of lynching in Nahualá were, on the one hand, a lack of access to the justice system and distrust of its efficacy, and on the other, the erosion of indigenous custom as a legitimate authority and system of control. The two outcomes differed because the members of the community were responding to and recalibrating the relation between the community's collective violence and the criminality and cultural breakdown that trigger this violence. They effected the change by reinvesting power in the town leaders (the mayor and town council in lieu of the once dominant principales), by inventing appropriate forms of local communal justice and labeling them as "traditional," and by reestablishing a codified system of public "indigenous" local punishments. To understand this transformation in detail, I begin with a general description of lynching in Guatemala and proceed to untangle its manifestations in the structural and cultural context of Nahualá.

Lynching in Guatemala

According to a United Nations study, between 1996 and 2002, there were 421 reported lynchings in Guatemala involving 817 victims, of whom 215 died (MINUGUA 2000, 2002). Handy provides a useful outline of the way these acts of collective violence typically unfold in Guatemala:

> A *linchamiento* often takes place spontaneously after someone is caught in the prosecution of a crime or believed to have been

> caught in such an act. A "mob" quickly gathers. While some mobs of more than 1,000 people have been reported, usually the instigators and perpetrators of the act are much fewer in number. Usually those reported to have been instigators of the crimes were adult males over the age of 35. Victims tended to be beaten after being tied up. In cases resulting in death, victims were occasionally hanged, but more frequently they were beaten or stoned to death and often burned. Victims varied, but there appear to have been two distinct types: known criminals or troublemakers in the community or outsiders suspected of crimes. In the case of known criminals or criminal gangs, the *linchamientos* were often spontaneous, but occurred after significant planning by a significant number of the people in the community. (Handy 2004:5)

As Handy indicates, details like the number of those involved and means of inflicting death can vary greatly. For the purpose of this study, I take lynching to be an extrajudicial process whereby a group of people severely brutalizes or executes one or various victims accused of a crime or act that has upset the community.

As academics and organizations have attempted to explain this growing phenomenon in Guatemala and elsewhere in Latin America, theories regarding the causes of lynchings have proliferated. The aforementioned UN study found a correlation between the number of violent incidents a region suffered during the war, its relative poverty index, and the number of post-conflict lynchings that occurred there. Handy (2004:1) indicates that the causes lie in "a collapsing peasant economy, insecurity of all sorts, and an unraveling of the social fabric in rural communities through the militarization of rural Guatemala," as well as the imposition of an "illegitimate" state legal system. Burrell (2009, 2010) similarly finds the rise in adult anxiety over gang violence and the increasing tendency of youths in Todos Santos to challenge local custom and authority to be related to structural transformations undermining local authority systems, though the gang members decidedly were not drawn from the poor. A study conducted by a Guatemalan judge emphasizes the role of the armed conflict and specifically the way that the army, the insurgents, and the civil self-defense patrols functioned as "schools of dehumanization" and became the "seed" of post-conflict communal violence (Fernández 2004:4).[1] Another study suggests that lynching is "an attempt by embattled communities to reassert their autonomy . . . [and] to reassert themselves collectively as agents rather than victims." (Godoy 2004:1).

As helpful as these and other interdisciplinary studies (e.g., R. Adams and Bastos 2003; Gutiérrez and Kobrak 2001; Torres-Rivas 2003) are in illustrating facets of the lynching problem at a macro level, the study whose general findings best correlate with the ethnographic situation in Nahualá is that of Mendoza (2004). In an extensive statistical analysis, Mendoza found that lynchings did not correlate significantly with poverty in a region or with the level of violence experienced in an area during the war. Rather, Mendoza found that the number of courthouses per hundred thousand inhabitants correlated inversely with the number of lynchings in a given area and that the percentage of indigenous people in an area correlated directly with the number of lynchings.

Lynching in Nahualá: An Issue of Access and Culture

My study largely substantiates Mendoza. I found lynching, lack of access to effective national justice, and indigenous identity to be closely interrelated. I shall first show how and why lynching flourishes when access to justice seems thwarted. Then I will show how access to justice articulates with indigenous cultural issues to either dampen or amplify the forces that lead to lynching.

Access to Justice

Interviews and survey data from Nahualá reveal a relationship between attitudes toward lynching and access to judicial resources. In the survey, for example, more than 90 percent of Nahualense respondents characterized the police, justice of the peace, and mayor as "corrupt" or "very corrupt," and more than 80 percent considered it "difficult" or "very difficult" to get help from them. More than 60 percent of the respondents indicated that the police, justice of the peace, and mayor were "ineffective" at doing their jobs.

The case of María helps us understand and vivifies the ineffectiveness that many experience in the justice system. María, a long-term but non-native-born resident of Nahualá, became involved in a land dispute when her neighbor began extending part of his house onto her property. What seems like a relatively simple legal issue is anything but in the context of highland Guatemala. At the time she was interviewed, María had spent more than six months meeting with the mayor, city council, and justice of the peace, and visiting various courts with a lawyer. When asked about the legal process, she expressed amazement at how slow and convoluted it was and said she would consider herself a "lucky woman" if the issue were resolved within a year.

María's tale of getting lost in Guatemala's confusing, lengthy legal process is not unique. What *is* unique about this story is that María is actually an American who has lived in Nahualá for twenty-two years, is fluent in English and Spanish, and possesses an advanced degree from the University of California, Berkeley. She reflected on what she had learned from the experience: "I'm trying to figure this out the way the ordinary folks do it to see if it can be done, and I'm not sure that it can be . . . I don't know how the ordinary person could ever get this solved . . . I mean, I can read and write and *I* can't get anywhere. Even with all of my highfalutin education—and I can read and write and I speak Spanish—I don't know how the ordinary poor folks who only speak K'iche' or Kaqchikel or whatever, who have this same problem, how in the heck they would get anything solved, what they would do, where they would go, anything. . . ." Her voice trailed off in exasperated frustration.

María's experience typifies the lengths to which even a highly educated person must go to get anything done in the Guatemalan legal system. For an indigenous person in Nahualá who doesn't have such resources, it isn't difficult to see how taking the law into one's own hands, individually or collectively, would seem like the only option. Indeed, 67 percent of respondents "agreed" or "strongly agreed" with the statement, "Lynching occurs when people get frustrated with the justice system," and 71 percent of respondents agreed with the statement, "People don't commit as many crimes because they fear getting lynched."

The first question explicitly probes for connections between the perception of an unresponsive judicial process and lynching. The second question suggests a tacit acceptance of the practice of lynching because these Mayas believe the threat of lynching lowers crime and remedies the inefficiency and corruption in the justice system—for they disregard as a technicality the crimes committed by the lynch mob. Indeed,

61 percent of respondents agreed that "Maya justice works better than state justice," and 55 percent agreed that "It would be better if the state didn't get involved in Maya conflicts."[2] Another 54 percent asserted that "State justice doesn't belong here." Even though some of these questions do not specifically mention lynching, they all make reference to the state system's inability to adequately address problems in Maya communities.

If experiences like María's were confined to one or two towns in Guatemala, perhaps extrajudicial means of seeking justice would not be as common, but, unfortunately, multiple studies have shown that the problem of access is widespread. A USAID study conducted in Guatemala City, using information from 1999 and studying only the office in Guatemala City, "one of the best" of Guatemala's 35 offices of prosecution, established that 450 cases per day were distributed to the 35 working prosecutor teams in the Guatemala City office, and that each team filed, on average, less than one case per month in court. In this one office, the case load accumulated at a rate of 90,000 cases a year (Hendrix 2000:837; 2002:16). From that total, 35,000 were rejected outright by a clerk for lack of merit (though no official criteria exist for such a determination), and another 30,000 were not pursued because the aggressor was not clearly identified in the documents. Of the 30,000 cases that remained, 2,800 were investigated, and in the three and a half months that the study lasted, only 328 actually went to trial. Of the cases that did go to trial, "no court was able" to bring to conclusion "even 6 percent of its already limited case load" (Hendrix 2002:16). In the USAID sample, zero percent made it into court.

Most complaints were dropped for various reasons. In many instances, the plaintiffs withdrew because of threats or because they grew tired of the lengthy court process. Researchers concluded that out of the 90,000 cases brought before the Public Ministry in the nation's capital each year, "actual success in prosecution in statistical terms for Guatemala City approaches zero," a result they called "catastrophic" (Hendrix 2002:16; 2003:837–38). The consequences, however, are ominous. "Criminals know there is little chance they will be found guilty in any court, and this knowledge encourages bold and outrageous conduct" (Hendrix 2002:17). Without knowing the cascade of exact figures, law-abiding Nahualenses, too, perceive this national judicial failure and react accordingly. Little wonder Indians found no use for the Ladino-operated legal system.

In addition to the incredibly ineffective judicial services manifested in Guatemala City, the scarcity of judicial resources in rural areas further marginalizes the country's indigenous population. According to a diagnostic study by the World Bank and Guatemala's Organismo Judicial (Judicial Branch) conducted prior to the start of a World Bank–financed judicial modernization program, about 30 percent of the country had absolutely no judicial branch presence (that is, no courthouse or justice of the peace). All of the civil, family, and labor courts were located in the capital (leaving 22 department capitals without such services). Criminal courts were more widespread, but 80 percent of criminal court judges did not have adequate space to hold hearings. This absence of courts, along with other organizational shortcomings of the judicial branch, led the researchers to conclude that Guatemala's justice system "did not have the capability to provide such basic judicial guarantees as equality under the law, effective dispute resolution, or access to services for the vast majority of the population" (Malik 2005:2).

Subsequent to the study, the World Bank program has done much to modernize the judiciary and improve its image in many parts of the country, including the initiation of community outreach programs, mediation centers, and mobile courts. Many in Nahualá, however, feel that the justice system is often corrupt and still too complicated and ineffective for anyone to get anything done through it.

In sum, even though it was a sensitive and somewhat abstract subject to address, published statistics, data from my survey, and interviews from this study triangulate to confirm a connection between national judicial ineffectiveness and local indigenous lynchings. The next section addresses the connection between lynching and indigenous identity.

Perceptions of Lynching and Identity

For a variety of reasons, it was difficult ethnographically to document Mendoza's statistical connection between being "Maya" (or partly Maya) and the practice of lynching. First, Nahualenses would understandably rather not admit a connection that reflected badly on their culture. Second, much of the academic literature on Guatemalan Indians seems to sidestep their participation in lynchings, presumably because of a combination of romanticization coupled with a strong sense of protective advocacy.

Mendoza (2004, 2006) found that whether or not someone is lynched in an area correlates more (by as much as five times) with its percentage of indigenous population than its level of poverty, past human right violations, and number of courthouses. Survey data collected in Nahualá for this study support the connection between indigenous areas and lynching. While 53 percent of respondents "agreed" or "strongly agreed" with the statement, "People from Guatemala lynch criminals," 58 percent agreed with the statement, "People from the department of Sololá lynch criminals," and 63 percent agreed with the statement, "People from Nahualá lynch criminals." The responses show that a higher number of Nahualenses agree with the statements that more closely pinpoint Nahualá, possibly because this place is known to be thoroughly Indian. Perhaps this indicates that Nahualenses see the lynching that occurred there as something that defines where they live or the people who live there; lynching is closely associated with and perhaps becoming iconic of Nahualá.

Regarding lynching and identity, 68 percent of respondents agreed with the statement, "Indigenous people lynch criminals" and 64 percent agreed with the statement, "Maya people lynch criminals." By contrast, 71 percent of respondents indicated that they "disagreed" or "strongly disagreed" with the statement, "Ladinos lynch criminals." A smaller percentage, 32 percent, agreed with the statement, "Lynching comes from Maya custom," which perhaps suggests a recognition that lynching is a modern response to the failed state in these recent decades of being drawn into globalized processes. In any event, these responses, overall, indicate a clear connection in the Nahualense mind between Maya identity and the practice of lynching. The perception that lynching is not associated with Ladinos further reinforces that connection.

On a more ethnographic note, a former mayor of Nahualá made a revealing comment. He described how, before the 1997 lynching, residents sensed that the next serious crime would trigger a lynching. "Everyone in the community knew that the next person to get caught stealing or committing a crime would be lynched. Delinquency was so bad in those days and people were tired of it . . . even though nobody said it, everybody knew that someone would be lynched because the people here felt it was the only thing we could do." This comment approximates Handy's remarks, quoted above, that lynchings often entail significant premeditation, if not actual pre-planning. When asked why lynching seemed like the only option, this former mayor said it was because those in Nahualá saw lynchings happen in other Maya communities and the consensus was that it would help lower crime. Fischer (2001:15) describes such collective consensus as "cultural logic": "Cultural logics are . . . dynamic, shared predispositions that inform behavior and thought. . . . Change is an integral part of culture, but such change must be reconciled with preexisting cognitive schemas in a manner that allows for an intersubjective sense of cultural continuity, even—perhaps especially—in the face of dramatic externally induced modification."

The change in the collective "cultural logic" of Nahualá described by the former mayor occurred in response to the "dramatic externally induced modification" of post-conflict lawlessness in the community. As Fischer indicates, these changes were "reconciled with preexisting cognitive schemas" by the collective recognition—from newspapers, radio reports, family members in other communities, indigenous leadership conferences, and even television and cable hookups—that lynching had occurred in other Maya communities and might therefore be a justifiable part of their own. However, although sufficient consensus in expectations existed for the Nahualá lynching to occur, not all Nahualenses agreed to or even knew what was happening that fateful Thursday evening in 1997.

EXAMINING THE 1997 LYNCHING AND ITS AFTERMATH

Having laid out the statistical connections and cultural logic of lynchings, I can now describe in detail the 1997 lynching and its indelible aftermath, for this aftermath altered the course of subsequent lynchings.

The 1997 Lynching

Although the 1997 lynching in Nahualá appears to accord in many respects with the aforementioned outline given by Handy, it differs in some important ways. Considering that the two young men had a history of delinquency in the community, that announcements were made over the radio, and that women were deliberately kept out of the plaza that evening, one concludes that the act was not totally spontaneous but involved premeditation and planning, as Handy suggests. However, simply because the punishment was premeditated does not mean everyone agreed about what it should be or its severity. When it became apparent that the boys' lives were in danger, a few objected and tried to intervene. One of those who tried to stop the lynching was the parish secretary of the local Catholic church, an older man respected by many in the community. Speaking of the mob, he recalled that, "when I tried to stop them, to reason with them, they got very angry with me. They wouldn't listen to me and told me that if I tried to stop them they would lynch me, too." Nahualá's police force was overwhelmed, and officers were called in from the department capital of Sololá, but they also decided not to intervene when they learned that the crowd they would be facing numbered in the thousands.

Although a large crowd had gathered, only a few individuals actually carried out the lynching. Eyewitness accounts give the sense that the majority of the spectators who went to the plaza probably had only a vague idea of what was going to occur and showed up not out of a desire for vengeance, but out of curiosity. Indeed, the idea that many fathers brought their young sons to see what was going on seems contrary to the image of an unruly, bloodthirsty crowd. No one will ever know how many in the crowd actually knew what would happen and objected (vocally or not) to what was occurring when they finally understood.

The 1997 Aftermath

When asked today about their feelings about the 1997 lynching, most describe a combination of shock and disbelief at what they had just witnessed and fear of its repercussions. Because the police did not come into the community until morning, the families of the slain boys could only cover the bodies and leave them lying in the plaza all night. In the days and weeks that followed, people in the community quietly debated among themselves whether or not the lynching was correct and postulated about its future effect on the community. While pastors denounced the act in their Sunday sermons, vendors selling at the street market going on outside said the boys deserved what they got. Perhaps the only people who were silent on the matter were the families of the victims, who kept quiet for fear more communal violence might be directed toward them.

When the Public Ministry from Sololá started to investigate the incident, it became apparent that what the prosecutors most wanted were culprits on whom to squarely pin the blame, regardless of whether there was solid evidence. Once the families of the lynched youths felt they had the prosecutors' support, it did not take long for accusations to begin in the months that followed. In what can perhaps best be described as a witch hunt, the fathers of both boys began to accuse and blackmail scores of individuals in the community in what some feel was an attempt to exact revenge and get rich in the process. According to one individual who was initially accused, the price for clearing one's name was 30,000 quetzales (about US$4,000), which some paid and others refused to. Unfortunately, and not surprisingly, we have no reliable information on whether any of the payments for exoneration made to the parents flowed through to any of the state judicial participants to further amplify the reach and power of the extortions. Informants also indicated that the fathers of the boys took suggestions from other members of the community about whom to accuse and blackmail. Some made accusations to avenge other wrongs: among the revenge cases, one man currently incarcerated for his supposed involvement in the lynching was accused by an employee he had fired. Another was accused by a jealous mistress.

At one point, the conflict in the community over the accusations became so intense that the first act of the incoming mayor in 1998 was to call a meeting with the parents of the boys and the accused (who by that time numbered twenty-eight) in an attempt to resolve the issue. The meeting failed because the accusing fathers did not show up and many of those whom they accused were either too afraid of capture to present themselves or did not take the charges seriously. Of all of the accused who went to trial, eight men were convicted and given fifty-year sentences, even though everyone in the community asserts that they were innocent.

A short while after the convictions, one of the accusing fathers, who was reportedly more vocal in his accusations and vicious in his blackmailing, was tortured and decapitated with his own chainsaw while in the mountains cutting wood. Since that time, no one else has been accused, blackmailed, or convicted for their involvement in the original lynching.

Seven years later, eight convicted men are still serving their sentences in the prison located on the outskirts of Quetzaltenango. Life is difficult for these prisoners. Some have had to learn new trades to help supplement the meager incomes of their now impoverished families. One man who now works in prison as a tailor indicated that the most difficult part was having his family suffer for a crime that he did not commit. Indeed, all of the men convicted in connection with the lynching emphatically denied any connection to it; many indicated that they were not even in the community when it happened.

In the decade since the lynching of the two youths, two things have become apparent. First, the lynching left scars on minds young and old that would be felt for years to come. One resident who was ten at the time described hiding in his room afterward and crying in shock and fear. The impression left on his mind was so indelible that, ten years after, when he heard of the aforementioned punishment of the three gang members, he was afraid to attend because he "didn't want to see someone else sprawled out, dead." Second, residents began to realize that any linchamiento that the Nahualenses committed in the name of preserving peace might easily lead to an aftermath of worse conflict.

Indeed, the conflicts, accusations, and legal interventions that tore Nahualá apart following the lynching help explain why the community wanted to avoid more communal violence and why they ultimately decided to initiate "customary" punishments in the community, punishments that were nonlethal but officially administered. They believed themselves protected by the Peace Accords injunctions to respect indigenous culture. Thus, even though the castigations in some ways were brand new, they were instituted under the cover of "traditional" Indian punishments. In order to understand the significance of this decision, we need some understanding of the way customary law works in Guatemala.

The Legal Basis of Maya Customary Law in Guatemala

In the absence of a fully functioning state system, Maya customary law may be the only recourse for indigenous people seeking justice. According to a study conducted by the Defensoría Maya (Maya Defense League), 98 percent of the legal problems in indigenous communities are solved through traditional means (Seijo 2006). How is customary, or traditional, law to be defined? Moore (1985:43) understands customary law as "a framework of organizations, relationships, and cultural ideas, a mix of principles, guidelines, rules of preference, and rules of prescription, together with conceptions of morality and causality, all of them completely intertwined in a web of ordinary activities. It is not a special domain of knowledge or practice, but a body of ideas known to all and used by all." By this definition, customary law has been the *de facto* form of governance in Maya communities since the time of the conquest. However, only since 1996 has "indigenous traditional law" started to be recognized as *de jure* and given the same legitimacy as the overarching state system.

The legal basis for the legitimacy of Maya customary law originates in the Agreement on Identity and Rights of Indigenous Peoples, part of the 1996 Peace Accords. After recognizing the essential role of indigenous people and their marginalization by the state, the document pledges that the government will develop:

> rules of law which would recognize the right of the indigenous communities to manage their own internal affairs in accordance with their customary norms, provided that the latter are not incompatible with the fundamental rights defined by the national legal system or with internationally recognized human rights. (1996 Peace Accords, Section IV, E)

The mandate that the state recognize indigenous "customary norms" reaffirms and gives international moral authority to Article 66 of the 1985 Constitution, which obligates the state to "recognize, respect, and promote the lifestyle, customs, traditions, and form of social organization" of indigenous communities as well as "men's and women's use of indigenous clothing, languages, and dialects" (*Diario de Centro América* 1985).

The legality of customary law was again upheld in 2005, when a man who was given a customary punishment for stealing a truck was then taken and tried according to state law and given a sentence of six years in prison. On appeal, the Guatemalan Supreme Court overruled the lower court's decision and upheld the legitimacy of the traditional punishment, stating that the man could not be tried twice for the same crime (Seijo 2006).

State recognition of indigenous culture has helped to legitimize Maya customary law. At the same time, the very processes of recognizing, legitimating, and codifying customary law make it, to a degree, non-customary because it no longer reflects Moore's definition of being an undifferentiated and nonspecialized thought system embedded in cultural practice. In the Mayas' case a processual movement is seen from customary law as felt traditional practice to customary law as a codified local invention. Through the protections of the 1996 Peace Accords, indigenous communities now have the capacity to invoke law by local referendum and local edict and have it receive court protection. For the first time in decades, the process has given the function of justice of the peace back to the mayor and to the indigenous community council members who advise him.

Nevertheless, in spite of local codification and state recognition, the present system retains some of Moore's definition of customary law in that it is embedded in everything—precisely because it is not yet fully invented or codified. Indeed, a lack of knowledge regarding what customary law is, what they can invent, and the extent to which it can be applied has been a difficult issue for many Maya communities. National organizations like the Defensoría Maya have been created to promote the use of customary law and the principles on which it is based. According to a Peace Ministry (SEPAZ) official interviewed by *Prensa Libre*: "Indigenous law has a framework of morals and values. It stems from respect for the wisdom of older people and tries to make up for those who've committed errors in their daily lives. . . . It's a way of practicing community service, repairing the damage one has committed, asking for forgiveness and offering reconciliation." An official of the Defensoría Maya added: "Also, it's an oral process, because words have the value of commitment. . . . The whole community can participate, including kids, so they learn not to commit the same errors. . . . It teaches us to resolve daily conflicts though dialogue" (Blas 2006).

In theory, indigenous customary law—whether descended from long tradition or newly invented—is consistent with the root cultural principles and structural experiences of a people. Yet it is also modified by context. Hence, different communities have different reasons for using or creating different forms of customary law. In the vast majority of cases, adapting and inventing customary law is simply the only alternative to a state system that many Mayas do not understand or feel works for them. In the Nahualá case, the return to so-called "customary" public punishment represents the Nahualense attempt at avoiding tragedies like the 1997 lynching and its divisive aftermath.

Customary Law and Public Punishment in Nahualá

The process by which the Nahualenses actively reconstructed their understanding of crime and traditional punishment was complex. Forces both external and internal to the community drove this process. I start with a contextualizing incident and proceed to analyze key vectors of political-legal reinvention.

Preliminary Incidents in 2005

In 2005, two incidents occurred in Nahualá that caused the town leadership to reexamine the issue of collective violence and how to deal with it in their community. Early in the year, two men believed to be drug traffickers were caught by the crowd and turned over to the police. After the officers released one of them, the crowd became irate, and according to one eyewitness, they began "looking for gasoline to lynch" the other, threatening the police officers as well. In the end, police reinforcements arrived with riot gear and tear gas to control the crowd. The "drug trafficker" escaped the lynch mob, but the group was so incensed that they burned his reportedly expensive car and also destroyed a police patrol car before they dispersed, mollified.

A few months later, another near-lynching occurred when two gang members came down from Quetzaltenango to cause trouble with members of a rival gang that lived in Nahualá. A fight broke out between the two groups on the town soccer field after a game, and the gang members were caught by the public and brought to the plaza to be punished. After beating and humiliating them for about an hour, the crowd began to debate what their official punishment should be. According to one witness, the gang members were standing in the town plaza in front of the municipal building, and the crowd that had gathered was shouting different ideas for punishing them. Some wanted to whip them, others wanted them to kneel on rocks, others wanted to beat them, and some wanted to lynch them. Juan Tzep, a respected *principal* in the community, and another of the community elders, reminded the crowd about the consequences of the first lynching in the community. In the end, they decided that a suitable punishment would be to strip the gang members down and throw water on them because it was night-time and very cold outside. After the public punishment, the gang members were then turned over to the police. The crowd, appeased by the punishment, went home.

Seeing how the public mob was appeased by the public punishment and how potential lynchings had been averted, the town's principales started working with the municipal corporation (in effect, the city council) and the mayor to increase security and formalize the penalty process. To accomplish those goals, the town leaders formed security committees in each neighborhood of Nahualá's urban center and surrounding hamlets. The committees were made up of people chosen and approved by a majority vote of those citizens present at each local community meeting. The role of the committees is still being defined in the community, but their job is basically to meet regularly to discuss the security needs of their part of the community and act accordingly. Those actions can range from having townspeople patrol the streets and rural paths at night (randomly throughout the year and especially during festival time) to supervising the public punishment of delinquents.

Reinvesting Power

One important and perhaps unexpected result of the process of forming effective security committees and reestablishing "traditional" punishment is that the town elders—the principales and other older men—have regained some of the power they had lost over the years. The term *principal* is a title given to older men in the community who have previously served either as mayor or in the municipal corporation and who function as informal advisors to the town leadership. The term has a decidedly political connotation compared with the older form of recruiting principales via the civil-religious cofradía hierarchy.[3] Older men in the community who are not principales also wield some influence, especially those who have served in the cofradías. The term "elder" will be used here to refer to both groups.

As Dracoulis has shown (see chapter 1), many factors contributed to a general decline in power among the elders in Maya towns, three of which pertain here. First, because the cofradías had functioned as a system of governance in communities like Nahualá, their breakdown impacted the power of the elders who had derived prestige from the system. Second, Guatemala's thirty-six-year civil war curtailed many forms of customary law, and by extension, the power of the elders who had been charged with administering the law. Third, the reforms in the 1985 Constitution limited the power of the principales because they no longer functioned as representatives of the community in electing the mayor. As Burrell (2009, 2010), J. Edvalson (chapter 6), and Call (chapter 7) show, these and other limits on the power of the elders, combined with failed power and authority in state institutions (especially the judiciary and security agencies), created an ambiguous space where no one was empowered to enforce community laws and norms.

In places like Nahualá, that space was filled by angry mobs who took the law into their own hands and committed acts of communal violence in the name of protection. However, since the current security committees are elected by majority vote, they are usually made up of town elders who have earned trust and respect. One security committee of more than seventy members, for example, included only a handful of young men and one woman—the rest were older men or principales. Thus, in Nahualá, power has again been vested in the hands of the elders, and the authority vacuum has been at least partially filled through the security committees operating under mayoral authority. In addition to removing power from the would-be lynch mobs, the committees also give Nahualenses a swift and effective alternative to the almost nonfunctioning state system. We note the irony that Nahualenses are thereby using models imposed on them by the military during the 1980s stages of the civil war to protect themselves from the effects of state ineffectiveness.

Reinterpreting Punishment

In order for the system of punishment to be acceptable to a town that had not seen earlier forms of customary public punishment for four or five decades, leaders and citizens had to reinterpret "tradition" into something relevant to present needs. When asked whether the aforementioned throwing of water on the offending gang members was "traditional indigenous custom," one informant replied that it was not, and that they did it because they "thought it would be a good idea because it was cold outside." This occurrence illustrates what Moore (1985:43, 51, 91, cited in Handy 2004:554) says of customary law: "custom is not synonymous with tradition but always in a state of flux, while maintaining its connection to the past." Nahualenses had to go one step further. They not only had to reinterpret what was traditional, they had to determine what was acceptable to the public, both local and national, and label that as traditional.[4] Yet the punishment would clearly be outside of national Ladino concepts of punishment.

The types of punishment currently being meted out as "traditional" are not like the types enacted fifty years before, as described by the elders in the community. Before the civil war, offenders were punished by being made to work on the construction of the church or through providing some type of community service. If any physical punishment had been applied, it usually would have consisted of whipping with tree branches or thorny plant stems. When asked why such earlier punishments were stopped, one former mayor indicated that human rights organizations had deemed community service a violation of the people's rights. Another of the principales said the new practice of kneeling on rocks was the punishment of choice because it seemed the most effective way to appease the public without being too harsh. Prior to the security committees, townspeople had only a vague idea of what traditional public punishments were and of their Peace-Accords–protected right to them. The resumption of customary law in their community has filled the "traditional" category with new practices deemed Indian-like, and has educated Nahualenses regarding both the practices and their rights. In short, to cope with their problems, Nahualenses are now, per Hobsbawm (1983), inventing traditions.[5]

Reinventing Customary Law

How does the invention of tradition or the reinvention of customary law occur? Guatemala's long civil war forced community leaders to suspend customary forms of justice. Indeed, the army and its allied institutions tried seriously to eradicate much of indigenous culture and not just its forms of local justice. Communities were erased, local leaders kidnapped and executed, indigenous cultural specialists persecuted, and forms of collective leadership and decision-making made lethal. Fear pervaded Indian communities as a "way of life" that forced cultural change (Green 1999). Whole communities were forced to drop their customary practices—economic, social, political, and religious—and march to the cultural clock of militarized communities called *polos de desarrollo*—concentration camps or reeducation camps, as it were. Indians acquiesced because they feared that the "inverse image" that Ladinos held of Indians might be equated with subversiveness (Hawkins 1984). Moreover, in the late Cold War idiom of anti-communist phobia, rebel groups indeed tried to recruit Indians (Stoll 1993). Today, more than a quarter century after the high point of the conflict, Nahualá's leaders find it difficult to reinitiate tradition. In fact, they must invent tradition because even the oldest principales and members of the security committee indicated that if they had even seen a traditional punishment carried out in their childhood, they only vaguely remembered it.

Several near lynchings had occurred previously and since, among them one that occurred in 1995 (detailed in Morgan 2005). But the public punishment of June 2006, authorized by the mayor, was literally—as far as any informants could specify—the first time such an event had occurred in Nahualá in almost fifty years. Moreover, from that date through the remaining two months that I spent in the community, leaders and townspeople mobilized seven times and meted out "customary punishments" to two thieves, three gang members, three runaway girls, twenty to thirty of the town's drunks, and two other groups of women and men for fighting and "kidnapping."

In Nahualá today, customary punishments generally occur in two parts—the first private and the other public. They follow a set pattern. Once the presumed culprit is captured—whether by deliberate rural mobilization, by more spontaneous mob action, or by officials designated to make an apprehension—community leaders instigate the private part of the process: the accused and their families meet with the rural hamlet or urban *cantón* security committee, principales, and members of the municipal corporation, who question the accused in a fact-finding session directed by the mayor.

During the private phase of interrogation, if those in charge find the accused innocent or their transgressions of little consequence, they are free to go. If they admit to minor wrongdoings, they are given the option of nonpublic and noncorporal punishment, such as a fine. However, if they are unwilling to admit to their crime, or they have committed something more serious, or they are repeat offenders, then the accused go through the second part of the process: the public punishment (fig. 2.1).

Public punishments now (in 2006) typically occur at midday on the balcony of the municipality that faces the town plaza, a layered quasi-amphitheater where Nahualenses gather to watch.[6] First, the mayor explains to the crowd the circumstances of the offense. Then, a *principal* or two will speak, giving counsel to the crowd and trying once again to get the offending parties to confess or renounce a specific crime or type of behavior. The accused are made to kneel on rocks or on the tiled balcony floor for a specified amount of time (usually one to four hours). During this time, those kneeling may be required to hold a lit candle of a size known to burn down in the time their punishment lasts. The principales further admonish the offenders to become reintegrated

Fig. 2.1. Crowd gathered in Nahualá's plaza to watch public administration of punishment. Photograph by Eric Ruiz Bybee, 2006.

and reconciled with their society and family, and they again invite the offenders to confess.[7] In addition, parents or relatives of the offenders come to the balcony microphone to justify or apologize for the behavior of the accused and also admonish them to reform. This admonishment to correct their behavior came not just from the mayor and the family, but from a number of other respected leaders; the whole community, as leading actors and audience, enters into the drama and process of attempted social reform and reintegration. After delivering punishment the prescribed amount of time, the mayor ends the public phase with admonitions to the community about the consequences of bad behavior, all blasted over the municipal address system audible throughout the town plaza.

In this invention of tradition, Nahualenses follow patterns deeply embedded in their cultural and symbolic practice. For example, at both Catholic and Protestant house weddings, the couple being married, and

Fig. 2.2. Nahualense girls receive publicly administered "traditional" punishment by kneeling on rocks on the mayoral balcony before assembled Nahualense citizens. Photograph by Eric Ruiz Bybee, 2006.

therefore in the process of changing their pattern of social relations to the community as a whole, kneel for hours on the unpadded floor of a simple house, often on concrete or tile, during which time they each hold a candle and receive admonishment from family, community leaders, and ritual guides on how to meld their new lives harmoniously into the community and make the transition from children without sense to responsible adults.[8] We note also that the indigenous judicial process of confession and admonition mirrors in body and commitment the stance of a person confessing before a priest in the mainstream Catholic Church; it mimes the kneeling, candle-holding petitioner who pleads before a saint and makes a promise to change in return for the granting of a petition in informal popular Catholicism; it replicates the kneeling supplicant in Charismatic Catholic healing ritual, and, sans the candle, in Pentecostal Protestant healings. This communal invention of new traditional public punishments is congruent with both traditional marriage and the public and private pursuit of confession, blessing, and healing in local religion in the way they symbolically change relations in the community. All draw on deeply shared cultural roots.

Codifying the New Traditional Norms

In reinitiating customary public punishment, Nahualense leaders have felt it crucial to write down and thereby establish norms and rules for traditional punishment in a formal code. Prior to punishing the gang members, the mayor read, to everyone present in the plaza, the code these elders had negotiated that established and authorized the actions of the hamlet and cantón security committees. The mayor, additionally, requested this audience of villagers to ratify the document as an expression of the will of the community. The mayor had previously sent these guidelines to the Ministry of Governance (Ministerio de Gobernación) for approval at the national level. Only after months without a response did the leaders in Nahualá decide to go ahead with punishment on the basis of local consent alone.

In addition to presenting the municipal code that established and authorized action by the local security committees, municipal leaders also encouraged each rural and urban territorial subunit of the municipio to formulate specific rules to govern their own areas and committees. For example, before punishing one of the aforementioned runaway girls, the community of Xepatuj (the Nahualá neighborhood where one of the girls lived) formed its own set of progressively harsher punishments. In this particular cantón, leaders agreed that after the first offense, the offending party would have to kneel on rocks. The second offense would require kneeling on a board with upturned bottle caps nailed to it. The third offense would generate a whipping with tree branches. The fourth offense would require a lashing with thorn-studded whips.

The written codification of norms, and the Nahualense attempts to approve them both locally and nationally, might not seem significant. But the effort accomplishes some specific objectives. First of all, writing down the customs defines acceptable, limited forms of punishment. Second, seeking approval at the national and local level gives the code a measure of legitimacy that is especially important when such procedures come up against internal and external criticism, as happened in Nahualá after the 1997 lynching.

Negotiating with State and Ethnic Expectations

While survey data indicate that a majority of Nahualenses support these traditional punishments and think they will reduce delinquency, these public events are not without their critics. The mothers of the girls punished on the balcony criticized the security committee that apprehended them and made their disapproval known during the punishment. Privately, the administrative secretary at the local justice of the peace office and courthouse likewise criticized the event and pointed out some of the difficulties inherent in dual systems of justice in one country. Being a Ladino, he said he felt discriminated against by the fact that he could receive a prison sentence for something like selling drugs, and yet, for the same crime, an indigenous person could get off with a public punishment. He also pointed out that applying indigenous justice nullifies the ability of the state to punish someone for the same offense afterward, because the Guatemalan Constitution prohibits double jeopardy. After the two girls were punished on June 28, for example, the mayor ordered that they be taken to the justice of the peace and put under house arrest under their parents' supervision. On arrival, the justice of the peace informed the mayor and the detainees that his institution could do nothing more because "indigenous justice had already been meted out" and that "the police were actually breaking the law by taking them into custody after the punishment."

Here one senses the full force of the embedded contradictions that Nahualenses must work with. Failure by the state plus an indigenous cultural thrust toward autonomy generated the move toward local "indigenous" punishment. Still, state authorities could have stepped in. But if Nahualenses had turned such cases over to the state, perhaps no punishment would have been enacted and certainly none that would have responded to indigenous notions of reconciliation within the community. While Nahualenses are not generally aware of Durkheim, they do understand the ritual and communal value of dramatic punishment. Indeed, in the way Mayas handled this case, they chose to discount the present value of the state, on account of its previous ineffectiveness in judicial matters of concern to the indigenous community, in favor of the present and future value of indigenous community.

Besides voiding the state's ability to act, some applications of customary law actually contradict or violate established national law and are inequitable in their application. The administrative secretary noted privately that the constitution contains special provisions for the protection of the rights of minors. Some of those provisions include minors not being compelled to confess and not to have their personal identity made public if they are involved in a crime. When youths were presented on the balcony, punished, and encouraged to confess, these traditional forms of punishment clearly violated the national and international norms designed to protect the rights of children. Yet, just as surely, the rights of these children were better protected inside their own community than if the children had been processed into state juvenile systems.

Regarding inequity in the application of punishments, the three girls who ran away for a few days and would not say where they went were twice made to kneel publicly on rocks—one for three hours, until she fainted. By contrast, the three boys, who had assaulted vendors on two occasions and had forged connections to gangs (including gang tattoos), were only made to kneel once for a little over an hour.[9]

Human rights organizations in Guatemala have to walk a fine line between promoting indigenous rights and punishments—to the benefit of communities bereft of the order of law—and maintaining respect for fundamental human rights. When asked if the application of customary justice violated human rights, one local human rights worker indicated that it did, but added, "just a little." Interviews with workers from other national and indigenous human rights organizations revealed conflicting perceptions. Some felt that indigenous rights should be subordinate to international human rights; others felt it should be the other way around (cf. Pitarch, Speed, and Leyva Solano 2008).

Finally, we should remember that Nahualenses and their leaders do not produce these cultural reinventions in a vacuum. Indigenous leaders communicate with each other through many avenues. They do so through the press; at nationwide meetings of mayors; and at conferences on indigenous affairs when drawn together by the state, by NGOs, or by international quasi-governmental organizations. What works in one place and seems tolerated by state institutions becomes generalized quickly. This flow of communication, too, is part of the emergent Maya consciousness that now competes with the preexisting municipal orientation.

Conclusion

Both informal interviews and survey data convincingly indicate that the people of Nahualá think public punishment is an effective way to deal with local crime. One might reasonably ask how effective these "traditional" public punishments are in preventing violent communal retribution under conditions where the crime is heinous enough to attract a lynch mob. Interview data and survey responses indicate that ordinary Nahualenses as well as their leaders feel these punishments are effective in deterring crime and inappropriate behavior, especially given the few options they have.

The first several public punishments recorded in Nahualá were administered under controlled circumstances for relatively benign crimes committed by local residents. The crucial test of whether the new system of mayoral-administered local justice could prevent the explosion of a mob-based lynching did not occur until late in the field study.

On August 12, 2006, in Palacal, a small hamlet on the rural outskirts of Nahualá, villagers suspected twelve people of being part of an illegal child-adoption ring. Nahualenses consider illegal adoption—and the kidnapping they believe is associated with it—to be heinous. Fear of child abduction runs high throughout Guatemala, and more than one foreigner has been lynched for merely being suspected of such a crime, notably, but not solely, in Todos Santos. Prior to the institution of traditional public punishment in Nahualá, one would have expected one or more of those accused to be torched in gasoline or beaten to death—or close thereto—by the crowd.

Instead, the Nahualense captors, under "Maya law" and mayoral oversight, required the twelve offenders to kneel on gravel, with the men having "burdens" or weights put on their shoulders. In addition, the local security committee had the offending women's hair shorn. Then, as one informant put it, after "applying Maya law so that this evil would disappear from the town/people," the committee handed the twelve over to the police.[10] The next day's national newspaper headline was: "*Se salvan de ser linchados en Sololá*—Saved from being lynched in Sololá." In total disregard of institutions of local justice, the newspaper made no reference to the punishment applied. Instead, it played to latent fears of the savage Indian and emphasized that the twelve were almost lynched (Morales and Rodas 2006).

Indeed, they likely would have been lynched under prior circumstances. What saved them from a near-certain violent end were the security committees and the newly available and codified alternative of public punishment. Fortunately, and contrary to both the cynical (American) aphorism (which any Guatemalan would understand instantly) that

"No good deed goes unpunished" and the lack of recognition displayed in the press, this good deed drew praise. In recognition of the way that Nahualá has used "customary law" to decrease delinquency and avoid collective violence, Guatemala's Presidential Commission on Human Rights recently honored Nahualá by declaring it an *Amigo de la Paz* (Friend of Peace) for its implementation of traditional law in the preservation of peace.

While the prevention of crime and communal violence is important, public punishment has deep cultural significance as well. In attempting to understand the motives underlying lynching, some have asserted that lynching represents an attempt by Maya communities to reassert their autonomy (Godoy 2002, 2004; cf. Goldstein 2004). There is some truth to that assessment. The autonomy argument, however, fails to examine the implications of what happens to a community that attempts to regain independence and order by incorporating violence and disorder—mobbing and lynching. The approach is intrinsically foreign to Maya culture, which focuses on negotiated consensus, harmony, and submission to law.

If lynching represents an attempt at autonomy, then it is a failed attempt. It fails because, like the post-conflict violence that preceded it, mob lynchings react to the failures of external state security and judicial institutions. Moreover, the violence of lynching fails to secure autonomy because it goads the state system into breaching the nominal autonomy of the municipio to deal with that lawlessness.

By contrast, the reinvestiture of power in the town elders, the reinterpretation of appropriate forms of communal justice as "traditional," and the reestablishment of a codified system of public punishment represent a return to the internal cultural logic and relative autonomy of leaders and community members of Nahualá. In particular, they respond to the sense of collective counsel in decision making, and the desire for equality and publicly shared communication, core values manifest in Maya culture (Jardine, in preparation). The process of deliberately organizing and codifying a community response—rather than tolerating or condoning the flare-ups of mob lynchings—represents a fundamental step toward reestablishing community-level autonomy and collective identity in the chaos of post-conflict Guatemala. It also steps firmly in the direction of Foucault's embodied self-discipline and governance he calls "governmentality." Here, however, the self-discipline adheres at the level of community—of municipality—the long-recognized master-unit of indigenous territorial control and ethnic identification (Tax 1937). We see, however, that this emerging govern-mentalité develops not at the level of the individual, self-disciplined mentality, as Foucault, locked in his Western cultural blinders, would have us expect. Rather, in indigenous Guatemala, emergent governmentality bubbles up within the social unit vastly more important to these Mayas: the municipio. Through the efforts of its leaders, the municipio seeks to discipline itself by codifying the actions through which it imposes bodily conformity on its sometimes culturally unruly and almost always frustrated citizens.

Precisely for this reason, Maya behavior has seemed, to Western eyes, rather inscrutable. Indeed, for many years, the personnel of outside countries and agencies have committed considerable resources to understand and combat problems like collective violence in the Guatemalan justice system, with little success. By contrast, the Nahualenses and the indigenous leaders of other Guatemalan communities—with precious few resources other than their deep cultural intuitions—have tried desperately to close the gap created by the corrupt impotence of the state judicial system and the previous withering of indigenous justice in the face of neoliberal "progress." They have done so by defining and creating—in their eyes, recreating—their own system of customary, "traditional," locally acceptable punishment hedged not by external notions of international human rights but by local understandings. In having done so, Nahualenses provide compelling evidence that the solution to many of their problems may lie closer to home than most outsiders have dared to think.

Notes

Fieldwork: 2006

1. The civil self-defense patrols were civilian paramilitary groups formed during the civil war starting in 1982. At their height they included almost one million indigenous men and boys; they were later implicated in anywhere from 18 to 90 percent of human rights violations and 35 percent of civilian massacres (Archdiocese of Guatemala 1999; Comisión para el Esclarecimiento Histórico1999).

2. The people of Nahualá and Santa Catarina all understand the term "Maya" as referring to traditionally oriented indigenous people. They commonly use the term *sacerdote maya* (traditionalist Maya shaman), for example. The uneducated more commonly use the term *indígena*, while the educated

and politically oriented commonly use the term "Maya" to refer to all Guatemalan Indians.

3. See Dracoulis (this volume, chapter 1), and Clay Larson (in review) for further details on the religious dimension of earlier principales.

4. For a comparative study, see Aida Castillo's (2002) research on women's rights among the Zapatistas in Chiapas, Mexico. She describes how indigenous leaders incorporated elements of state and international law into their indigenous system to create more-inclusive roles for women.

5. Here we follow Hobsbawm's notion that local people invent tradition by creating a set of acts, concepts, or symbols with which they "attempt to establish continuity with a suitable historic past" (Hobsbawm 1983:1). We recognize, but do not intend here Wagner's (1981:1–16) more postmodern anthropological notion that culture is invented when anthropologists assume the term as an analytic concept used to make other peoples understandable. Wagner, however, also recognizes the local invention of culture for local use in evolving cultural negotiations (Wagner 1981: 103–106, 335–41).

6. The setup for the Nahualense judicial punishment drama mirrors the structure of the colonial Spanish mission churches that held religious plays and masses on a balcony facing the mission's interior plaza.

7. Student fieldworkers have additionally witnessed the requirement to kneel, bare-kneed, on the upturned cleats of metal bottle caps.

8. See Araneda (2005:105–109) and Ajpacajá Tum (2001) for discussion of the marriage admonishments while kneeling as a rite of passage and Watanabe (1992) for discussion of the Mam Maya concept of knowledgeable adult perceptiveness and responsibility.

9. Call's argument (this volume, chapter 7) appears to apply here. The community is more concerned about the breakdown of traditional norms of gender behavior and cultural respect than about national or international notions of crime. Community leaders punish female-gendered disrespect more than male-gendered disrespect. Moreover, they appear to be punishing women for acts that would not be a crime at all in the national or international system. Such gender inequality will no doubt pit external advocates for gender equality against the community's concern with cultural disintegration in some future round of culture wars. Durkheim manifests his analytical potency again. Mayas depend on women to symbolize cultural integrity, especially through clothing and preservation of the domestic domain. Therefore, women receive greater punishment for their offenses, which consist of disobedience against the community's boundary-maintaining standards and disrespect for parental authority.

Men receive less punishment for their offenses, because they have only committed acts of violence against the culturally less-valued individual persons, not against the boundary mechanisms that maintain ethnicity and community. Nevertheless, the community can easily respond toward men with lethal lynching if they sense that the local basis of communal subsistence or reproduction has been tampered with by theft, personal assault, or external adoption.

10. One might ask why the twelve were handed over to the national police if already punished under Indian customary law and not subject to double jeopardy. Here we can only speculate: The process is so new that community leaders may not have realized the full implications of their liberation from national law via the mechanism of protection for indigenous customary law. Perhaps they understood, or hoped, there might be other offenses committed that were not dealt with under their indigenous judgment and punishment. Finally, perhaps they simply wanted to test to what degree respect for indigenous culture, and the laws preventing double jeopardy, actually held up. Or perhaps it was a simpler matter: there remained an abiding sense of subordination to national authority, regardless of its ineffectiveness.

CHAPTER 3

A Land Divided without Clear Titles

The Clash of Communal and Individual Land Claims in Nahualá and Santa Catarina Ixtahuacán

Curtis W. Dabb, James H. McDonald, John P. Hawkins, and Walter Randolph Adams

Land disputes in and between the municipios of Santa Catarina Ixtahuacán and Nahualá occur with frequency and lethality today, as they have for 150 years. Such long-term quarrels are by no means rare in Guatemala. Hawkins (1984:67–80, 121–28) records a three-century conflict between San Pedro Sacatepéquez and San Marcos that was still unresolved in 2010. Hostnig (1997a, 1997b, 1998) has transcribed and compiled hundreds of cases—bundles (*legajos*) of documents recording the disputations and petitions of the litigants in decades-long disputes in and between southern Mam and K'iche' municipalities in the departments of Quetzaltenango and Totonicapán. In volume 1, for example, Hostnig adduces sixty-three cases involving five Mam municipios. One municipio alone, Concepción Chiquirichapa, produced twenty-five cases spanning the years 1712 to 1952. Volume 2 presents eighty-six cases spanning the years 1601 to 1930 regarding five municipios, and an additional forty-six land dispute documents from San Juan Ostuncalco's municipal files. Volume 3 focuses on San Miguel Totonicapán's litigation with surrounding municipios and Indian and Ladino parties to the disputes, with more than fifty-six cases and fifteen-plus documents spanning 1567 to 1993. Each case often includes dozens of lengthy documents.

Nahualá and Santa Catarina have disputed their mutual boundaries and hamlets at least since the time of their separation in the 1860s. Nahualá's official recognition as a municipality in 1872 (Asociación CODEIN 2008:4), however, did nothing to clarify titles and boundaries. Since 1998, at least one Nahualense has died and several people in both communities have been seriously injured in continuing land-related altercations. We suggest that these conflicts will escalate in frequency, ardor, and lethality because of increasing land scarcity driven by population growth. Competition for land is intensified in an environment where a weak state and its often corrupt administrators try to establish their new cultural, legal, and neoliberal market hegemony in Indian communities that were once relatively autonomous and communal.

This chapter explores current changes and contradictions in the ownership and tenure of land, and their effect on the indigenous communities of Nahualá and Santa Catarina Ixtahuacán. By implication, these processes extend to Mayas and their communities throughout Guatemala. First, we briefly sketch the history of the two communities and outline the fundamental elements that help illuminate the administrative and physical divisions. These steps enable us to examine the processes that drive intercommunity tension. Second, we discuss the way land policies have been manipulated to justify and support rival claims of ownership between residents in each of these two municipios. Despite officially trying to maintain communal tenure, they are in the process of inadvertently shifting from communal tenure to private holdings. Third, we present three cases of usufruct privatization whereby commons areas are converted into individually administered and quasi-privatized holdings. Fourth, we explore the problem of fuzzy boundaries that has led to long-term conflict between Nahualá and Santa Catarina Ixtahuacán, a problem that in part results from the political manipulation of these mixed and conflicted land tenure concepts and systems. In short, we explore the dynamics of land policies that unintentionally encourage conflict and set the stage for present and future disputes, as individuals and communities vie to manipulate local communal and national private-tenure systems to their own advantage.

COMMUNAL LAND AND PRIVATIZATION: THE BUILDING BLOCKS OF CONFLICT

Access to land has been a significant part of religious and social life in Maya culture for centuries. Both Brintnall (1979) and Watanabe (1992) describe the senior generation's control of access to land through incrementally allocated inheritance, wherein parents distribute portions of their estate at several key points in the children's maturation cycle, based on their obedience. Such inheritance rewards and maintains traditional respectful, obedient behavior in the family, in the community's cofradía system, and in municipal governance (see also Dracoulis, chapter 1).

Of course, the principal crop, maize, sustains people in both communities and provides offerings to Maya religious deities for religious traditionalists, past and present. One hears informants say they, and Indians in general, are *hombres de maíz* (men of corn), a phrase recorded much earlier by Valladares in another municipio (1957, 1993). Indeed, maize remains integral to Nahualá and Santa Catarina society, which underscores the importance of access to cropland. Residents plant the majority of their fields in maize during an eight-to-ten-month growing season. They plant the corn sometime between March (at low elevations) and May (at high elevations). During October through December, the crops are harvested and the land is then left fallow or sown with other crops.

People delineate plot boundaries with natural and planted shrubs, bushes, or trees, as well as rocks, pathways, and other landmarks. Over time, hand hoeing and furrowing leave raised, packed footpaths, little ridges, or dirt terraces that mark identifiable plots. Except around the yard of a house, one rarely observes wood-slat or wire fences (fig. 3.1).

In spite of the visible plot boundaries, the leaders of Nahualá and Santa Catarina Ixtahuacán claim that their municipios have maintained a long and successful tradition of *communal* land tenure. By this, they mean they have acted as stewards of the lands in their municipio, all of which are held as a communal resource for regulated exploitation by those belonging to the municipio by birth. Leaders and residents also explain that they only hold use rights, or usufruct, to their land; they cannot sell the lands they farm or the houses they occupy to outsiders. Outsiders are defined as persons not born to parents who have lived their lives in Nahualá or Santa Catarina Ixtahuacán. They can, however, sell their rights to use land or houses to others born to the community and descended from past generations also born there.

Under the communal system, an individual or family obtains use rights to land from the municipality and its custodians, the mayoral council. Leaders of both municipalities explain that the right to use land under current "customary law" means individuals have stewardship over a piece of land as long as they cultivate it. A person receiving an allotment of land must invest time and resources to improve or cultivate the area. If land goes uncultivated for several years, the family forfeits its right, and anyone wishing to work the land is free to do so, advocating for their claim before the municipal authorities if contested.

Fig. 3.1. Nahualá: a hillside with informal land boundary demarcations. Photograph by Curtis Dabb, 2006.

One resident of Nahualá, a former mayor, recounted that he had cultivated a parcel of six *cuerdas* in an area that was formerly pastoral rangeland. He had found that with chicken manure, the land produced. One year, however, he let it lie fallow. Someone else planted the land. When the former mayor returned, he found it under cultivation. Municipal leaders upheld the rights of the subsequent cultivator and the former mayor stood without recourse.

Thirty years ago this use-right provision applied to all of the municipality of Nahualá. Thereafter, to the present day, lands near the municipal seat (*cabecera municipal*) and in the intensely cultivated flatter areas in rural hamlets—that is, lands in corn cultivation from time immemorial—could not be captured by another tenant even if left in periods of disuse by the longtime users. In effect, they had social title to use rights. But lands in clearly municipal commons usage, such as improved pasturage and sometimes forest land, could be cleared, put into corn production, and defended by use right.

The communal system also has a quasi-private dimension whereby usufruct land users may register their plot with the local Municipal Property Commission, which grants them an official municipal license for use to protect against competing claims to that plot. Registration also allows users to lease their plot to other farmer-renters without fear of the renter or sharecropper making a claim based on several years of use.

The Municipal Property Commission requires registrants to demonstrate that the individual, their parents, or grandparents made improvements to a parcel of communal land and worked it a number of years in order to record their use-right in the municipal registry. Given the scarcity of land, many families tried to prove their claim to any available parcel. Others depend solely on the (unregistered) social recognition of their family having farmed a plot for generations.

Nahualá and Ixtahuacán are relatively unusual in the highlands of Guatemala because their municipal governments declare *all* land within their jurisdictions to be communal, although their ability to enforce that assertion is rapidly weakening in the face of encroaching market forces. Of this communal land, some is treated as a commons resource, administered by the municipal corporation for the benefit of the community as a whole. Such commons use is now limited primarily to communal forests, where municipal residents are allowed free access to collect dead wood for cooking and others are granted licenses to extract lumber (see Brown, chapter 4, on communal forest management). Thirty years ago, the commons included pasturage areas to which one could freely take one's animals. Today, the pasturage has largely disappeared in the face of individual plot cultivation made possible by the availability of manure trucked in from large-scale chicken farms supplying eggs to Guatemala City. By contrast, most other municipios hold some land as communal (for example, non-arable forest reserves for firewood collection) while arable land is held as formal private property, preferably registered at the national property registry office located in each department capital.[1]

Communal tenure like that of Nahualá and Santa Catarina Ixtahuacán has long been under pressure from post-colonial liberal reforms that have sought to establish private property and individual entrepreneurship. Throughout Guatemala, communal landholding has been under assault since the introduction of coffee in the early 1800s turned the mid-mountain Boca Costa (piedmont) from an indigenous forest largely ignored by Ladinos into prime agro-export land avidly sought by them.

Even before coffee came, Ladinos have tried to confiscate or buy Indian lands for cattle haciendas and other purposes (Hawkins 1984:74–83). A cursory check of the card files and record bundles in the Tierras section of the Archivo General de Centro América reveals hundreds of land disputes between municipalities contesting their boundaries, between indigenous municipalities and Ladinos expanding their estates, and between Indians or Ladinos within a municipio contesting field boundaries and use rights. Such disputes occurred in virtually every municipio, and McCreery (1994:151–57) gives a detailed historical account of a half century of land disputes between Santa Catarina and all its neighbors, including, in particular, Nahualá.

Later, during the liberal Barrios regime (1870–75), for example, aggressive legislative moves sought to abolish communal landholdings and replace them with a private tenure system. This legislation sought to transfer land into the open market and thereby into Ladino hands. Such privatization supported the overarching liberal project of civilizing and incorporating Indians as laborers in the national agro-export system. At the same time, land privatization fueled a major struggle regarding race/class/ethnicity that threatened indigenous life-practice and sought to eradicate the identity category of Indian and replace it with the *mestizo* (mixed heritage) identity category, as occurred in other parts of Latin America.

Mexico offers an interesting comparison case. Describing Juchitán, Oaxaca, Binford, for example, shows how changes in land tenure from communal use to "a system of private property" created "insecurity of tenure." These insecurities had economic consequences and gave rise to politicized debates about "which form [of tenure] was 'correct,'" one's position regarding correctness, of course, determined by one's place and assessment of advantage in contested structures and political discourses (Binford 1985:180–81). Although the origins and history of Guatemala's indigenous communal lands and Mexico's ejidos differ radically, both communal holding and a movement toward privatization reveal a number of significant structural and processual similarities.

Land ownership in the Guatemalan highlands is and always has been fuzzy and difficult to enforce, resulting in a history of political and social conflict arising out of disputes over access to land. Several factors contribute to this condition of fuzziness.

First, concepts of tenancy vary, as does individual knowledge of what one might need to do to secure title to a particular form of tenancy or resolve a dispute. In addition, regardless of the form or knowledge of tenancy, uncertainties of measurement have bedeviled participants, scholars, and state administrators. There are, for example, at least two indigenous concepts of the length of a *cuerda*, the cord or chain used to measure length, which gives its name to the square unit of land surface that all peasants use to calculate their landholdings. Some municipalities use a 40-vara standard, so that a cuerda is a square of land measuring 40 varas by 40 varas. Most use the 25-vara standard, so that a cuerda is 25 varas by 25 varas. In either case, a vara measures some 33 inches. Nahualá and Santa Catarina Ixtahuacán use the 25-vara standard.

Further adding to the confusion, state surveys and census reports use the official metric system and divide surface areas into hectares. Of course, when the state intervenes with the metric system, its agents may scramble the conversion rates by not knowing the local length of the cuerda. Even more likely, local citizens seldom understand their land in metric quantities, which renders state pronouncements less intelligible (see Brown, chapter 4, on the "illegibility" of the state).

Finally, at the point of inheritance or internal sale, most cuerdas are measured and transmitted by estimate, guesstimate, informal measurement, or oral family lore, not by actual chaining, let alone by competent use of accurate survey instruments. Such procedures create much room for interpretation. And interpretation in a matter so crucial to peasant survival is fuel for dispute in a family or village, between municipios, and between Ladino and various Indian ethnicities that have different access to local and national government land-registry systems.

Registration of land has created a number of problems throughout the highlands as the national and local governments facilitate the move toward formal privatization through registering individual title in a national property office. The national property offices commonly use the municipality's record of an established usufruct claim as a basis for issuing a nationally valid deed of private and saleable ownership. Such practices clearly place a local communal tenure system and its municipal use-rights registry at odds with the national private property registry system.

Thus, today, we witness a breakdown in the clear claim of communal stewardship that municipal leaders once had to municipal lands. To start with, urban sites and long-farmed milpa land can now be bought and sold among the life-long residents of a municipio, and whether they are use rights or clear title matters little. Second, residents can homestead municipal areas that once were commons and then gain title by municipal registration. The municipal registration effort designed to reduce land conflict has, ironically, jeopardized the municipal leadership's cultural claim to communal ownership, because the parcels it registered to individuals are now the basis for private titles. Finally, the relatively new practice of taking out mortgages on one's land to finance projects has further eroded the claim that residents have use rights only. For example, a resident wishing to secure the forty or fifty thousand quetzales needed to pay a *coyote* (smuggler of migrants) for transport to the United States mortgages a piece of family-held land to the coyote or his backers. If the person does not secure gainful employment in the United States, the land reverts to the coyote, often an outsider. These outsiders then sell the land to whomever. Since approximately 2005, parcels are frequently sold to relatively wealthy Mayas of nearby Totonicapán. Likewise, one can mortgage to a bank to secure funds for a project. In short, from about 2005 to the present, the land has been commoditized, whether the municipality approves or not. The old tenet that only native-born residents can own use rights is eroding. In Nahualá and Santa Catarina, in the 2010s and 2020s, illegal nonresident coyotes taking mortgages for migration will finish the privatization program that President Barrios started, and so desired to complete, in the 1870s.

This shift in ownership and tenure practices has resulted in several unresolved property disputes between residents in the two municipios we studied. The shift in ownership registry has also fostered renewed tension and conflict between Santa Catarina and Nahualá. We will argue that these disputes and conflicts will continue as long as local communal tenure, local use-right registry, and national private tenure with registry coexist in unrecognized, unresolved opposition to one another and until a dominant system fully emerges.

Nevertheless, dependence on land, competition for the land between families, and a growing population on a fixed amount of land have spurred many people to record their usage. One of my informants summed it up: "The communal way of doing things is no longer a viable option because of overpopulation. People will have to look to other methods besides farming to provide for themselves." By "overpopulation" he referred to the extraordinary population increase of the last thirty years relative to the capacity of the land. The "other methods besides farming" meant taking jobs, mostly outside the community, either as laborers on export-oriented plantations or as factory or service workers in Guatemalan cities. Thus, the proponents of the emerging neoliberal economy have tried to marketize indigenous land and convert it to export- or market-oriented purposes. The few communities like Nahualá and Santa Catarina Ixtahuacán that have resisted marketization have done so through strict municipal maintenance of a communal tenure regimen. But their efforts are now rapidly breaking down under the twin assaults of government registry and the possibility of financing globalized migration, or other economic opportunities, through pawning one's land.

Land Conflict in a Municipio and the Move toward Quasi Privatization in the Communal System

In Nahualá and Ixtahuacán, desperate efforts to obtain and secure one's claim on scarce land have generated the increasingly common process of quasi privatization through usufruct registry at the municipal level. Such registry protects the cultivator from other use rights claims on that land. In a convenient fiction, it gives the user protected (or at least registered) usufructuary rights nearly equivalent to private property, and it gives the municipality the right to claim that all its territory is held in common. This formal, local recognition of use rights also helps ensure the next generation may inherit the use rights, though such registration has not been necessary in the past.

Besides registration, land-use practices have been moving toward privatization. One man recounted the change with respect to animal grazing: "In the past there were goats and sheep everywhere, and they got into everything. They even came up to the front of the house, and you couldn't say anything. That's how the culture used to be. I think that it is becoming more privatized, a form more respectful of neighbors."

Under conditions of significant demographic pressure, people, as well as goats, encroach on the commons and compete to secure scarce land for agriculture and wood for fuel.[2] The following cases suggest the ways communal land has been quasi-privatized within Nahualá's communal system. The first case outlines the process by which plots of communal land are registered with the Municipal Property Commission and receive quasi-private status. The second elaborates the priority of witnesses over formal documentation. The third case underscores the social and property dynamics that encourage local registration and formalization through quasi-private licensure with the municipality.

Case 1: Nahualá
I (Dabb) observed a parcel of land being prepared for division among three sisters as an inheritance. The land formerly had been a forest preserve, communally accessed and held in common, but their father had cleared the land for cultivation about forty-five years ago, encroaching on the preserve, apparently without permission. To divide up the parcel, the family had to file a claim application with the municipality's land registry. To be successful, they needed a respected witness, an elder man who was familiar with the boundaries of the property. The witness, an uncle of the inheritors, had to be able to confirm that improvements, and more importantly, cultivation had taken place on the plot of land being registered.

Addressing the two brothers-in-law who were preparing the application papers while standing on the property, the witness gave a history of different locations where wheat had been grown and pointed out a tree where, forty-six years before, a shelter had been built to watch over the fields. While surveying the perimeter of the property, the witness identified tree trunks that had been felled at various times for firewood by different family members. The witness had not visited the property in twenty years, yet he could point out trees that had been planted, trees that had been cut down, and other features on the land that indicated the family's right to claim ownership.

Once the witness had established the general area, the family measured the property lines using a length of rope purchased from the local hardware store. Thick undergrowth made the task difficult (fig. 3.2). As we conversed, they indicated that if a problem or disagreement with neighboring holders had arisen regarding the boundary, it was customary for the parties to meet and resolve the issue with little or no legal representation. They said disputes rarely occurred because there was some leeway between the land parcel boundaries and informal methods of measuring sufficed.

Case 2: Nueva Ixtahuacán, before the Elected Alcalde
During a mayoral council meeting, several men disputed the rightful ownership of a plot of land. One man claimed that his father had given him the land several years before, but he did not have any

Fig. 3.2. Measuring the land informally using a rope. Photograph by Curtis Dabb, 2006.

papers or a witness. The other party, a group, had documentation that said the land was theirs. In addition, they had a witness who had worked the land during the past sixteen years. The council made the decision in favor of the group based on the witness's testimony, ignoring the written documentation. This underscored the importance of witnesses in litigating claims to local land. A reliable witness can actually supersede documentation.

Case 3: Antigua Ixtahuacán, before the Alcalde Indígena
One informant detailed the origin and transformation of his landholding as he gave testimony before the alcalde indígena, the informal governing representative of Antigua Ixtahuacán. Of the five plots of land that his family owned, he had inherited three from his grandparents, rented one from a neighbor who had moved to another community, and purchased the other. As in case 1, the inherited plots had been carved out of communal forest land. During the

process of dividing the land among the next generation of inheritors, it became necessary to register the land with the municipality to ensure future access.

These cases illustrate the processes whereby land to which all in the community share access and which is communally administered, is transformed into a quasi-private holding of use right tenure. Cases 1 and 2 highlight the importance of witnesses. When resolving land issues at the municipal level, it was often more effective to have a witness than to have legal documentation. Indeed, a city official involved with land registration confirmed that the testimony of a witness often takes precedence, even over proper documentation.

Relying on a witness affirms the communal and consensual element of Maya culture and speaks directly to the matter of use and improvement that underlies use rights. By contrast, documents cater to the external, legal, and Ladino elements and bespeak individuation and possession, regardless of whether the land is used. Quite apart from the Indian community's emphasis on orality, its residual illiteracy, and its suspicion that documents have been manipulated throughout its colonial history—all good reasons to trust witnesses over documents—the use of witnesses instantiates community and is therefore more Indian than referral to documents.[3] In effect, relying on documents subjects the community to the document-oriented gaze claimed as the purview and mechanism of state control. Worse yet, documents frequently are, or are feared to be, fabricated. Thus, for several reasons, witnesses reign.

As the remaining communal land is infringed on—with or without municipal permission—and then registered for purposes of inheritance, sale, or protection of one's claim, tensions over control of land have escalated. Referring to the growing scarcity of communal land, one informant said, "Our ancestors thought they would always have enough land. [In the past, people] grabbed bit-by-bit. But, now they don't grab bit-by-bit. They grab large quantities. Now they make the land private so you can't enter. That wasn't the purpose of this land."

Katz (2000:114) theorizes the difficulty of maintaining the communal purpose of a piece of land when property rights are not clearly established. "Without clear and enforced property rights, everyone is afraid that neighbors will reap the fruits of one's own restraint in resource use, so user costs (the present value of possible future profits forgone by using a resource unit today) are ignored." In sum, the residents of Nahualá and Ixtahuacán register use rights with the municipality to both formalize their claims to land and fend off potential counterclaims by other community members.

The mix of different approaches to tenure has confounded the ability of municipal custodians to regulate and restrict access to land inside the municipios and has generated conflict between municipios. So, on the one hand, families vie for land or use rights by selectively emphasizing the tenure perspectives that most accrue to their advantage. On the other hand, adjacent communities clash over ill-defined municipal boundaries. This latter problem has fueled intercommunity tension. It has also drawn the attention and intervention of the state, which leaders of both communities have called on to help secure landholdings through formal, state-sanctioned land titling as a means to consolidate an improved position and then suppress intercommunity tensions. Nahualá's and Santa Catarina's leaders are currently engaged in one such dispute arising out of the decision by Santa Catarina's leaders to resettle the municipal cabecera on safer land. Many other such disputes fester throughout the country and from time to time result in fights, injuries, and deaths.

LAND CONFLICT BETWEEN MUNICIPIOS: THE RELOCATION OF SANTA CATARINA'S CABECERA

While there is tremendous tension *within* communities over the distribution of the scarce land base, conflicts also arise *between* municipalities, especially under conditions of poorly defined boundaries and vague titling, both of which invite opportunistic transgression. Conflict over municipal boundaries has been smoldering in the municipalities of Sololá since the 1700s (Cardona 2002:40–41). Here, we relate the details of a long-term land conflict between Santa Catarina Ixtahuacán and Nahualá but focus on the recent flare-up resulting from the fission and resettlement of most of Santa Catarina's cabecera municipal population.[4]

The municipality of Santa Catarina Ixtahuacán first fissioned in about 1865 as a result of political differences. Its offshoot, initially called Santa Catalina Nahualá, achieved formal municipal status in 1872. However, no respected arbiter established an agreed-upon boundary between the Nahualá branch and the Ixtahuacán branch, and disagreement persisted—and was festering—in 2006. The two municipalities attempted to create a formal boundary in 1905, resulting in partial agreement to establish select parcels of land as territory pertaining to each. The agreement left approximately 56 *caballerías*, approximately 6,240 acres, *mancomunada* (jointly administered) between both municipalities (Administración Miguel Tzep Rosario n.d.; Cambranes 1992:349). *Mancomunada* meant joint stewardship by the two entities over the same area of land.

Unfortunately, each tried to satisfy its population's desperate need for land by accessing the mancomunada communal land, and that led to a "tragedy of the commons"—the unintentional depletion of environmental resources by farmers acting in their individual interests. Because of the land shortage, by 1986 the citizens of Nahualá had begun cultivating a portion of Chwipatán, a rural area in the joint-administration (mancomunada) commons located astride the highest point of the Pan-American Highway, just outside what was usually thought of as Nahualá's municipal holdings. Ixtahuaquense leaders challenged this usage of the shared area, and a political struggle ensued. In 1989, upset by Nahualense cultivation in Chwipatán, a supposedly neutral area intended for sustainable mutual use, the municipal leaders of Ixtahuacán retaliated by registering a large portion of the mancomunada land as Ixtahuacán property in the National Property Registration Office. Predictably, Ixtahuacán's registration action angered the citizens of Nahualá because much of the previously shared communal land would legally cede to the municipality of Ixtahuacán.

Tension continued to fester between the two municipalities through late 1998, when the onslaught of Hurricane Mitch spurred and escalated the conflict. The devastation Mitch wrought drove many Ixtahuaquenses to ask for government aid to relocate their town to safer and more stable ground. Indeed, Ixtahuacán's cabecera municipal had been hit hard with landslides and flooding, forcing many people to abandon their homes and crops. In the face of government inaction, Ixtahuaquenses engineered a secretive mass migration, which, from the point of view of Nahualá, constituted a land invasion.

Early on the morning of January 11, 2000, a five-sixths majority of Ixtahuacán's cabecera residents stripped their homes of belongings, loaded them onto trucks, and hiked or rode the sixteen kilometers to Chwipatán, relocating and forming a new community and municipal cabecera. They called the new site Nueva Santa Catarina Ixtahuacán. About one-sixth of the population had chosen to stay behind in what would come to be known as Antigua Ixtahuacán, all in the aftermath of the destruction caused by Hurricane Mitch. In other words, the Ixtahuaquenses invaded land in the mancomunada zone, a territory already subject to cultivation use-right claims by squatters from Nahualá.

Faced with a fait accompli, the national government acceded to Ixtahuaquense demands to legalize the settlement, which Ixtahuacán claimed as ancestral, which both municipios had managed as mancomunada, yet which had numerous squatters from Nahualá who had been cultivating the high, cold, bunchgrass tundra for some years. These latter, therefore, had some expectation of squatter's use-right permanence.

The government promised to secure title to three and a half caballerías, approximately 390 acres of land, for Ixtahuacán's new housing settlement and municipal seat, by paying off 1,000 quetzales per cuerda to squatters who had registered their cultivation in the Nahualá land office. Unregistered squatters got nothing. The government authorities assumed that buying out the Nahualense cultivators would ameliorate, if not end, the tensions between the two municipios. Clearly they did not understand the passions or persistence of the unregistered farmers.

Between 1998 and 2000, the government had proposed at least two other sites to relocate the people of Ixtahuacán. Ixtahuaquenses, however, had rejected them because none was near the Pan-American Highway, a key element of their leader's goal for community progress. One was not even inside the boundaries of Ixtahuacán as most broadly conceived; moving there would have inserted Ixtahuacán into another municipio entirely. So Ixtahuaquenses were set on going to Chwipatán because of its proximity to the highway, which they felt would give Ixtahuacán's cabecera access to development, education, jobs, and markets. Moreover, they felt they had claim to the land as an ancestral communal area of their municipio and that they needed to occupy the area to confront and stop Nahualá's continuing flow of squatters who cultivated, quasi-privatized, and placed on Nahualá's municipal property rolls the formerly mancomunada area—now registered at the national level to Ixtahuacán.

Other than providing access to the international highway and offering a chance to challenge Nahualá for hegemony in the area, conditions in Chwipatán were not ideal for settling a new town. At 9,500 to 10,000 feet in elevation, Chwipatán bore the nickname "Alaska" because of its frigid climate.[5] Altitude, combined with poor soils, made it difficult to grow the common varieties of maize and forced growers to use expensive, high-altitude-adapted seed. Compounding matters, there were few nearby trees for firewood, little access to water, and little shelter from the often harsh, cold climate.

All of these factors contributed to further conflict, in some cases violent, because Ixtahuaquenses had trespassed private and municipal boundaries to collect what they needed to survive. "The people were not thinking about all of that when they insisted on moving there," one Nahualense informant said. "They thought that by being closer to the highway, they could quickly establish a market to compete with the one in Nahualá, creating many economic opportunities. They did not think about the things they were leaving behind." Indeed, conditions were so harsh that a few of the citizens who were part of the original mass migration returned to their old community, where maize grew better and where water, electricity, and other infrastructure already existed.

The town center and all government offices were relocated from Antigua Ixtahuacán to Nueva Ixtahuacán. The new town was organized according to a grid that the national government established with the help of international aid groups. Unlike typical Maya hamlets, this one had straight, concrete streets and new, modular houses organized by defined blocks, all of which lent the community an urban feel. In contrast to the pines and thriving vegetation surrounding Nahualá and Antigua Ixtahuacán, the main vegetation around the settlement of Nueva Ixtahuacán was *pajón* (bunchgrass), suitable for little more than thatching roofs in the now-abandoned style of building.

At the center of town, opposite the municipal building and facing a municipal park, stood the Catholic church, waiting to be completed when more funding became available. The remainder of the city emanated from that nexus. Six years after relocating, people had become settled in their new homes.

In summary, land scarcity, coupled with a heavy reliance on maize production for subsistence, had heightened tensions between the two municipios and between Antigua Ixtahuacán and Nueva Ixtahuacán by fueling the move toward registering, and therefore quasi privatization. Land registration finally broke down the fiction of shared access to a commons in the mancomunada. The increase in quasi-privatized land clashed with the communal concept of openness and access based on need. Quasi-private property involved cultivation, which physically and symbolically marked the land by furrowing, terracing, and other indications of controlled use and investment, and these landmarks restricted access to what was formerly commons. The unrestrained pioneering and subsequent registration process pursued by each municipio clashed with the notion of jointly administered and joint-access commons.

CONSEQUENCES OF UNCLEAR MUNICIPAL BOUNDARIES AND TENURE

A number of tumultuous consequences flowed from the lack of clear boundaries between municipalities. Here we comment on the physical, social, structural, cultural, and symbolic violence attendant to the unclear division of Santa Catarina Ixtahuacán when Nueva Ixtahuacán fissioned off, and of Nahualá, continuing from its unclear fission 150 years ago.

Violence Occasioned by Imprecise Survey Techniques

For centuries, the use of imprecise survey techniques to demarcate land boundaries between municipios such as Nahualá and Ixtahuacán has fostered conflicts. Under conditions of extreme scarcity and dependence on land for corn, ill-defined and contestable boundaries invited members of each jurisdiction to grab what land they could and defend it fiercely.

Unfortunately, informal estimation techniques were used once again to gauge the size of the area originally allocated for the resettlement of Ixtahuacán's cabecera. Historically, such informal estimating techniques frequently involved measurements being calculated by walking the perimeter of an area, marking it off without any formal surveying equipment, and estimating distances between trees, hills, and other natural landmarks.

In that manner, an engineer accompanied the mayor of Nahualá in 2000 to estimate the size of an area that included the provisional sheet-metal-clad sheds built in the immediate hours of the Ixtahuaquense migration—the area to be offered to the displaced citizens of Ixtahuacán. The unfriendly and unstable political conditions of the resettlement, however, did not permit adequate measurement. Nahualense informants said Ixtahuaquenses brandishing machetes were ready to defend their new settlement with whatever force was necessary. "It was extremely hostile up there," Nahualá's mayor said of his trip to the Chwipatán area with the government surveyor. "I went up with the engineer, and we did not want to stay there very long. He asked me how much land I estimated there to be in an area he pointed out. I told him I thought there were about three and a half caballerías. Then we left." No official measurements were made, and the legal documents were signed using the estimated amount. The mayor later told Hawkins that he did not actually set foot in or walk the perimeter of the area they "surveyed," but observed it and estimated it from a nearby hillside viewpoint.

The estimated amount, however, was grossly inaccurate. Shortly after settling into their new homes, the local leaders of Ixtahuacán discovered the discrepancy. With legal documents in hand, they requested the remainder of the three and a half caballerías they felt they had been promised and to which they felt legally entitled.

When a team from the national government finally officially surveyed the originally allocated area with instruments, they discovered that what was supposed to be three and a half caballerías was only about half that. But by then, the whole relocated population had ensconced itself on allocated plots, living in a mix of provisional and formally built structures. Once again, informal methods of measuring and marking land had contributed to prolonging intercommunity conflict and violence.

The government concluded that a second area must be acquired from Nahualá to bring the area ceded to Ixtahuacán up to the three and a half caballerías promised. During the second acquisition from Nahualá, all Nahualenses who held vetted titles to land in the area to be redistributed to Nueva Ixtahuacán residents were paid 2,500 quetzales per cuerda,[6] plus compensation for the loss of the current crop, if any. Again, anyone who was cultivating land but had not registered it received no compensation. That payments were made only to registered holders infuriated the unregistered holders, whose passions flared. Moreover, many of Nahualá's citizenry felt betrayed that "their" land was again being ceded to their competitor, Ixtahuacán. As a result of such intense feelings, the former mayor of Nahualá narrowly escaped being lynched by an angry mob in Nahualá shortly after the discrepancy and resulting second land exchange were announced. Several informants referred to him as "the mayor who gave away our land." Having received multiple death threats, the mayor felt forced to migrate quickly and illegally to the United States. He supports his family in Guatemala with remittances.

Violence Spurred by Interdigitation and Multiple Registry of Land

The recent process of squatters encroaching on the mancomunada commons to cultivate, followed by registering their cultivation in their own municipality, has resulted in considerable interdigitation and overlapping of personal and municipal claims along the border zone, especially in areas that had been held jointly as "mancomunada."

Because Nahualá and Ixtahuacán share access to a large area of communal land, the increased registration and privatization inside the shared communal area has created enclaves and overlap between the territories of the two municipalities. Use-right privatization requires the claimant to register the pioneered land in the person's municipality of birth. This process undermines the convenient fiction of joint management in common—the status called "mancomunada"—and forces municipal leaders to extend exclusive municipal claim over whatever land individuals register at that municipality's land registry office. The result is a patchwork of enclaves that individuals have registered at their respective cabeceras, as well as contestable claims for the status of certain rural hamlets. Each municipio would prefer to be the sole authenticator of quasi privatization and the nominal administrator of the territory associated with a hamlet. As one advisor to the governor of Sololá lamented, "If a border were drawn between the two [municipios of Santa Catarina and Nahualá], it would be very difficult to determine where to place it. People from Nahualá would have lands in the territory of Ixtahuacán and vice versa, creating something resembling a checkerboard."[7] The essence of this problem was officially inscribed in a hamlet's roadside name placard: "Welcome to Pak'awex hamlet. Santa Catarina Ixtahuacán *and* Nahualá, Sololá" (emphasis mine) (fig. 3.3). The maneuver enables the hamlet to "cover its bets" with both municipios and perhaps gives it a double network to access or manipulate. One resident explained: "the two municipalities frequently try to function as though they were one, even though they are two separate political entities."

The relocation of Santa Catarina's cabecera continues and exacerbates this interdigitation of the two municipalities and checkerboard of plots claimed by one or the other. Moreover, Guatemalan state buy-out of the Nahualense squatter-cultivators validates Nahualá's claim over Ixtahuacán's in the mancomunada area. The buy-out creates further overlap of or enclaves in the two municipios by setting the new municipal headquarters in an area with three levels of land claimants. First, individual Nahualenses claimed and farmed the land, some of which they registered in the Nahualá land office. Second, the two municipios affirmed an equal right to share the area as "mancomunada" commons. Finally, Ixtahuacán claimed the land by original colonial title, recent registry at the national land office, and current land-invasion occupation.

Fig. 3.3. Lacking clear municipal affiliation because of unclear title and boundaries, a hamlet covers its bets and perhaps gains a double network to access or manipulate. Curtis Dabb stands next to a sign for Pak'awex hamlet, in photograph by hiking companion Pascualino Tahay, 2006.

None of these claims or their implications has ever been settled definitively—and how could they be settled? That is, who would be the respected arbiter and guarantor of a definitive agreement? The corrupt state? The compromised judiciary? The untrusted police? The hated army? Self-help threat of violence is the only protection for one's personal and communal assets. The threat of violence at once isolates the communities by turning them into enemies and protects the weak state against the rise of a coalition of towns under a shared ethnic identity as a political bloc that might undo Ladino control. The former consequence, however, anticipates the next section.

Violence Engendered by Defense of Community Resources

The resettlement of Santa Catarina in an area bereft of the water, forest, and land needed to sustain a Maya community has had unforeseen consequences for Santa Catarina and its neighbors Nahualá and Totonicapán. In the first place, some Ixtahuaquenses have felt forced to steal, a new and conflict-inducing phenomenon. We noticed this transformation in the first months after the relocation. "Trees are not the only thing that has been stolen," one informant said. "Crops and other goods have also been taken by desperate individuals who cross the border and carry them away."

In response, and to preserve its integrity, the leaders of neighboring Totonicapán municipality have had to protect its municipal boundaries. Its municipal corporation assigns residents to patrol its borders, watching for violators and reporting them. A Nahualense teacher explained the process of boundary maintenance using the example of goat herding: "Maybe you have seen the goats that graze in the mountains? [A shepherd from Nahualá] would never be allowed to cross the border of Totonicapán because there's always someone watching, guarding the border. [If someone crosses] they will go straight to jail, where they will have to take care of the problem. On the other hand, [a herder from] Totonicapán crosses the border of Nahualá and Ixtahuacán because there is no punishment for it." In 2006, the residents of Nahualá and Ixtahuacán responded in kind by organizing groups to protect their own forests and patrol for violators. Trespassers intent on theft would often use violence against anyone who happened upon them. Thus, if ordinary residents (as distinct from authorized patrols) found a tree cut down or in the process of being cut, they typically would not report the theft out of fear of reprisal. Numerous informants told of incidents of property holders losing eyes, limbs, and sometimes their lives in violent altercations with adjoining property holders or thieves from out of the area.

The outcome is a quasi militarization of municipal boundaries patrolled in the expectation of offense. This occurs precisely because notions of open access to commons invite people to use untended resources, while at the same time, boundary integrity is so ill-defined and misallocated among multiple levels of government entities. These include municipally sustained quasi-private use rights, state-sponsored programs of private titling, municipal claims, and untitled squatting, all involving culturally and ethnically diverse sectors of the population.

Economic Disruption Affecting Displaced Nahualenses

A member of Nahualá's land registry commission explained that Ixtahuacán's relocation obviously created "significant conflict," especially with those Nahualenses displaced from their long-held squatter holdings in the Chwipatán relocation zone. Informants from Nahualá repeatedly complained that the national government failed to take into account the important role access to this land played in their livelihoods, when the government sided with Ixtahuacán on a relocation site and bought out the registered Nahualenses. Moreover, a number of Nahualá's citizens who had been cultivating in the commons but had not yet registered with Nahualá's use-right land registry office lost their only landholdings when the government bought out the registered claimants in the invaded area (and later in the expanded error-correction area) in an attempt to reduce the prospect of violence between Nahualá and Nueva Ixtahuacán. Indeed, Dabb easily located ten Nahualense informants between the ages of forty and seventy who had not registered their land and who said this was the only land they had and that it was forcibly taken from them, without compensation by the government, in order to relocate the Ixtahuaquense disaster victims.

In a world of scarce resources and even scarcer options, these Nahualenses had to find new ways to support their newly vulnerable households. Many of the older individuals who lost their land had been forced to live with their children or extended family. Some of the younger ones felt obliged to go abroad looking for work—principally to the United States—or to send family members to work as wage laborers elsewhere in Guatemala. One man ran a small store out of his home, which he used for income after his only landholding in Chwipatán was "taken" from him. He told of the loss he had suffered during the relocation. "They invaded our land," he said. "The government had a list of people who had titles and some of those who did not, and they gave everyone on the list 1,000 quetzales [approximately US$125] for each *cuerda* [approximately 4,700 square feet] of land. I had five cuerdas, but now I have nothing. The money is gone, too." Yet he considered himself fortunate because he still had his shop to generate some income by selling basic goods, in partial compensation for the loss of his land.

The Problem of Population Expansion and Sense of Entitlement

In 2000, when Ixtahuaquenses moved into provisional tin sheds and began building small homes with government and international aid, the plots of land allotted to each family fully used up the original 1.7-caballería (about 190-acre) land allocation. With marriages and unions, the residents of Nueva Ixtahuacán needed more land, both for house building and for corn milpas. They got it when the state made arrangements to purchase the remainder of the three and a half caballerías promised.

Many in Ixtahuacán felt that the second distribution of land should go to the same family units that had received the first distribution—to those who had originally dared to make the migration in 2000. But new couples had hived off, or desperately wanted to hive off, from the original stem families; they and a few other people from Antigua Ixtahuacán who had joined the community after the initial move demanded land.

With the second distribution, Ixtahuacán's leaders at first intended that every original migrant family (those who moved in the year 2000) would receive two additional plots of land. These could then be given to their children through inheritance, if they so wished. But many of the children complained and demanded land for themselves.

In response to these complaints, the mayor charged cantón neighborhood leaders on Nueva Ixtahuacán's *traslado* (relocation) land committee with the task of distributing the land. Each family would be given three scattered, non-adjoining plots of land. That procedure promoted equality and minimized complaints about receiving all of one's land in a less valuable location. An appeals procedure was in place through which one could complain regarding one's allocation. After the land had been divided and the allocation known but not yet formally distributed, some families indeed complained about the allocation. They petitioned the mayor and his council in the following week, and the mayor's office made adjustments. In one concession, they agreed that every new couple that had not received a home and parcel of land in the initial move would receive one plot in the second distribution.

To compound the distribution problem, a number of newcomers to the town had built their homes wherever they wanted, just outside the defined perimeter of the original land allocation. When the second distribution came up, some of the plots that were supposed to be divided among the original year-2000 families had preexisting, unauthorized structures built by the new squatters. Neighborhood leaders approached the mayor to question the fairness of land being usurped by newcomers when it should have been distributed among the existing community members.

Thus, in this second allocation, amid confusion, complaints, and promises from political leaders, the land was surveyed, measured, marked, and distributed to each family in the community. To avoid the same problem that had occurred in the initial land division, the national government sent professional surveyors, "engineers" who drafted a plan and divided the land, creating a grid that accounted for varying planes and slopes. Each lot comprised a 25-meter by 18-meter rectangle. The engineers marked each corner with a small concrete post and assigned each plot a number. When asked about the process of distributing the plots, the engineers said that the majority would be distributed among the community members, but a certain number of plots, located near the highway, would be retained as municipal holdings for commercial development.

Marking land plots with concrete posts introduced a new complexity into future land-dispute resolution. Will concrete posts be more official or desirable than witnesses, documents, or the old, accepted furrows, paths, and trees that had marked boundaries for decades? Likely so. This process may insinuate the state ever deeper in a process that municipio leaders once handled internally, based on respect for leaders, municipal registry, and socially respected witnesses. Finally, will the insinuation of a weak state—ethnically alienated from the municipio's residents and widely believed to be corrupt and uncaring—help resolve land disputes, or further complicate and inflame them? We feel virtually certain the result will be increased complication and exacerbated conflict, including violence.

The Transformation of Indigenous Identity

The individual and communal struggles to define land tenure and to clarify title are also, surreptitiously, transforming indigenous identity.[8] Dracoulis (chapter 1), and to a lesser degree Bybee (chapter 2), has indicated that certain interactions with national political processes distance Indians from their ethnic roots and "Ladinoize" them.[9] To a degree, we suggest, this happens also with property registry procedures. Communal landholding (as opposed to private property; see Hawkins 1984) is an indigenous practice, because communal discussion and decision-making as a community in open counsel with one another are indigenous modes of political action, distinct from Ladino caudillismo leadership by hierarchical fiat. Nevertheless, the intermixture of various modes of property tenure, and the history of Ladino progressives trying to introduce marketable private property and marketable Indian labor into the national sector, has a tendency to Ladinoize the indigenous participants. Put another way, communal holding by the municipio is a mode of indigenous resistance, and forced national property registration is a mode of trying to break down that resistance.

Both Dracoulis and Bybee (this volume) suggest that this process affects indigenous mayors. They show how political practice alienates mayors from their social and symbolic roots, and in making them more Ladino, makes these select individuals less respected. Property, however, affects almost everyone. To the degree that full privatization occurs via state intrusion and registration, the ordinary citizen engages in a Ladino act and violates the initial premise of the municipio: that land stays in the municipio and is not sold in fee simple to outsiders, but must be re-allocated in usufruct within the municipio with municipal leadership oversight and authentication.

One sees subtle evidence that recalibrating land tenure Ladinoizes. When the citizens of Nueva Ixtahuacán built their homes on their newly issued plots, many of them built right up to the road, in violation of a city ordinance mandating an easement of several feet (the preferred rural Indian pattern of having a house placed away from immediate frontage on its property lines, though frequently violated when population pressure expands housing in a dense neighborhood).[10] The municipality established a commission to take measurements to assess code compliance. To encourage compliance, the mayor and his committee threatened to withhold allocation of the two additional parcels of land promised in the second distribution. The matter had to be dropped. How does one obtain compliance when the houses are made of rebar and block and the ubiquitous Ladino image of urban modernity and rising status entices one to place dwellings and protective walls close to the road?

The lack of respect for a city ordinance suggests the customary form of enforcement has also weakened, resulting in conflict and sometimes violence. Under the Maya traditional justice system, social pressure and the threat of mayoral punishment were enough to protect the rights of an individual who merely used communal land for crops and resource procurement. The economic stress caused by land scarcity, along with the transformation of communal land into private property and the intervention of the state, has arguably changed the way people create, maintain, and perceive borders as well as their evaluation of what it means to be both "communal" and Indian.

The Violence of State Intervention

Although the state is clearly called upon to intervene and even to referee and decide boundaries and assets allocated to each municipio, state intervention does further violence in two senses. For one thing, buying out the tenants of one municipio to reallocate their land to the residents of another municipio accelerates privatization as prices are formalized, boundaries are marked with concrete, and marketable ownership is registered in and backed by a system outside the municipio. For another, intervention by a weak state, suspected of corruption, further disrupts relations between municipios.

The state's pay-off solely to those who had registered their squatter cultivation in the municipality greatly enhances the value of squatting—as long as it is followed by registration. Squatting (in this case, cultivating without living on the plot) therefore speeds up privatization. The municipality of Ixtahuacán may have conducted the land distribution, but the state provided the pay-off to buy out the land from the previous squatters. Thereby, the state-mediated process injected the full personal property expectations of the state into the municipio, substantially weakening the municipio's claim of holding all land in communal tenure with use-right registration. In the name of reducing violence, the state's action will end up further breaking down the communal tenure and indigenous identity of the two municipios. Finally, the state pay-off to registered squatters in the mancomunada area—done in order to avoid strife—invites repeated land invasion and further strife in the remaining mancomunada areas shared by these two tensely related municipalities and their residents. In effect, we can expect people to invade any jointly administered land without clear title, register in their appropriate municipality, and blackmail the state with the threat of violence if the state does not buy out and rectify their claims.

A lack of confidence in the efficacy of the weak state, when it does intervene, encourages strife between municipios. In July 2006, the local police were driven out of Nueva Ixtahuacán by an armed mob that accused the mayor and police of corruption and abuse unrelated to the land dispute. This followed earlier occasions when the police had been driven out in 1999 and 2000, events observed by earlier field school students. These incidents demonstrate the utter weakness and lack of authority of state institutions, and they underscore the state's fundamental inability to adjudicate or ameliorate land disputes between or within municipalities. As Bybee (chapter 2) has shown, frustration with impotent state institutions, an ethic of communal self-help, and in this case, indistinct boundaries and desperation for land make for volatile crowds and spontaneous self-help violence.

Continued Festering of Intercommunity Conflict

When Nahualenses relate the story of the relocation of Ixtahuacán's cabecera, they underline the hostility and violence that flowed from the Ixtahuaquense seizure of Nahualense land:

"Even before any documents had been signed, people started moving to the area of Chwipatán. Farmers from Nahualá who had been cultivating land in that area went up there to work in their fields. When they arrived, they were met by an angry mob with machetes and other weapons. Voices emanating from the mob told them to leave because it was not their land anymore. One [Nahualense] boy [in Maya culture a 'boy' can be twenty or thirty years old] stood up to them and asked why they were doing this. Outraged, several of the mob members attacked and killed him. One other man lost an eye that day, too." This type of aggressive violence instilled fear in many of the individuals who lost land to the relocation effort.

Nahualenses recounted other incidents of intercommunity hostility. For example, they reported illegal tree-cutting by Ixtahuaquenses on Nahualá's land. Lacking nearby resources, Ixtahuaquense resettlers allegedly crossed the ditch marking the boundary to pillage firewood from Nahualá's communal preserves. During a routine check for illegal felling of trees, said an informant, "I went up there once to make sure that trees were not being illegally cut down and found several men with machetes and a chainsaw cutting down a tree. They told me that if I reported them or tried to stop them they would kill me with the chainsaw. I listened, and left as fast as I could."

Another informant told of a friend who went up to his land to harvest firewood and did not return. Several days later his family found his decapitated, mutilated body in the forest. Around him were the remnants of recently felled trees that the thieves had cut down with the chainsaw murder weapon.[11] In such cases, if the offenders are apprehended, the accuser is often threatened with violence and occasionally attacked. Landowners in Nahualá said they feel helpless and disempowered to retaliate, with no support from local leaders or state authorities.

The Prospect of Further Municipal Fission

The fission of Santa Catarina Ixtahuacán in 2000 has stimulated the growth of boundary ambiguity and conflict. As noted above, at the time of the fission, some five-sixths of the population, about five hundred families, moved to Chwipatán. But a few, about one hundred families, stayed put in the originating town site, remaining in their homes in what became known as Antigua Ixtahuacán. The leaders of those who moved, however, considered it essential that *everyone* move together, in unison. Not only was it more indigenous, but how could Ixtahuaquense leaders justify the "emergency necessity" of the move if some remained behind? The leaders believed unity was essential to convincing the government and aid agencies to release funds to mitigate their plight.[12]

For several months, the leaders of Nueva Ixtahuacán succeeded in hiding the fact that some residents had stayed behind. They had the original area declared a safety hazard zone. That disallowed development or any restoration investment in the area by government or NGOs operating in the nation. They had the electricity turned off to the area. After all, nobody lived there, or so they said. Eventually, the residents of Antigua Ixtahuacán made their presence officially known. After much suffering, they succeeded in having essential services turned back on. But Antigüenses resented the leaders of Nueva Ixtahuacán, many of them their kin, for having made them suffer.

Recently, the leaders of Antigua Ixtahuacán have turned that resentment into the possibility of a sophisticated political play. By August 2006, very little had been done to support and compensate the citizens of Antigua Ixtahuacán who had stayed behind to rebuild their homes and cultivate their fertile lands. Rumors circulated in Nahualá that Antigua Ixtahuacán's remaining residents were angered by their post–Hurricane Mitch treatment. Antigüenses, they said, talked about leaving the municipality of Ixtahuacán to join Nahualá. Moreover, the governor of Sololá was simultaneously making plans to split off a new Boca Costa municipality from the inaccessible southern half of Santa Catarina Ixtahuacán.[13] Thus, when Dabb visited the governor of Sololá, the governor mentioned his "plans to divide the two municipalities" to create a new, third municipality in the Boca Costa. When asked about the lack of political boundaries dividing what would then be three municipalities, he said, remarkably, "The issues that citizens are more worried about are things like economics and education. People aren't worried about land issues and whether or not there is a border." He obviously does not fully understand his citizens.

Adding further complexity, if a new, third municipality were split off, Nueva Ixtahuacán might no longer have a sufficient hinterland population to be considered a municipal headquarters or even a separate municipality. Nothing would please the inhabitants of Antigua Ixtahuacán more than to see the source of their pain and political isolation—Nueva Ixtahuacán—itself become isolated and collapse. The intrigues, rumors, and politico-administrative possibilities become byzantine. Here are just some of the possibilities:

- Santa Catarina Ixtahuacán might remain united, to include Antigua Ixtahuacán, Los Guineales (an *aldea* of Santa Catarina Ixtahuacán), and the southern Boca Costa region
- Santa Catarina Ixtahuacán might officially divide again and split off the southern Boca Costa, with Los Guineales as the likely new municipal seat
- Such a split might also foment a parallel division of Nahualá's lowland Boca Costa, most likely generating a fourth municipio
- Antigua Ixtahuacán might join Nahualá to spite (and weaken) Nueva Ixtahuacán
- If any of the above fissions or defections take place, Nueva Ixtahuacán might still manage to maintain its headquarters status despite its losses
- If not, Nueva Ixtahuacán might join Totonicapán to spite Nahualá for considering or completing the accessioning of Antigua Ixtahuacán

Regardless of which politico-administrative route the members of these communities take, or have foisted on them by the state, the border conflicts and bloodshed in a land divided without clear boundaries or clear titles will continue indefinitely. Moreover, the conflicts will probably escalate in stridency and violence.

Conclusion: Unclear Boundaries as a Source of Real and Symbolic Violence

The problems of violence—symbolic, structural, and real violence of humans at blows with each other—flow as a corollary of Douglas's proposition (1966) that matter out of place creates uncertainty and ambiguity. Matter out of place is disconcerting, fear-provoking, and therefore, dangerous.

For matter to be "in place," there must be clear boundaries—left and right, clean and unclean, right and wrong. In the case of property, there must be ways to understand and symbolize what is "yours" and what is "mine." For communities of identity, there must be clear delineations of what is "ours" and what is "theirs." This requires identifiable, clear, respected boundaries and ways to maintain them. Moreover, there must be a trusted arbiter to resolve any remaining disputes. Such would seem to be the responsibility of the Guatemalan state apparatus, but it has largely failed in the task. Human misery and violence have been the inevitable results.

Indeed, rivalry and conflict have long festered between Nahualá and Santa Catarina, a rivalry thrown into stark relief by the population relocations attendant to Hurricane Mitch. Shortly after the hurricane (1998) and the subsequent relocation of much of Santa Catarina's cabecera municipal population to higher, more stable ground, accessible by road, tension flared between Nahualá and Nueva Santa Catarina Ixtahuacán over their territorial boundaries. Recent instances of informal boundary delineation amplified long-existing tensions between the two municipalities, and their conflict was exacerbated by the limited political intervention of a weak state government. The result was violence between municipalities.

Under colonial and post-colonial conditions, Maya land tenure systems have been subjected to transformative pressures by the larger national and international political economy. Most notably, these pressures flared in the late 1800s under Barrios's liberal reforms and again in the wake of the 1996 Peace Accords, when neoliberal globalizing market reforms swept into the country under international pressure. While communal forms of tenure have survived into the twenty-first century, they are now seriously challenged by pressure to quasi-privatize communal landholdings by registering use rights in the municipio or to fully privatize them by registering land at the national land registry offices in department capitals.

The history of Nahualá and Ixtahuacán is one of division and conflict both within and between municipalities. Although pressures for liberal land-reform measures have historically ebbed and flowed, the communal landholding claim of the entire municipio has endured in these two municipalities. But, as we have seen, it is now under severe pressure. Residual portions of the communal systems still influence the mentality of many individuals in the highland area, and, on occasion, conflict with private property rights. In Nahualá and Santa Catarina, the communal system is now juxtaposed with state-privatized and municipally vetted usufruct claims for securing land tenure, resulting in boundary disputation and conflict. As the two systems collide, tenure will be hotly contested until a dominant or fully synthesized system emerges.

What would a "fully synthesized" system look like? We have no idea. Whatever the outcome, however, for it to work, the state and the municipality must have the power to enforce claims they have registered and vetted. Moreover, both state and municipality must have the reputation of reliably honest brokers and enforcers. Finally, all concerned must agree to a shared set of definitions and procedures regarding land tenure.

We do not foresee any of these three conditions appearing in the near future. Nevertheless, perceptions of ownership and restriction of land access will continue to evolve through contestation as long as the communal, quasi-private, usufruct, and private tenure systems coexist at familial, municipal, and state levels (Durrenberger and Palsson 1987: 514). It is not surprising, then, that as demographic pressure places a premium on the relatively inelastic land supply, families will seek to codify their usufruct right to communal land through local licensure at the municipal level, whether as a hedge against the claims of others or as a defense against the arbitrary intrusion of the state as it referees between municipios.

The custom of communal property continues to influence Maya thought and action. The many residuals of that custom influence these Mayas as they move toward quasi and full privatization in a land-scarce but highly marketized neoliberal world. Unfortunately, neither full communalization nor full privatization seems likely to reduce the threat of conflict between families or hamlets within a municipality, or between municipalities within the state, because a culture of corruption vitiates the state and renders it an untrustworthy and impotent arbiter.

The intercommunity violence Nahualá and Ixtahuacán exhibit is but one example of conflicts between municipios and between individuals that have erupted throughout Guatemala, a country characterized by ill-defined territorial boundaries within an ill-equipped state. For anything to be different, state and local leaders must demarcate, adjudicate, resolve, and enforce tenancy and boundary issues. If they do not, these two municipalities and their residents—and all Guatemalans—face escalating outbreaks of hostility and violence within and across their unclear and therefore hotly contested borders. For here, land is life.

The case of Nahualá and Ixtahuacán underscores the relatively limited reach and ability of Guatemala's central government to establish a consistent governance of space through the routinized practices of title establishment and registry. In this case, the central government has been ineffective in moderating boundary disputes in and between communities, disputes exacerbated by its poor management of relocation efforts after Hurricane Mitch in 1998. The new community of Santa Catarina Ixtahuacán was established in what had been communal land ostensibly under joint, sustainable management but in fact registered to Ixtahuacán at the state offices but homesteaded by cultivators registering their use-right claims locally in Nahualá. The two communities were thus pitted in direct rivalry with each other and with the state. In the wake of both internal and external conflicts over land, the state has shown scant ability to exert its authority over space or to define the nature of rightful ownership by citizens or communities. This is not to suggest that the state's precarious authority, control, and reach make its role insignificant. Clearly, the state is seeking to imprint its form, logic, and practices on localities. It is the job of empirically oriented ethnography to explore the development of ever-shifting local-state relations in the imperfect, conflictive, and fragile governmentality that characterizes Guatemala (see Ferguson and Gupta 2002:995).

The situation analyzed here—of land boundaries and the cultural processes and bureaucratic institutions that surround land titles, claims, boundaries, and contestation—provides a counterexample to the growing literature on the governance of space that draws heavily upon Foucault's notion of governmentality (Ferguson and Gupta 2002; Merry 2001). Those works show the operation of new forms of security, control, and the disciplining of space through regulatory and surveillance modalities that focus on space rather than on individual potential offenders. In the case presented here, we see that the reach of the state and its proxies has not thoroughly penetrated indigenous rural Guatemala via effective neoliberal management of space, thus exposing rural Mayas to ongoing risk, threat, and violence. Further, we are reminded—in keeping with Ferguson and Gupta—that processes of state verticality and encompassment, whereby states legitimately hold authority over localities through rituals of everyday bureaucratic practice, are poorly developed at best in Guatemala's Maya Western Highlands.

Notes

Fieldwork: 2006

1. Registering the land protects a smallholder against claims of others equally weak (that is, of one's peers in the municipio). But it exposes one's land to the depredations of the powerful, who have more access to lawyers and to the possibility of forged claims, and who thereby can find (or assert) that an Indian's registered claim is on a piece of land to which they have (or have fabricated) an older or colonial title.

2. What constitutes overpopulation? In a culture oriented to subsistence—the Maya, for example—one must have enough land to feed the household throughout its life cycle and enough additional wage labor capacity or land whose production can buy products not produced on the land but deemed essential. Brintnall (1979) gives figures that one must have 40 cuerdas of unirrigated land "to avoid the dreaded seasonal labor migration." The average holding in Aguacatán at that time was 30 cuerdas, but Brintnall does not specify how much of this average is irrigated. A few cuerdas of irrigated land can produce enough garlic cash-crop to alleviate land shortage and feed the family. Other ethnographies maintain a lesser holding will sustain a family. Nevertheless, Early (1982) asserts that virtually all of the 1930s–1950s ethnographies show evidence of severe land shortage vis-à-vis family subsistence needs. In spite of fertilizers, the problem has only gotten worse in the recent period.

3. Documents that authenticate the whole community constitute a different class and are widely revered and carefully preserved in semi-sacred *cajas*, the "royal coffers." Hawkins never was allowed to see the communal titles of Santa Catarina Ixtahuacán, held, he was told, in a box. Oakes (1951) describes the reverence among residents of Todos Santos Cuchumatán for communal land titles, also held in the royal coffer.

4. A number of useful Internet sites, including Wikipedia references, can be accessed using "Nahualá" or "Santa Catarina Ixtahuacán" as search terms. Academically, however, these documents reflect the positions of partisans to the land and administrative disputes. Anthropologically, they constitute analyzable versions of several of the groups' mythical charters of foundation/justification. Hawkins and Adams hope to provide a more permanent record of the relocation in the near future (see Hawkins and Adams, in preparation). This study offers a political-economic history of events leading to the fission of Santa Catarina Ixtahuacán and the relocation of five-sixths of its population to Nueva Ixtahuacán in the *mancomunada* territory here discussed that was being diverted to agriculture by Nahualenses.

5. Throughout the summers of 2000 and 2002, Hawkins slept in one of the provisional tin sheds that served for homes. He slept in a middle-grade synthetic-filled sleeping bag with a heavy canvas tarp draped over it. He always went to bed fully clothed (except for boots), wearing an alpine ski parka. He still nearly froze.

6. During the first buy-out, the government reportedly paid Q1,000 per cuerda. After they discovered the surveying mistake, they had to pay Q2,500 per cuerda to secure the additional land to make good on the original promise of land.

7. The fission of municipios and their subsequent disputations are not unique to Nahualá and Santa Catarina. Carey (2001:58–70), for example, records the origin myths of Poaquil's separation from Comalapa.

8. We treat identity transformation more extensively in Hawkins and Adams, in preparation.

9. See also Hawkins (1984:173–212) for a study of the impact of institutional position on identity transformation in San Pedro Sacatepéquez, San Marcos.

10. The pattern is long-standing, in spite of its many "violations" in urban settings, or, put differently, in spite of the Ladinoizing impact of urbanity on Indian urbanites. La Farge (1947: figure 9, facing page 34; see also 33) observes, "Ladino houses front on the road, with patios behind; Indian houses are set back, with patios in front."

11. Whether this incident is the same decapitation as that described by Bybee (chapter 2) we cannot ascertain. If it is the same man, it is possible that he came upon a theft and was decapitated, in which case Bybee's informants interpreted it as just deserts for extortion; or that he was assassinated for extortion and wood theft was used as a cover-up. Or it may have been a different person.

12. Nuttall (in preparation) thoroughly describes the logic of feigning unanimity of response to danger in order to secure the funds needed to succeed in relocation.

13. The Boca Costa is an area distant from the municipal heartland of Ixtahuacán and Nahualá (approximately a nine-hour hike or four-hour bus ride). Individuals who reside there are far removed from the center of political decision-making that affects them. Yet they represent a significant portion of the population. Traveling along the road to the Boca Costa, one sees the villages alternate between the municipalities of Ixtahuacán and Nahualá in a confusing checkerboard. This has caused problems for these distant small villages. When problems arise in them, neither municipality claims responsibility.

CHAPTER 4

"They Do Not Know How to Take Care of the Forest

Analyzing State-Sponsored "Decentralization" of Forest Management in Santa Catarina Ixtahuacán

Jason M. Brown, John P. Hawkins, James H. McDonald, and Walter Randolph Adams

The preservation of forests rightly stands at the fore of global concern and study.[1] An array of interpretations, declarations, and strategies express multiple social values, agendas, and paradigms for dealing with the earth's forest lands. Biodiversity, poverty, and global warming are all intimately linked to forest management and the social values that accrue to forests. As evidence of the tight connection between forests and global well-being, the World Bank (2006) asserts that 90 percent of the world's 1.5 billion poorest people depend directly on forests for some critical aspect of their livelihoods. For multiple reasons—social, economic, and environmental—the processes of and impacts from decentralizing forest management worldwide have received considerable attention in recent years.

The Mayas of the Western Highlands of Guatemala have used traditional ecological knowledge to successfully manage their forests to provide for diverse uses and values under multiple formal and informal institutions. Some scholars think they have done so for hundreds, if not thousands, of years (Anderson et al. 2005; Berkes, Colding, and Folke 2000; Posey 1985). In addition to sophisticated ecological knowledge, many indigenous communities throughout the world have also developed institutions to regulate the use of communal or common-pool forests that provide basic sustenance materials such as fuel wood, medicine, fertilizer, animal fodder, and building materials (Agrawal 2001; Anderson et al. 2005; Gibson, McKean, and Ostrom 2000).[2] Some communities, such as the Yucatec Mayas of Quintana Roo, have successfully adapted to changes brought on by globalization (Anderson et al. 2005); others have not (Richards 1997). Maya ecological land management practices and institutions have been successful in managing and preserving forests, as Veblen (1978) and Utting (1993) have shown. Wittman and Geisler (2005:65) show that traditional land tenure has contributed to the preservation of the remaining forest cover in the Western Highlands of Guatemala: "While privately owned land in the highlands is almost completely deforested, a recent study of 22 highland municipalities (FLACSO 2001) found that 80 percent contained forest under customary communal tenure although some of these areas were simultaneously subject to management claims by municipalities." In other words, communal tenure has tended to preserve forests; private tenure has tended to deplete them. To be sure, there is no guarantee that communal tenure management by municipios is the most efficient possible mode of forest preservation. But it has preserved forests and managed them, and in the cultural and political context of Guatemala, it is the only management institution and practice so far that has worked.

The 1996 Peace Accords recognized the long-standing unequal distribution of land and sought to better enfranchise indigenous Maya peoples by exhorting the Guatemalan government to promote rural development programs, mediate and solve land disputes that had erupted during the civil war, establish lands for the resettlement of displaced communities and the landless, and seriously address inequities in land distribution (Wittman and Saldivar-Tanaka 2006:23). That general state movement is explicitly called "decentralization." In the area of forest management, the National Forestry Institute (Instituto Nacional de Bosques, INAB) claims it is decentralizing its forest management to the municipal level.

In this regard, Article 5 of the Forestry Law (Congreso de la República de Guatemala 1996), passed just before the final signing of the accords, states that the newly created Forestry Institute will be "autonomous" and "decentralized." The law specifies that forestry officials are "required to involve communities in planning and executing forest policy, and that the institution [INAB] and its personnel comply with the decentralization and deconcentration plan" (Congreso de la República de Guatemala 1996, Forestry Law no. 101-96, Title 2, Chap. 2, Article 19).

INAB's decentralization program has proved controversial. The plan involves opening municipal forestry offices throughout Guatemala. INAB offices in the municipalities are supposed to manage forest operations by adhering as closely as possible to rigorous and centralized protocols. As a result, university-trained INAB technicians have found themselves less than welcome in many of the Maya communities that INAB has sought to advise. Little surprise there. K'iche' and other Mayas have long viewed government programs and officials with skepticism. In Guatemala's cultural context, Ladino and Indian interests have often been opposed, and Maya communities have suffered exploitation, condescension, and discrimination at the hands of Ladino officials.

Santa Catarina Ixtahuacán, with an indigenous population greater than 95 percent, is one of many municipalities where INAB has implemented forest management decentralization. In 2004, INAB opened a municipal forestry office in Nueva Santa Catarina Ixtahuacán, the recently established municipal *cabecera* approximately sixteen kilometers from the considerably depopulated former municipal center (now referred to as Antigua Ixtahuacán).[3]

Regarding the recent entry of this state agency into the municipal scene, I develop this thesis: in spite of INAB's ideology or stated policy of "decentralization," the program's implementation in fact *increases* the centralization of forest management and escalates state control in an area that was previously decentralized via traditional indigenous autonomy. This chapter thus confirms the findings of Elías and Wittman (2005) and Wittman and Geisler (2005). In theory, decentralization should increase the decision-making power of local people. In fact, as I and others argue, despite being under the auspices of municipal authorities, INAB forest technicians operate under a highly centralized and upwardly accountable protocol that actually *decreases* local decision-making power and threatens traditional management institutions, norms, and the ecologically sustainable practices that indigenous communal institutions encourage. Furthermore, INAB's protocol criminalizes the gathering of fuel wood essential to all Maya households by imposing a licensing system that is required for larger wood harvests. Unfortunately, given the ambiguity of poor communications and a persistent fear of the state, some residents feel the INAB licensing requirement applies to *all* wood harvests and deadwood collecting (Elías and Wittman 2005:291), in effect criminalizing (in people's perceptions, anyway) the entire project of sustenance wood collection.[4]

This chapter is thus a case study of the potential problems that INAB faces if it ignores traditional forest management strategies and the social arrangements that surround them. While the details here are specific to Santa Catarina Ixtahuacán, the strategies INAB must employ to deal with local specifics are generalizable throughout Guatemala. Despite valid critiques of INAB's centralized protocol, however, the knowledge and resources that INAB possesses can certainly benefit communities. Therefore, it is my view that INAB should better incorporate traditional local knowledge and expertise and encourage participation in the forestry institute's management process. Once meaningful gains have been made in these areas, INAB could become a more equal, accountable, and effective partner in forest management at the municipal and national levels.

DECENTRALIZING FOREST MANAGEMENT IN GUATEMALA

Many developing countries have undergone some aspect of political, financial, or resource management decentralization in recent years (Montero and Samuels 2004). Anne Larson (2005:33) defines decentralization as "the transfer of power from central government to lower levels in a political-administrative and territorial hierarchy." Decentralization implies a redistribution of decision-making responsibility from central government posts to regional and local ones (Blaser, Küchli, Colfer, and Capistrano 2005:8). Despite Latin America's long history of centrist and often authoritarian states, Latin American countries have decentralized in significant ways (Willis, Garman, and Haggard 1999). For example, between 1980 and 1995, the number of Latin American countries that allowed direct election of mayors increased from three to seventeen (Montero and Samuels 2004:4).

Decentralization is a complex process that involves political, fiscal, and administrative dimensions (Montero and Samuels 2004:5). Some scholars have argued that the impetus for decentralization comes from the increase in International Monetary Fund (IMF) structural adjustment programs that have been imposed on the region (Bird and Vaillancourt 1998:4; Oates 1993). However, Falleti (1999) suggests that decentralization became a part of IMF structural reform only after 1988 and shows that decentralization trends were well established in several regions prior to that date. Some point to urbanization since the 1960s as a key factor in Latin American decentralization (Diamond 1999). However, despite the more pragmatic reasons, such as easing highly centralized administrative and fiscal burdens, much of the recent wave of decentralization is happening in the language of rights-based democratization (A. Larson and Ribot 2004). Ideally, decentralization efforts in the resource management sector empower local people with a greater measure of "downward accountability" regarding natural resource use and allow localities to make decisions based on local priorities (Blaser, Küchli, Colfer, and Capistrano 2005:8; A. Larson 2005:33, A. Larson and Ribot 2004:3).

According to Agrawal (2001), more than sixty countries are in the process of decentralizing some aspect of resource management. Brazil, Honduras, Guatemala, and Bolivia, among others, have all implemented some level of decentralization of forest management in recent years. The decentralization of forest management is becoming more common as national governments face failure of centralized management policies, pressure for multi-stakeholder participation, and administrative necessity (Blaser, Küchli, Colfer, and Capistrano 2005:2). Some authors have anticipated a positive outcome from forest management decentralization (Ferroukhi 2003). But as Tacconi (2007) suggests, efforts to correct the problems associated with centralized forest management by decentralizing it do not always lead to better management, or, as in the case of Guatemala, to an empowered local population of forest users.

In 1996, after a bloody civil war left Guatemala in ruins, government and insurgent leaders signed peace accords that included provisions to increase indigenous access to power, land, and natural resources. Along with the accords and other reforms, the government instituted a new Forestry Law (Decree no. 101-96) (Congreso de la República de Guatemala 1996) designed to clarify the national government's role in resource management in those forests that fall outside the jurisdiction of the National Council of Protected Areas (Consejo Nacional de Áreas Protegidas, CONAP). To that end, the National Forestry Institute, INAB, was created to replace a legacy of previously unsuccessful programs such as the General Directorate of Forests (Dirección General de Bosques, DIGEBOS). The 1996 Forestry Law made INAB an independent institute charged with increasing the economic productivity of the Guatemalan forestry sector and decreasing rampant deforestation (FAO 1999:8; Loening and Markussen 2003).[5] INAB has opened municipal forestry offices in more than one-third of Guatemala's (then) 332 municipalities. In most cases, a single forest technician staffs a town's municipal forest office in order, as one technician put it, to "be closer to the people." Nine regions and thirty-three subregions that extend throughout Guatemala manage these municipal forestry offices. Technicians run the municipal licensing system to regulate tree harvesting and manage the Reforestation Incentives Program (Programa Incentivo de Forestación, PINFOR), and they are the only persons legally authorized to write forest management plans.

Licensing Woodcutters

In 2004, INAB opened a municipal forestry office in Santa Catarina Ixtahuacán with the support of the mayor. The office began issuing domestic use licenses for harvests of ten cubic meters or less, and licenses for commercial felling, which includes lumber or firewood harvests above ten cubic meters. Such licenses must be procured both for felling in the municipal commons forest and for felling on one's private (use-right, whether registered or not) land. These licenses are issued and authorized by the municipal forestry technician, who monitors each licensee and verifies that each licensee is the legal owner of the land where harvests have been proposed. A family consumption license costs sixty quetzales, a prohibitive sum for most residents with scant cash income. Taking out a license also requires that one interact with the municipality's offices and, preferably, that one be at least semiliterate so one can determine that the papers issued are what they claim to be. Such is not always the case among residents of Ixtahuacán. As both the literature and my informants suggest, imposing a licensing system criminalizes the felling of trees on small parcels where sustenance farmers have tenure but no money, while allowing those who can pay—usually large landowners and commercial woodcutters with access to cash—to cut down trees at will (Elías and Wittman 2005:289). Moreover, the external regulations place in doubt the traditional household gathering practices that have allowed municipal residents free entry to the municipal forests to collect deadwood—dried and fallen branches or dead trees—in quantities of human backpacked or animal-carried loads.

Records at the Municipal Forestry Office indicate that only seven licenses were taken out in 2005 for felling trees by residents of Antigua Santa Catarina Ixtahuacán. By contrast, the municipal headquarters issued seventy-eight licenses to residents of Nueva Santa Catarina Ixtahuacán

(Oficina Forestal Municipal 2006). The large difference in number of cutting licenses could be explained by several factors. For one, Antigua Ixtahuacán was massively depopulated following the relocation to Nueva Ixtahuacán, retaining approximately one-sixth of its former population; it has, at best, only one-fifth of the population now living in Nueva Ixtahuacán. Thus one might expect a fifth of the licenses to be from Antigua Ixtahuacán; here we see a tenth. The discrepancy may reflect the difficulty of getting from Antigua to Nueva Ixtahuacán to obtain a license. It might also reflect the belief that the distance from the forestry office protects them from the need to get a license. In addition, residents of Antigua Ixtahuacán feel (and encourage) resistance to the administrative dictates of Nueva Ixtahuacán, a feeling stemming from disputes over the relocation process and the old town's subsequent suppression by leaders in the relocated municipal seat.

Another factor explaining the disproportionate number of licenses is that many residents of Nueva Ixtahuacán still retain holdings in Antigua Ixtahuacán. The area around the old location is much more densely forested than barren Nueva Ixtahuacán. Before settlement in 2000, the new area was used exclusively for communal sheep grazing in the 1970s and 1980s and only began to be farmed, with extremely spotty (and stunted) corn plots and some wheat, in the late 1980s and 2000s. Thus, Nueva Ixtahuacán residents must travel far to secure wood. As a result, they are more likely to use vehicles and harvest in quantity at less-frequent intervals. Both the quantity and the mode of travel increase the likelihood of getting caught if involved in unlicensed gathering or fresh woodcutting, because municipal and national police watch the road choke-points but seldom patrol the foot trails. Therefore the residents of Nueva Ixtahuacán have more reason to obtain licenses.

Reforestation Incentives Program

The Municipal Forestry Office in Ixtahuacán also runs PINFOR, the reforestation incentives program. Participants must agree to reforest preapproved parcels at their own expense. After one year, PINFOR incentive payments begin: Q10,000 per reforested hectare, paid in graduated monthly installments over a six-year span. Participants, however, must pay substantial up-front investment costs. They must buy, fertilize, and plant INAB's required tree species, provide for fire suppression and prevention, and ensure sapling survival by clearing competing vegetation until trees achieve dominance. To ensure compliance, INAB technicians regularly inspect PINFOR projects.

Given that one hectare contains, in the local idiom, 22.9 or effectively 23 cuerdas, each cuerda of reforested land under the plan generates Q72 of income per year ($\frac{\text{Q10,000}}{\text{23 cuerdas x 6 years}}$), without counting initial investment costs. By comparison, a cuerda of good land in a temperate Ixtahuaquense location would yield two *quintales* (hundredweight) of corn, plus additional intercrop harvests, the corn alone being worth Q75 to Q95 per quintal (2006 prices). Thus, a cuerda planted in corn generates Q150 to Q190 of income per year. Both calculations exclude certain investment costs, such as fertilizer.

A farmer can minimize production costs by procuring seed from the previous harvest and supplying labor input from family. The only significant cash outlay is for chemical fertilizer, and that pays back in higher yields within a year, if it is purchased. We do not have figures on corn harvests at the Nueva Ixtahuacán altitude, but what we saw growing seemed quite stunted. Compared with milpa corn production using traditional technology, the reforestation incentives are economically quite unfavorable for the first six years and difficult, if not impossible, to estimate over the subsequent life of the timber harvest cycle. It is doubtful any peasant can survive the years that the land will be out of corn production while the timber stand matures, let alone calculate the profits that might accrue from waiting. At best, one can only justify the reforestation incentives on land utterly unsuitable for hoe agriculture or by people not dependent on corn for life—which is to say, large owners and municipal corporations (see fig. 4.1).

Finally, because reward (if any) is based on inspection, and inspection is, ultimately, a judgment call, one's hoped-for cash crop from reforested land can easily be undercut by the arbitrary judgment of a stringent and unsympathetic forestry official whose goal is to reduce costs by demanding strict compliance to a rigid protocol. Thus, the risks of participation are great—assuming no investment costs—and the prospect of reward vanishingly small and much too distant when initial investment costs are considered. Note that this risk is mitigated for large owners or municipal corporations because they can maintain close social contact with and even power over inspectors and thus favorably influence their behavior. The program, in fact, is designed

Fig. 4.1. Reforestation with *ciprés* (*Cupressus lusitanica* [Mill.]) on municipal land in Nueva Santa Catarina Ixtahuacán. Photograph by Jason M. Brown, 2006.

for large landholders, though there is no required minimum land size to participate. In practice, while some reforestation projects in the municipality have succeeded, others have failed to meet the rigid INAB requirements, leaving participants without compensation.

The Myth of Decentralization

Despite the official rhetoric of decentralization, INAB is for the most part an upwardly accountable institution with a highly centralized protocol. Elías and Wittman (2005) and Wittman and Geisler (2005) have shown that instead of decentralizing, the INAB "municipalization" process in fact *centralizes* INAB's role in municipal forest management. Wittman and Geisler (2005:1) assert that "decentralization policies at times diffuse centralization and actually increase state power at the local level, putting at risk and even weakening successful village-level forest governance structures and local livelihoods." Ribot and colleagues (2006) have called this trend "recentralizing while decentralizing." For instance, in regard to licensing, one INAB technician reflected on the new top-down mandates, "People must register and do what INAB tells them: 'You must do this, this, and this.' Then the people do their cutting, but with commitments, and INAB is constantly supervising to see that the commitments are carried out."

INAB technicians act under the direction of the alcalde (mayor). The municipality pays the technician's salary until the office becomes self-sustaining through the revenue it generates from its fees and programs. However, as this technician indicates, the municipality has little say in what he does: "I am an employee of the municipality but under the direction of INAB. The rules I follow [are those] INAB indicates to me. The municipality basically has no knowledge of what my work is. I inform them of what I do and how I do it, but they do not give me orders."

The so-called decentralization of INAB is in reality a co-optation of the municipality into INAB's centralized protocol. Far from being downwardly accountable to the municipality and its citizens, technicians are upwardly accountable to the subregional and regional directors of INAB. In the end, Ixtahuacán citizens pay for INAB's management either through municipal funds or fees for use or felling in municipal forests or on one's "own" quasi-private usufruct lands. It is, at best, a newer form of colonial extraction in a program not of Ixtahuacán's making.

THE IMPORTANCE OF TREES IN SANTA CATARINA IXTAHUACÁN

Trees figure significantly in Guatemalan Maya life. Today, speakers of K'iche', including the residents of Ixtahuacán, parse their language as *k'i* (many), and *che'* (tree[s]). In the Western Highlands, the forests have been continually utilized and managed for thousands of years. White pine (*Pinus strobus* var. chiapensis [Mart.]) and cypress (*Cupressus lusitanica* [Mill.]), dominant species in the Western Highlands, are even mentioned in the first lines of the Popol Vuh, the K'iche' creation story (Tedlock 1996:66). While Mayas make a sharp cultural distinction between cultivated fields and uncultivated forest, Utting (1993:60) points out that the distinction is not as sharp in practice regarding sources of biosustenance, because they have continually harvested the forests for medicines, herbs, animal forage, and fuel used in daily life. The acquired knowledge that created these multi-use forest-gardens has long been ignored, first by Ladino colonists and now by Western agricultural developmentalists (Berkes and Folke 1998:17; Greenpeace Central America 1997:10).

The Traditional Maya Forest

Many Maya communities have developed sophisticated institutions and norms for managing communal forests and regulating forest use (Anderson et al. 2005; Gibson, McKean, and Ostrom 2000). Indigenous models of forest management in Guatemala have been studied most notably in the neighboring department of Totonicapán (Elías and Wittman 2005; Greenpeace Central America 1997, Tiu López and García Hierro 2002; Veblen 1978; Wittman and Geisler 2005).

In Totonicapán, as in much of Guatemala, communal forests are remnants of colonial land divisions that were designed to create self-sufficient pools of cheap labor and government tribute (Annis 1987; Elías and Wittman 2005:284; Hawkins 1984). Traditionally, forest committees or assemblies governed communal forests and coordinated management activities, such as fire suppression, reforestation, and felling. They also employed the use of *guardabosques* (forest guards). Guardabosques are volunteers who patrol the communal forests to avert illegal felling of trees and prevent and fight forest fires.

In traditional Maya belief and practice, forests are a source not only of daily sustenance and of wood for cooking meals, but also of spiritual power (Utting 1993:63). The flora and fauna of the forest were said to possess a *nahual* (protecting spirit). Therefore, a Maya priest typically officiated at a ceremony in which sacrificial incense and candles were burned so the tree's spirit would not scream when cut down and to ensure no one would be hurt when the tree fell. In traditional Maya belief, the forest is alive with spirits both benevolent and malicious.

After the introduction of chainsaws and vehicles to haul away trees in quantity, such beliefs and practices passed into the annals of folklore. However, forests continue to hold an important place in K'iche' spiritual practice. Pine needles (*uxaq chaj* when on a tree) and incense derived from pine sap accompany most traditional and many Catholic religious ceremonies such as blessing and divination, Catholic Mass, the *novena* funerary rite, and All Saints' Day festivals. Pan-Maya activists seek to restore the importance of the forests as sacred sites for ceremonies (Utting 1993:61) and accordingly use traditional forest products in ritual performances. Similarly, recently harvested pine needles (*xaq chaj*) typically carpet the floors of homes celebrating any kind of fiesta. Similarly, special political events are decorated with recently harvested branches and pine needles that provide a pleasing aroma and festive presence.

To Ixtahuaquenses, as I heard many times, forests are the *fuente de la vida* (source of life). As one informant observed, "trees—they bring the rain; they protect the springs; when there are no trees, there is no rain." Ixtahuaquenses know the forest protects the soil from erosion. They harvest forests for livestock fodder, edible herbs, medicine, and mushrooms. Forest duff scratched up from the forest floor provides fertilizer for crops. Pitch (*chaj* or *ocote*) is collected for incense and fire starter. The trees render timbers for making houses, and of course, fuel wood. A corn farmer who also served on a local forest committee mused on the forest's mixture of pragmatic and spiritual properties: "The trees are like us. We need air just as they do. They help us a lot. For example, when we go to the forest, if there is a tree, we sit down for a bit to rest. What we breathe is air that comes from the trees; it is very pleasant. It is not like the air in other places, where you inhale the air from trucks that is contaminated. Trees have spirits—they have life. They are just like us; we have a life and so do the trees."[6] Despite the opening of an INAB municipal forestry office, Ixtahuacán retains much of its traditional forest use and management practices, the most important of which allows families access to gather dead fuel wood in the surrounding forests. INAB's perceived authority, however, may threaten the effectiveness of these norms by undermining traditional authority and practices with regard to forest use, due to INAB's inability to enforce its own protocol and the presumption that users need licenses.

Fuel Wood Collection Norms

For many of the world's poor—including Mayas of Guatemala who rely on wood as a primary source of cooking fuel—gathering wood is a daily chore. Nearly all Ixtahuaquense households use wood as a fuel for cooking, preparing the *nixtamal* (dried corn cooked to soften it for wet-milling), and heating water for bathing in the traditional sweat bath, the *tuj*. While riding in the back of a pickup truck down the steep, bumpy dirt road that descends from the Pan-American Highway to Antigua Ixtahuacán, one cannot but notice the small groups of men or young boys hunched under the burden of large loads of firewood hanging from a *mecapal* cinched across their foreheads (see fig. 4.2). This laborious daily task is an essential sustenance activity. As one informant stated, "If we don't plant corn, what will we eat? And if we don't gather wood, what will we cook with?"

As discussed above, INAB regulates the felling of whole trees through a licensing program authorized under Forestry Law no. 101-96. Lawmakers sought to prevent the rampant illegal deforestation occurring throughout Guatemala. The Forestry Law does not regulate downed or deadwood, which in theory makes up the bulk of fuel wood gathered by residents of Ixtahuacán. Nevertheless, INAB criminalizes the large-scale collection of deadwood, variously stated as "more than ten cubic meters a year" or "a pickup truckload at a time" or "more than a *tarea* at a time." What this inspecificity does, however, is put all collection, even a backpack load at a time, under a cloud, especially for the uncertain, the illiterate, and the unconnected. In short, Ixtahuaquenses cannot easily get a clear notion of what is legal and what is not, with the net result that a traditional and socially regulated practice essential to sustenance has been criminalized.

INAB could decrease illegal felling if its administrators paid attention to the local systems of regulation prevalent throughout Guatemala. Previous to INAB (National Forestry Institute) and the earlier DIGEBOS

Fig. 4.2. In Nahualá, men and animals take fuel wood for daily use home or to market. Photograph by Jason M. Brown, 2006.

(General Directorate of Forests), the municipality effectively regulated the gathering of dry wood for fuel by face-to-face social relations. As one informant explained: "We forgive one another. Why? Because of our needs. If we are going to be very rigid and privatize everything, what happens to those who do not have any land? For example, my father has one cuerda of land that has trees; if we are going to be very private about everything, where are those people going to go to get firewood and plant corn? It is very damaging to make laws that enforce private property, because of the people who don't have any." This arrangement functions as a system of common consent that allows for all members of the local community to collect *leña seca* (dry wood), which comes from dead branches and fallen trees in municipal commons forest. Green branches on living trees are officially off limits, though they do sometimes get harvested for fuel wood. Ixtahuaquenses believe that wood is necessary for survival, and to deny someone access to it would be immoral. Hence the

Fig. 4.3. A mountain scene in Santa Catarina Ixtahuacán suggests the extent of deforestation on steep slopes. Note the effects of limb-lopping. Photograph by Jason M. Brown, 2006.

common-law right of free scavenging for deadwood on municipal forest land in daily-use (backpackable) quantities.

Katz (2000) suggests that shared Maya identity, history, and lifeways constitute a form of social capital that effectively regulates forest resources. In recent years this capital has been put to the test by natural disasters, population pressure on fuel-wood resources, and the increased mobility and considerable speed with which illegal loggers can pillage trees.

In any forest in Guatemala, one can observe trees with several whorls where branches were lopped off near the bole of the tree, leaving them looking somewhat like palm trees or umbrellas. To some degree, this results from cutting live limbs for fuel wood (see fig. 4.3). However, the cutting of green branches that is ubiquitous in the Guatemalan highlands has more to do with providing materials for the various religious ceremonies described above than with the illicit harvest for fuel purposes alone. Green branches do not make good fuel because of their high water content. In addition, they are much heavier to carry.

Because fuel wood is becoming more scarce, conflict has erupted over even the most innocent trespassing on another's property. In one case, while out with his brothers harvesting fuel wood, the son of a local farmer cut the branches of a neighbor's tree. The neighbor exploded at the boy and went directly to his parents, demanding cash compensation for the damage and attempting to blame other damages on the brothers' mischief. The neighbor threatened to take the matter to the municipal justice of the peace.

Most Ixtahuaquenses said they would much rather resolve conflicts over forest resources face-to-face. "If you understand what I say, there is no need to go to the municipality, [but] if you are going to scold me, I will go to the municipality to complain." People frequently spoke of "chastising" or "telling someone off" as a tactic for convincing someone that they had done wrong. Many informants used the term *regañar* in talking about incidents of conflict over forest use.

Just as in the gathering of dry wood, felling of whole trees has traditionally been left to local enforcement. Problems arise, however, when the offending party is from outside the community. These parties have no stake in nor allegiance to the community and are simply attempting to maximize profit under the noses of legal and village authorities. In these cases, as will be seen, there is little local authorities can do. Loggers from outside the community come at night and are long gone before stumps are discovered. In 2004, municipal officials established a checkpoint where the gravel road to Antigua Ixtahuacán separates from the Pan-American Highway. The checkpoint was manned twenty-four hours a day, and each passing vehicle was checked for loads of timber and proper documentation. Apparently, as I heard repeatedly, one could easily bribe the guards, and illegal felling of whole trees continues.

In Ixtahuacán, the chaos surrounding the relocation of communities in the municipality has also had an impact on forest resources.[7] In the year 2000, when Nueva Ixtahuacán relocated, its residents stood in desperate need of timber. They made frequent trips to harvest in the nearby forests under cover of darkness. In response, a small group of men from Antigua Ixtahuacán began patrolling the forests. At one point, the group blockaded the road and confronted a group of armed men who were hauling a load of freshly cut logs in the back of their truck. One participant in the conflict said that the police, municipal leaders, and INAB were unsupportive of their claims. Although the incident did not result in violence and residents successfully confiscated the load, the group of loggers returned. This time they carried formal documents signed by INAB. That left a bitter taste in the mouths of Antigua Ixtahuacán residents, who believed INAB to be in collusion with woodcutters. When those patrolling found that the cutters had obtained licenses from INAB, the group lost motivation and the preservation effort ended, opening the road to further timber poaching.

Despite the complexity of forest issues in Ixtahuacán related to illegal logging and municipal politics, social capital in the form of reputation preservation remains a powerful regulator of day-to-day wood gathering. As this incident indicates, however, residents are increasingly looking to INAB as an authority for the enforcement (or lack thereof) of tree harvesting norms. INAB, however, has no legal authority to enforce its protocol against illegal loggers. It can only grant licenses (for a fee), which legitimates woodcutters, leading to a deep suspicion of collusion between two kinds of outsiders—the INAB technician and the loggers—in the unauthorized depredation of local resources.

Municipal Legal Structures

In Santa Catarina Ixtahuacán, the municipal justice of the peace is the legal authority who adjudicates conflicts over municipal forest use. In Guatemala, however, the penalty for illegal felling of trees is very lenient.[8] When a person is caught cutting down trees on someone else's property, the first offense generates a warning. Second offenders are fined the value of the timber harvested, but the money goes to the Organismo Judicial (Judicial Branch) in Guatemala City. Thus, the offended party does not receive compensation for the loss, and the money leaves the community. Because of this, illegal cutters are rarely "denounced" in the municipal court system because victims know they will not be compensated. Moreover, because local judicial authorities cannot conduct investigations of crimes committed, they must rely on eyewitness accounts. Witnesses, however, might not present themselves because of intimidation or because they know that the offense is treated lightly, even if proven, and pressing the case will only sour local relations with no obvious worthwhile outcome.

The inability of the justice of the peace to investigate locally contradicts the notion of decentralization of authority. If forest resources are to be managed sustainably, local people must have a stake in protecting them from illegal felling. By choosing to ignore the importance of communities in enforcing the forestry laws, INAB misses the benefit of authentic decentralization. If local people do not feel they are benefiting from INAB policies, even the most eloquent management principles will not bear fruit.

Legibility and Environmentality in Forest Management

The "decentralization" advocated by INAB presents deeper problems than simply a new layer of bureaucracy regulating forest resources. The differing paradigms with which INAB technicians and Maya people think about and use forests causes tension and conflict. University-trained INAB technicians are taught to quantify, measure, and manage the forest as a resource that yields commodities and environmental services. Rural Maya farmers, on the other hand, relate to the forest in a fundamentally different manner. To Maya people, the forest renders products for use in daily living, primarily fuel wood, fodder, herbs, and medicine. Secondarily, forests yield construction timber for homes and other local buildings. In addition, forests provide environmental services of soil fertility, water supply, and clean air (Greenpeace Central America 1997:11).

In *Seeing Like a State,* James Scott (1998) describes the way many states have come into conflict with local systems of management as the state seeks to standardize practices and thus render the landscape "legible" to the state apparatus. Just as scientific forestry took hold in Europe under an expanding state, so too, it would seem that INAB's model of forest management seeks to expand in post–civil war Guatemala under the guise of "decentralization" (Elías and Wittman 2005; J. Scott 1998:14). INAB forestry technicians render the forested landscape legible to modernism's eye by mapping, measuring, and planning. This "high modernism" leads INAB technicians to assume superiority over local people and to discount sustenance practices as primitive or backward. The approach reproduces the ethnic relations of Ladino over Indian and outsider over indigenous villager (Hawkins 1984; Hawkins and Adams 2005).

In talking about development organizations, Nolan (2002:234) observes that the "technicist mindset" can cause projects to fail because of its narrow view of reality: "What is considered real and therefore important is almost wholly confined to that which can be measured. Further, the reductionism in this approach encourages a divorce of measurements from context. The implicit forms of knowledge contained in a specific cultural context are all too often ignored or overlooked. . . . Growth is axiomatic; more, bigger, stronger, [and] further is better." INAB technicians frequently denigrated local people in my presence, revealing their perception of them as ignorant, lazy, and clinging to local traditions that hindered their own "progress." They frequently sneered that "they do not know how to take care of the forest." Conversely, local people distrusted INAB officials due to the reputation of government bureaucrats as being corrupt. The inability of most INAB technicians to speak K'iche' made communication difficult and hindered effective collaboration.

As another clue bespeaking their modernist worldview, forestry technicians used metric measures for all statistics, not the widespread system of *varas*, *cuerdas*, and *tareas* that most Mayas use. According to the forestry law, family consumption of deadwood less than ten cubic meters per year is unregulated. Rare is the Ixtahuaquense who could tell you how many cubic meters of wood he or she consumes per year, let alone abide an outsider's rule limiting culturally essential consumption. But Ixtahuaquense men and women can tell you, easily, how many tareas of wood they need each day or week. INAB technicians also employ GPS and GIS mapping in their projects and keep meticulous statistics about forest cover. The use of standardized measurements, sophisticated computer technology and mapping, and statistical record-keeping render the forested landscape legible to INAB technicians, but to them alone.

James Scott's concept of legibility leads us to Agrawal's concept of "environmentality." Agrawal's study of Kumaon, India, expands on Foucault's concept of governmentality by tracing the changing attitudes of Northern Indians toward their forests. Agrawal observes two shifts in local attitudes related to the forest: now humans are separate from nature and thus a danger to it (whereas before they were not), and now nature needs protection by government (whereas before government had no involvement) (Agrawal 2005:201).

The so-called "technologies of environmental government" in India during the nineteenth century included control of forest lands through central management agencies that relied on numbers and statistics to represent and control forests. The forest council rules of 1931 enabled villages to create forest councils that were allowed to manage certain forest areas. Power over forests in India thus became scattered, and emanated from multiple locations. Where Kumaon villagers decided to create village councils, those councils now have the right to decide how to allocate the products of the forest they oversee. While the "binary of domination and resistance can no longer be mapped onto the forest bureaucracy and locality, respectively" (Agrawal 2005:90), Agrawal points out that this dispersal of power allows the state to produce new "environmental subjects" who care for the forest by rewarding the communities with the products from the forests they oversee. This entices them to regulate daily activities that the state is incapable of regulating.

In the case of INAB in Guatemala, however, there is currently only a nominal decentralization, one that does not share power with local communities, but, rather, imposes INAB's management protocol on local communities. It could thus be said that INAB wants to produce a new kind of Maya by attempting to convince Maya peasants that their use of the forest is irrational and that only through the knowledge INAB possesses can the rational use of trees as economic resources be achieved. In the case of Kumaon, villagers have successfully decentered forest management to a significant degree. By contrast, INAB's "decentralization" dictates what locals must do to manage forests appropriately, using statistics and numbers, with little regard for local culture and history.

By imposing Guatemala's state protocol for forestry management, derived from the high-modernist paradigm that renders the forest legible, measurable, and usable only by the state apparatus, INAB provides further evidence that it has not engaged in decentralization in any meaningful sense. Appropriate accountability in a truly decentralized institution would actively seek to incorporate local language, customs, worldviews, and institutions into its forest management protocol. Indeed, terms like "environment" and "nature" emerge from the environmental discourses of high modernism. They inform INAB's efforts to produce new subjectivities more closely aligned with external and technical cultural assumptions about forests than with local cultural assumptions about forests.

Conclusions and Recommendations

After just two years of operation, it is difficult to fully evaluate INAB's impact on municipal forest management in Santa Catarina Ixtahuacán. One can say that the worldview and practices of residents of the municipality have not been included in INAB's decision-making processes related to forest management in Santa Catarina. Protocol and licensing are centralized through INAB, and most communities have not received significant benefits from reforestation efforts, management plans, or INAB technical expertise.

INAB has criminalized tree felling (whether for sustenance fuel wood or commercial extraction) without providing a mechanism of enforcement. It has also undermined the community norms and community-wide observation procedures that formerly regulated such uses. This derives from INAB's having assumed regulatory responsibility at the same time that it is manifestly unable to either conduct surveillance or enforce its own rigid protocol and avoid accusations of collusion with illegal loggers.

Finally, INAB has thrown the daily gathering of dry wood into doubt by criminalizing quantities over an abstract annual limit (ten cubic meters) rendered in a measurement incomprehensible to local residents. The quasi criminalization of Maya customary practice makes Mayas reluctant to seek help from or report to forestry officials or other municipal officers when they see blatantly illegal harvesting activities, because they fear they may themselves be illegal or marginal in their forest harvesting. To gain the force of all residents as collaborators, INAB must learn to navigate municipal politics, work to find adequate means of gaining the trust of residents, and develop mechanisms to equitably enforce forestry laws.

INAB prides itself on its professionalism, independence, and technical precision. If INAB would incorporate local knowledge and participation in its forest management, it could potentially live up to the democratic decentralization it has claimed as its hallmark. It is hard to say exactly how a decentralization scheme would look, work, or better achieve its given ends except to suggest that specific approaches will depend greatly on the local context of each municipal forestry office. This may seem like a dodge; however, decentralization doctrines require context-specific approaches and downward accountability. INAB management plans must adapt to, and to some degree embrace, municipal and community forest values. For example, some municipalities may readily accept management plans oriented toward the extraction of timber; other communities may emphasize the importance of forests to sustaining local water supplies; still others may focus on sustainable fuel-wood harvesting.

Institutional Reforms

With the increasing recognition of the importance of local and indigenous knowledge (Berkes and Folke 1998), civil society organizations, such as Familia a Familia, EcoLogic Development Fund, and Ulew Che' Ja',[9] could be appropriate mechanisms for bridging the cultural gap that now stands between INAB and many Maya communities. Civil society organizations could facilitate a context-specific approach to forest management. INAB staff, from top to bottom, must also learn to respect traditional forest management institutions and should work with—not against—the social capital that many communities possess. This follows the principle that "local peoples are more likely to follow their own rules" (A. Larson 2005:49) and would make INAB an equal, accountable, and effective partner in forest management at the municipal level rather than an aloof, technocratic overseer.

INAB must also become more downwardly accountable. Village committees that oversee forest protection and reforestation efforts should be consulted and respected—and encouraged where they do not exist. To achieve its goals of sustainable forest management, INAB will need to collaborate with local communities to enforce the forestry laws. "Social capital can, to some extent, substitute for the costly monitoring, supervision, and enforcement of the rules governing property rights and resource use in both private and common property regimes" (Katz 2000:117), but that requires paying attention to and respecting local social capital.

By incorporating participatory processes into municipal forestry office protocol, INAB could become a resource for semi-autonomous forest management institutions, rather than standing as an obstacle to them. It could complement local knowledge with technical assistance and financial resources (including credit), thereby achieving the goals of protecting valuable environmental services, contributing to economic productivity, and preserving local self-reliance.

Such approaches can occur and could be generalized. Anne Larson (2008), for example, describes a successful case in which the municipal forestry office of Cotzal, Guatemala, implemented a forest management plan with the help of 180 community participants. Among other things, they used a participatory process to identify local problems and needs. The plan also included elements of traditional Maya forest practices by synchronizing cutting with the cycles of the moon and giving thanks to trees before they were harvested (A. Larson 2008:42). Such success stories, unfortunately, tend to be the exception rather than the rule, perhaps because most INAB technicians do not consider it their job to pay attention to Maya culture or institutions, but to manage the forest according to agency protocol (A. Larson 2008:43).

INAB protocol must be accessible and beneficial to local indigenous people, in this case to K'iche' speakers. Technicians should be required to have at least a working knowledge of the local language. INAB could hold regular workshops and forest committee meetings to discuss forestry protocol with village committees and other interested parties. Such meetings would help to familiarize community members with the technician's role in forest management, educate members in forest ecology, and discuss local forest management problems. At the same time, and reciprocally, such meetings might educate INAB technicians and familiarize them with local ecological and cultural conditions. Forest management scholarships could be awarded to exceptional village forest stewards so that the Maya might eventually make up a sizable percentage of INAB technicians in their own villages. Such a program would be modeled after the state bilingual normal school system that has trained Mayas as teachers and has tried (with only partial success) to deploy teachers in each village who speak that village's Mayan language. In addition, PINFOR should extend incentives to smallholders through microcredit loans or by special needs assessment grants.

The state must approve fundamental changes in the INAB licensing system to decriminalize fuel wood collection. Municipal authorities and the state apparatus should also work to guarantee that all fines for illegal felling compensate victims and stay in the community. Identified illegal tree-cutters, especially those from outside a community where the felling occurs, should be subject to more-punitive fines and to traditional punishment systems (short of lynching; see Bybee, chapter 2), as well as to compensatory community reforestation work. This would also encourage residents to utilize official legal channels and give them a say in compensation for damages and appropriate punishment. The licensing program should also create incentives for complying with the system by giving away tree seedlings or some other appropriate reward with every license.

Unfortunately, in concrete terms, such inclusion of local opinion would require a major ideological reorientation on the part of INAB *técnicos*. Up to now, they have embraced a Western development-oriented model that is further supercharged by the insidious race relations in Guatemala. As a result, INAB administrators see indigenous Maya peoples as backward and wrong-thinking. They do not see them as having tremendous social capital. The perspective of INAB's técnicos parallels what McDonald (2003) found and struggled with in western Mexico between small-scale dairy farmers and state agricultural extension agents. The latter embraced a Weberian notion of development problems and challenges as merely technical, while disregarding the cultural, social, geographical, and environmental context and knowledge of the farmers themselves. In sum, they saw farmers and their knowledge as wrongheaded and backward—something to be actively disregarded—rather than as resources to understand the complex challenges they faced in their struggle to survive in a poor, marginalized place.

Forestry Projects

In addition to these institutional changes, INAB should consider a number of project-based changes that could also increase its credibility with local people. Community-based enterprises created through microcredit loans that seek to add value to wood products could create an effective local lobby for continued forest cover and forest law compliance, as it did with Totonicapán furniture- and cabinetmakers during the early twentieth century (Veblen 1978:423). INAB could also explore agro-forestry practices that incorporate trees into food production zones and vice versa. Intensive intercropping or coppice woodlands of fast-growing trees and other perennials could also produce biomass for fuel wood on small parcels of land in a relatively short time, freeing up larger species for producing timber. Community-based native tree and plant nurseries could also be encouraged so that forest committees could organize community educational and service activities supported through the sale of tree seedlings.

INAB's future success in fostering improved forests depends on its ability to secure widespread local participation. To achieve that, INAB officers must endeavor to respect, cooperate with, and learn from local communities. But does the political will exist to respect the lifeways of the Mayas, who have already suffered enormously at the hands of government-run programs and schemes? Will INAB become a more equal, accountable, and effective partner in forest management at the municipal level? Or will it continue to impose a centralized protocol guided by high modernism, which ignores local values and wisdom as well as highly effective, local, face-to-face monitoring of resource use? Unfortunately, this last option will be the likely outcome if technicians maintain, teach one another, or are taught the belief that "they"—meaning the local residents, seen as third-person aliens—"do not know how to take care of the forest." To a great degree, the outcome will depend on whether INAB continues to seek to transform Maya peasants into subjects compatible with modernist assumptions of forestry through various "technologies of self," as Foucault puts it, or if INAB moves in a different direction that admits a more active role for local communities in managing their forests.

Notes

Fieldwork: 2006

1. I thank my Maya host family, the INAB forestry technicians who allowed me to tag along and gave me access to municipal forestry statistics, and the municipal leaders of Santa Catarina Ixtahuacán, who trusted me. I also thank the forests in Western Oregon for giving me strength to press on while I banged out several "final" drafts of this paper.

2. I (Brown) deliberately use the word "sustenance" over the more common, anthropological "subsistence." "Subsistence" comes loaded with a Euro-American, culturally assumed superiority of marketized forms of livelihood over self-provision by agriculture or hunting and builds in a judgment that simply providing for one's life-maintenance needs is less than adequate. It comes from Latin *sub-*, connoting (per Webster's Ninth) under, below, beneath, subordinate, secondary, inferior, less than completely, less than perfectly, less than normally; and *-sistere*, to stand. The combination suggests a less-than-adequate standing or existence. The dictionary proceeds to a somewhat negative definition as "the minimum (as of food and shelter) necessary to support life" and then provides one neutral definition: "a source or means of obtaining the necessities of life."

3. See Hawkins and Adams (in preparation) for a description of the politics of the village's fission into two locations.

4. Like the ambiguities of land measurement Dabb discusses (chapter 3), multiple measures apply to wood. A license is required for felling a tree, whether on municipal communal land (i.e., in municipal forests) or on one's own land held in usufruct. The cost of a license depends on the use of the wood. A tree felled for household non-commercial firewood requires a Q60 fee. A tree felled for construction timber or planks, or for commercial sale of firewood, demands a fee of Q100 per tree, a considerable sum in local lives (two to three days' wages for a peasant farmer). Collecting fuel wood for one's household is free, provided that only deadwood is collected. However, collecting "in quantity" demands a licensing fee. The problem is, the estimate of what constitutes "in quantity" is variable. Municipal forestry officials suggest 10 cubic meters. Local residents suggest "a pickup truckload" or a *tarea.* The tarea, however, is variously understood as a day's work, or a 1 vara by 4 vara stack of cut or split wood (from fingertips to elbow in length) akin to a cord, or eight human backpack loads. (A vara is a measure equivalent to about 33 inches.) As we shall see, the variability in measures contributes to the conflicts.

5. The official INAB slogan is "More Forests for the Development of Guatemala." It is estimated that from 1990 to 2000, approximately 54 thousand hectares were cleared annually in Guatemala, due to illegal logging, cattle ranching, cutting for firewood, and the expansion of the agricultural frontier (FAO 2005:233).

6. The close association and even substitutability of air, breath, spirit, and life among the Classic Maya is well represented in this quote.

7. Antigua Santa Catarina Ixtahuacán was relocated in the aftermath of 1998's Hurricane Mitch; others in the municipality were subsequently relocated after 2005's Hurricane Stan.

8. A former mayor of Nahualá indicated that if an unlicensed local were caught felling a tree, he would be required to pay a fine equal to the licensing fee. While this makes woodcutting a good gamble, there are further social capital costs: the municipality would not extend a license for six months or a year to a prior offender.

9. Literally, "Earth, Trees, Water," naming an NGO network of villages that manage a watershed in Totonicapán.

CHAPTER 5

Barriers to the Political Empowerment of Nahualense Midwives

Rebecca A. Edvalson, John J. Edvalson, John P. Hawkins, James H. McDonald, and Walter Randolph Adams

The relationship between pregnant mothers, midwives, and modern medical practitioners raises a number of complex issues relative to attitudes and perceptions about reproductive health on a global scale (see Craven 2007a, 2007b; Hunter 2004). Central to these debates is the midwife, often cast as an unpredictable and untrustworthy agent in state-sponsored efforts to promote standardized prenatal practices and assert control over the birthing process. In the United States, these efforts have resulted in the transfer of childbirth from the domestic sphere of the home to the public sphere of the hospital, where modern forms of medical surveillance are thought to result in better outcomes for mothers and children. Many developing nations have sought to follow a similar model in an effort to create more modern institutions (Hyde and Roche-Reid 2003).

However, in cases where coverage by trained doctors is inadequate to replace midwives, some nations have sought to incorporate midwives into the public health system and to provide them with training to standardize practices and more effectively promote birth success. Guatemala is now implementing this model of training for traditional midwives, which conforms to biomedical standards of practice. This chapter explores the implementation of state-based training and certification of traditional midwives in Nahualá, a K'iche'-speaking indigenous *municipio* in the Western Highlands of Guatemala. Nahualá provides a case study of the tension between biomedical personnel and traditional midwives, given state efforts to control prenatal care through a "partnership" with midwives. In their recent medical volume on Nahualá and Santa Catarina Ixtahuacán, Adams and Hawkins (2007a) treat an array of cultural and structural issues embedded in medicine and health, relating to the confrontation between ethnomedical ("Traditional") versus biomedical ("Western") medical practices. This chapter adds to that discussion by exploring the *political* implications of Guatemala's national health policy as experienced by midwives practicing in Nahualá during the study period in 2006.

Guatemala's Ministry of Public Health and Social Welfare (Ministerio de Salud Pública y Asistencia Social, hereafter referred to as the Ministry of Health) has been training midwives sporadically since 1955. In the 1980s, Guatemala went one step further by adopting the model of midwifery training espoused by the World Health Organization (WHO). The WHO model emphasized integrating midwives into the formal health care system. But it was not until the health system reforms resulting from the 1996 Peace Accords that health care leaders began to emphasize midwifery as a key to fulfilling the Peace Accords' objective of lowering maternal and neonatal deaths and improving standards of health among indigenous groups in Guatemala (Maupin 2008:355–56).

Neoliberal decentralization served as the foundation of these health care reforms because the Inter-American Development Bank (IADB) financed the reforms and therefore assumed part-authorship of the restructuring plans. So, although sporadic midwifery training programs had been in place for more than forty years, in 1996 the IADB pushed for health care decentralization that refashioned the role of midwives from that of side players to that of key health care workers within the national health care system. Midwives were now workers who must be trained to responsibly and competently fulfill their role as the central means of complying with international health standards in an effort to decrease infant and maternal mortality (Maupin 2009:1458).

Consequently, as the national training system over the past decade has conveyed a formal recognition of midwives' importance nationally and globally and has conceptualized them as an organizable category, efforts of Nahualense midwives to organize themselves politically have dramatically increased. Even before the Guatemalan government ratified the Peace Accords, NGOs and segments of the Ministry of Health deployed the principles outlined in the accords to structure several national health policies. In the process, midwives in Nahualá have gradually been made to feel that they are important players in the larger health care system.[1]

Administrators of the Ministry of Health's midwifery training program said they believe the training of midwives has helped increase medical knowledge and decrease maternal and natal deaths. Unfortunately, we have not found a reliable study of the mortality outcomes of trained traditional midwives in comparison with untrained traditional midwives delivering services in rural homes. Goldman and Glei (2000) come close by indicating that they see little difference in behavior between certified and uncertified midwives.

State training has, however, made otherwise traditional midwives aware of the possibility of imprisonment if their patient should die in labor. This is the extent of the legal knowledge conveyed in the training. As one midwife said when asked about legal liabilities associated with midwifery, "I don't have any idea. What I do know is [you can be put in jail] because of a death. Other things that may exist, I don't know." Such limited legal understanding has led midwives to feel ignorant of their legal rights and liabilities and fearful of the consequences of that ignorance—a fear that comes from the knowledge that there is heightened state monitoring of midwifery practice (and malpractice). These Nahualense midwives confirm Hinojosa's (2004) discussion of how midwife trainers in San Juan Comalapa, Guatemala, instill fear and insecurity in midwives and disparage traditional practices in favor of approved practices, thereby subordinating midwives to the state hierarchy. Clearly, one sees here an unconsciously Foucauldian project of bodily discipline that subjects midwives to the state and to the state's high modernity project, as the Guatemalan state positions itself before world health-monitoring organizations.

Amid their worries of imprisonment for mistakes or deaths that might not be of their own causing, midwives feel an urgency to advocate for themselves. They claim they need to lobby for legal protection from unjust imprisonment, make legal orientation part of the required training sessions, obtain more opportunities to do hands-on work at the hospital in Sololá, and receive funding for monetary incentives and supplies (gloves, scales, stethoscopes, and so on.).[2] Many midwives say, however, that they do not pursue these political goals, because they lack formal education, do not speak Spanish adequately, suffer discrimination from non-indigenous medical and political leaders, and risk incurring the envy (*envidia*) of other midwives if they do become political advocates.

Each of these barriers prevents midwives from forming an effective and confident political bloc. Thus, state-mandated training has made midwives feel they need to become politically involved, but the courses have not provided them with the legal knowledge or organizational skills to do so. In addition, language barriers limit the ability of the most traditional midwives, who are monolingual K'iche', to communicate with midwives or advisors in Spanish or other indigenous languages. Discrimination further discourages many, but by no means all, and limits them to local horizons of practice. Finally, fear of envy discourages traditionalist women from trying to overcome gendered, ethnic, educational, and leadership barriers and expectations. All of these contribute to the political ambivalence Nahualense midwives feel toward advocating changes in the state's protocols for interacting with indigenous midwives.

To frame this argument, we first review how the training program has created a perceived need for greater political activity. We then discuss the above-mentioned barriers to political involvement and present the solutions or recommendations proposed by Nahualense midwives. Finally, we discuss the implications of state-sponsored efforts to subsume midwifery practices and how those practices may influence Nahualense perceptions about childbirth and the role of midwives.

The State-Mandated Training Program

In a 1996 pamphlet co-published with MotherCare (MotherCare 1996, see also 1999), Guatemala's Ministry of Health reports that "in 1992, 77 percent of all births occurred outside of [biomedical] health facilities. . . . In more outlying areas [which would include all of indigenous Guatemala], midwives attended close to 90 percent of all births." An associated technical report notes that the southwestern region of Guatemala—which includes Nahualá—has the fewest professional medical personnel and highest rate of midwives as attendants to pregnancy and delivery in Guatemala (Bocaletti et al. 1999:11).

Guatemala's high rates of maternal and neonatal deaths have largely been attributed to a lack of knowledge on the part of the attending midwives. In fact, Bocaletti and colleagues (1999:9) suggest that "close to 50% of the 4.3 million fetal deaths estimated per year are a direct consequence of mishandled deliveries [by midwives], as is also the case with millions of neonatal deaths."

Even before the signing of the 1996 Peace Accords, Guatemalan midwives' lack of familiarity with Western medical practices relating to labor, delivery, nutrition, and other lifesaving information led to the institution of a state-mandated midwife training program (MotherCare 1996). Their training integrates midwives—including traditionally apprenticed and spiritually "called" midwives as well as women who choose to become midwives—into the formal medical system. The program, implemented through training, leads to certification. This places all midwifery activities under the political jurisdiction of the state medical system, which seeks to comply with international health standards (Maupin 2008:354–55).

Shortly after the 1996 Peace Accords, the Public Health Ministry set forth the current national guidelines for midwife training to be conducted by local *centros de salud* (health centers) and *puestos de salud* (health posts). The guidelines required "a formal recognition of midwives, establishing a registration system, granting them licenses . . . carrying out training courses and indicating that part of the work of the midwives is to promote the use of contraceptive methods" (Bocaletti et al. 1999:11–12).

Via the registration and licensing systems, midwives receive a *carnet* (training certification card). Midwives in Nahualá possessing this identification card believe it shows that the Guatemalan state officially recognizes them as certified and authorized medical workers. As one midwife explained: "It [the carnet] is what we use to help and protect ourselves. . . . It is like a legal document that says we are authorized to work in this profession. Also, we always carry it with us when we bring our patients to the hospital because they [the hospital personnel] ask us for it." Hinojosa (2004) shows that Comalapa midwives share the same confidence in the carnet, which they call a *permiso*:

> Midwives . . . sometimes showed me either a certificate or a carnet (pocket license), which was earned by attending midwife training sessions. Celedonia displays her framed certificate recognizing Adiestramiento de Comadronas Tradicionales, "Training of Traditional Midwives." She has difficulty reading the rest of the certificate, but explains that it certifies her to work openly. . . . The acquisition of such a permiso, [the] work authorization, marks an important moment for both the midwife and the Health Center. For the midwife, she can rest assured that, so long as she abides by the tenets of the trainings, or keeps a

> low profile when she does not, she can legally perform as an ambulatory midwife. For the Center, to authorize a midwife means that she can be monitored and called upon to share insights with other midwives. That is, she can share insights that agree with the Center's teachings. (Hinojosa 2004:642)

The training sessions that midwives must attend to obtain their carnet focus on life-threatening situations such as abnormal fetal position, premature births, inability to expel the placenta, prolonged labor, and infections of the mother or newborn (Bocaletti et al. 1999:13; Maupin 2008:357). The purpose of these training sessions, as stated in the Ministry of Health's published guides, is to insert "[t]he midwife [as] the principal health provider sought by the rural indigenous population. . . . She is the nexus with formal health services, which is why it is necessary that she be included in any intervention [i.e., training] tending to decrease perinatal mortality" (Bocaletti et al. 1999:132).

Whether intended explicitly by Ministry of Health policy or not, public health workers have tried to instill a sense of fear into the midwives if they attempt any practice that might put the life of a mother or child in danger. One local state-employed health worker and trainer explained, "This fear is part of what we have tried to inculcate in them or make them understand: that if a woman dies under their care because of their malpractice as a midwife, they can end up in prison." This fear has made Nahualense midwives revere the training sessions and their carnet as protection from incarceration. Again, Hinojosa shows that the structural conundrum, the fear imposed, and cultural responses are quite generalized. Thus, for example, "health authorities mandate use of horizontal birth positions without critically examining why," and "instead, they teach midwives to fear birthing in any other way" (Hinojosa 2004:644). Indeed, they actively discourage the indigenous preference for squatting, which has proven superior.

One Nahualá midwife expressed her faith in the training as a means of legal aid in case of maternal death, saying: "What would protect us would be the trainings that they have given us. And, at the same time, the people at the Health Center could help us, just like the trainers could. They could say, "Well, this midwife has always attended the trainings, so we have the obligation of defending her because she is doing a good job."[3] Nahualense midwives believed that by attending the "trainings" and maintaining good relations with Health Center personnel, they would be spared from imprisonment. For some, the training imparted knowledge, which they appreciated. For others, sitting through the poorly understood courses until certified served as a strategy that enabled them to continue their practice as a traditional midwife. It is notable that these midwives spoke in an uncertain, conditional voice: "what would protect us *would be* . . . " and "the people at the Health Center *could* help us." Nahualense midwives are not at all certain they can rely on the state, in part, as Hinojosa (2004:643–45) also demonstrates, because state health trainers and physicians thoroughly berate indigenous midwives, denigrate indigenous health practices, and threaten them with the law, even in a difficult health environment where some babies surely will die.

Midwives have good reason, however unconsciously understood, not to trust too much in the state. Nahualá's Health Center personnel report that indigenous faith in the protective power of licensure may be misplaced. When asked if the training sessions provided midwives with any measure of legal protection, one local health worker said: "Not necessarily. I think that it is to the contrary—the more training one receives, the more ability and answers one has to have. Because if she [the midwife] fails and is trained, then I don't believe her carnet will be of much validity. . . . They have the idea that it [the carnet] can save them from prison." This health worker establishes that attending the training does *not* serve as legal protection, contrary to midwives' understanding. Clearly, state-connected health care professionals and trainers are aware of the midwives' common misinterpretation, yet they do not explain this vital law in an understandable and culturally contextualized way during training sessions. Hinojosa (2004) reports a litany of similar misunderstandings held by Comalapa midwives, while Goldman and Glei (2000) confirm with survey and interviews the range of impediments midwives face.

One locally based physician involved with training sessions explained the interplay of culture and law: "I don't see it [the imprisonment of a midwife] as something that is very probable. I believe that it is going to be something difficult, not from the point of view of the law but rather from the point of view of the denunciation. There is not going to be anyone who is going to denounce the midwife. As long as there is no one who will denounce her and provide follow-up to a case, I don't believe it could happen. The people in the communities don't say anything because . . . they view the midwife as someone distinct or special. And who's going to go against a midwife? So they don't do it."

Midwives throughout Guatemala, including Nahualá, believe they are chosen by God (Paul and Paul 1975:449–50). Kevara Wilson (2007) details the process—generally by finding a sign or recovering from an illness—and its similarity to the call of an *ajq'ij*, the traditional "daykeeper," the shaman-diviner. Because of their divine calling, midwives receive respect and prestige. The special nature of their profession makes it unlikely that a family would even begin the legal process leading toward imprisonment. If a family did want to press charges against a midwife, it would require financial resources and legal knowledge possessed by very few in the community. Even if knowledge of the legal system existed, the generalized Nahualense lack of faith in the legal process, as well as the social stigma of prosecuting a midwife, would make litigation against a midwife unlikely. Nevertheless, the pain experienced over the loss of a child, generalized envy, and the previous experience of blackmail or extortion might overcome such scruples (see Bybee, chapter 2, this volume).

The state-mandated training and certification program explicitly seeks to bring traditional midwifery under the umbrella of the state. The state is co-opting the traditional medical system now, much as it previously sought to co-opt the mayoral election system, or the mayor's judicial functions, or the municipal management of forestry. In fact, we find here another instance of control by centralization; through protocol imposed on behavior, with no analysis of or appreciation for the merits of traditional midwives' behavior.

The physician's comment, above, suggests that, in Nahualá, a midwife's divine calling served as her greatest protection from negative legal consequences. But informants did not feel protected by their calling, because the monthly training painted imprisonment as inevitable if one of their patients were to die. And women do die in childbirth in Nahualá. Thus, the midwives' ignorance of the legal process of pressing charges leads them to have greater fear than may actually be warranted. Because of this inculcated fear, midwives expressed a need to mobilize politically. Unfortunately, language differences, lack of formal education, outright ethnic and gender discrimination, and interpersonal envy impede their progress toward joint or individual political action. These will be explored in turn.

EDUCATIONAL AND SOCIETAL IMPEDIMENTS TO THE EMPOWERMENT OF NAHUALENSE MIDWIVES

A number of entwined impediments continue to disempower Nahualense midwives. Among them, the social value of formal education and the communicative power of controlling the language of state—Spanish—stand out. Combined with discrimination, fear, and other factors, they make it difficult for Nahualense midwives to form the networks necessary to advance their interests, personal and professional, inherent in their practice of midwifery.

Education and Language Barriers: "We Can't Express Ourselves Well in Spanish"

Most adult women in Nahualá speak K'iche' only. Because these women did not enroll in public elementary school as children, they lost their principal opportunity to learn to speak and read Spanish. Their lack of formal education has caused a sense of political disempowerment. One midwife commented: "We really can't fight for others because of our situation that we can't express ourselves well in Spanish and we don't understand what is being said to us. We couldn't solicit the help of other people outside of our own community because we can't express what we have in mind." Some of the non-indigenous medical personnel interpreted the midwives' inability to speak Spanish as an expression of political apathy, a misinterpretation or illusion given that the majority of informants shared specific political commentary and sound ideas when allowed to speak K'iche'.

Carey (2006:4–5) elaborates this theme, referring to "historical silencing" among Kaqchikel Maya women: "Monolingual Kaqchikel women's acute sense of how their inability to speak Spanish handicaps them nuances theoretical conceptions of silencing. The act of historical silencing is active and deliberate—even if not recognized as such by its perpetrators. 'We are blind because we cannot speak, but I am not the only one. *My whole generation was kept out of school* [emphasis in original] so we all struggle to speak Spanish,' notes Ixchipix, a seventy-three-year-old campesina." Similarly, for a variety of reasons, the majority of Nahualense midwives could not attend school; this places them at a disadvantage when asked to present their knowledge or express their views in official settings where Spanish is the operative mode of communication.

A physician in the area commented on how the inability to speak Spanish translates into a political handicap: "They leave Nahualá to go to Sololá [where regional midwife training is held] . . . and they don't speak Spanish. They have many problems, many limitations, because there is no one to translate for them. And the trainings outside of the district [Nahualá] are all in Spanish, they aren't in K'iche' and they don't translate them. . . . *The indispensable requirement is speaking Spanish to be able to leave [and operate effectively outside of their community], to be able to participate in the political system*" [emphasis added]. This language barrier keeps midwives from moving forward in their political designs outside their community.

Carey (2006:4–5) shows that Maya women's silenced political voice is not only the result of not learning Spanish but also a sign of a government that does not wish to hear: "Mayan women's silence was also a product of their audience's inability and unwillingness to listen. Ixq'in, a sixty-eight-year-old weaver . . . notes, 'It really hurt us. We could not talk to Ladinos or Ladinas because we did not know the language.' In recognizing her own silence, Ixq'in also highlights the deafness of Ladinos (and by extension the state) who did not speak Kaqchikel or other Mayan languages." Nahualense midwives experienced the same difficulty in communicating with Guatemala's Spanish-speaking public health officials due to a similar construction of relationships that has led to the historical silencing of Nahualense midwives.

Education and Ladino Discrimination: "They Look Down on Us"

Ladino discrimination, in combination with language inability and education deficit, fuels a feeling of political disempowerment. As one woman explained, "We don't speak another language [and] we must remember that the Ladinos always treat us poorly, they look down on us and they tell us, 'Don't listen to her. She's not worth anything.'" This sense of discrimination by those in power causes the midwives to feel reluctant to pursue political change.

One might ask why the senior health-system officers in places such as Nahualá do not often speak the local languages. The matter boils down to discrimination and prejudices that impact both recruitment and placement. Medical jobs, especially that of physician, carry high prestige. To be a medical officer who is also a competent speaker of an indigenous language, one must be born and raised in a family that speaks an indigenous language in the home *and* complete an advanced education in a system that under-resources and discriminates against indigenous students. That student must then not be attracted to the urban center and its preferred comforts, and can only serve in a limited set of municipalities that speak the particular language she or he has learned. Such a medical practitioner has to be fairly altruistic and proud of his or her role in rural service because the income opportunities will not be as good in the indigenous village as in a city.

Alternatively, one must be a Ladino willing not only to get a medical education but to learn a difficult language over a period of years. That same Ladino student must not be seduced by urban comfort, wealth, or ethnic prejudice. Hinojosa (2004:638) gives a structural explanation for the overwhelmingly Ladino emphasis of professional medical training: "Guatemalan Ladinos occupy a structurally advantageous position over Indians. Not only do they tend to have a higher income than Mayas and benefit from operating solely in the national language of government and education, Spanish, but they concentrate in places where formal health services are located: urban and semi-urban areas. The providers of these services, in turn, come largely from Ladino backgrounds. This situation has often disfavored Indians in terms of affordability, treatment, and inter-ethnic regard." In short, persons of either ethnicity must overcome a great deal of social prejudice, their own bias against working in a remote area, or both. In addition, Indians and poor Ladinos must overcome severe structural impediments to getting any education above primary school. Consequently, neither ethnicity yet serves Indians frequently enough.

Education and Connection to Networks of Power: "They Have Put It in Our Heads to Fear Authorities"

The majority of Nahualense midwives interviewed were willing to support legal change but felt that it was beyond their capability to approach those in power. They had no trustable networks, for all the above reasons. As one explained:

> Those who could make or generate change in our community would be those people who have more knowledge because if the person is educated, they have received orientation. Also, if they speak Spanish well, I believe that the person is called to

> make changes in our community. We're not able to do anything, but I believe that we can support them [that is, Spanish speakers from the midwives' community]. *But [for us] to have a conversation with high officials, they would just laugh at what we are saying* because we don't speak Spanish well. On the other hand, the young people, as well as those who have had good academic preparation, I believe are the ones chosen to realize changes in our country and in that way help us in our own town [emphasis added].

In addition to speaking powerfully to the topics of education and language competence in Spanish discussed above, this midwife's observation illustrates the chasm that exists in Guatemala between educated *profesionales* (professionals) and non-formally educated *campesinos* (peasant farmers) when it comes to social empowerment. Because the midwives' profession does not require even a primary school education, they fall in the category of campesino. The educated reflect their sense of empowerment in the way they speak about social change, demonstrating their confidence via detailed plans that involve personal action to obtain change. Those with little formal education, in contrast, speak of social change as something they wish for but feel is nearly impossible to obtain. So, if change is to be, the program to obtain it must be headed by someone with formal education who can effectively negotiate with people in positions of power. As more people become educated in Nahualá, the potential of a professional class of Nahualenses to possess the social capital necessary to broker with public health officials on behalf of Nahualense midwives may increase. For the moment, however, inadequate education—and gender bias—make that advocacy unlikely. In short, Nahualense women lack the social capital that Bourdieu and Wacquant (1992:119) define as "the sum of the resources, actual or virtual, that accrue to an individual or a group by virtue of possessing a durable network of more or less institutionalized relationships of mutual acquaintance and recognition." In Nahualá, the ability to connect with personnel from development organizations and institutions of state power derives from formal education. Nahualense midwives lack that education and, consequently, that connection.

Formal educational access has been improving in Nahualá. Many of the town's biggest buildings throb with public and private educational institutions. With this access, and because formal education leads to higher-status jobs and provides skills to deal with the public health bureaucracy, a growing number of young Nahualense high-school graduates and even college graduates can, as "professionals," interact with government officials within and beyond the community. However, the emerging class of professionals is unlikely to interact with or take interest in midwives, and may draw social, educational, and economic distinctions between themselves and "traditional" midwives, thus maintaining midwife isolation. Consequently, these less-educated Nahualense midwives experience limited social and physical mobility and do not have access to the resources necessary to allow them to function officially within political and social fields that would benefit their profession or protect them from negative sanctions of the Guatemalan state.

In part, this inability to form social networks derives from discrimination and prejudice, and in part, from an imposed fear. One informant explained her reluctance to form networks in terms of fear of authority: "I think that [our fear to make political petitions] is because from a long time ago they have put it in our heads to fear authorities when asking for things. Because if we ask them, all of a sudden they may get mad at us and say, 'it's better you don't come anymore.'" The problem is long-term and deep-seated; Waldemar Smith (1977:115) describes an informant who evidenced his bravery by asserting he was not afraid to enter any government office.

Education to Deal with Corruption

Yet, even when the midwives have overcome their fear of authority figures, they have met with corruption and its attendant lack of transparency. Presumably, education would help midwives demand transparency and thus deal with corruption. Consuelo, a Nahualense midwife, reflected:

> We had a committee so that we could start (about six or seven years ago) to solicit help from the government. The government approved our petition and gave us, the midwives, one and a half million [quetzales]. But what happened to the money on the way? It ended up with the doctor, or the doctors, or the nurses. I don't know where it ended up. The doctor told us to sign a paper because the money was coming for us to do shifts at the hospital. We signed the paper. . . . But what happened is that the doctor had a lot of meetings so that she wouldn't have to

> give us the opportunity to have shifts at the hospital. They just gave us a few trainings. But the trainings that they gave us weren't new trainings; we had already received these trainings in the Health Center.

When asked if the doctors put in charge of dispensing the money were Ladino or Mayan, Consuelo replied that they were Ladino.

Consuelo had interacted with Ladinos when she did shifts at the hospital in Sololá on another occasion years ago. She gave a detailed account of the racial discrimination she and other midwives received during those hospital shifts. The discrimination took on the form of name-calling, referring to the midwives as *xuka* (dirty), making them do the more difficult work at the hospital while the nurses rested, and overworking and underpaying them.

The midwives received a small stipend for their time, but Consuelo might have forfeited her wage had not other Spanish-speaking Nahualense midwives included her in their efforts to ensure payment of the money owed them. Consuelo believed that the Ladinos kept the wage and project money because, according to her, Ladinos thought they could take advantage of poor, monolingual indigenous people. Although it was not possible to confirm this account, the indigenous perception of widespread Ladino discrimination seemed to deter many Nahualense midwives from political activism. Despite this discriminatory and corrupt treatment, Consuelo and other midwives considered working at Sololá's hospital a valuable experience because they increased their medical knowledge and helped translate for K'iche' patients.

Envy as a Deterrent to Political Action

Not only did the midwives report discrimination on the part of Ladino officials, but also on the part of their fellow midwives, in the form of *envidia* (envy or jealousy). The prime causes of envy were the holding of leadership positions and having a high number of clientele—both guarantors of prestige. Midwifery in and of itself grants a woman great prestige because she is not only an important medical figure but also a religious figure (see Paul and Paul 1975:449–50; K. Wilson 2007). One might assume that a midwife with many clients is envied because she accumulates a bit of wealth. Not so. Midwives affirm that they rarely are paid much, if anything. Often the only payment the family offers is food and lodging as the midwife holds vigil with the laboring woman. It is prestige that fuels the envy, prestige rooted in leadership positions and number of clientele rather than material gain.

Concerning envy of leaders, Spanish-speaking ability (and thus education) again came into play. Not only did midwives relate that they felt looked down upon by the Spanish-speaking midwives, but also that their inability to speak Spanish had impeded access to positions of leadership, and therefore to community prestige. One midwife explained: "There are some [midwives] who understand and speak Spanish well, and they make us feel like we are less than them. It's almost always [the midwives] who speak Spanish well who have more power than us, just because we can't speak or understand Spanish."

Though not explicit, this midwife expresses envy of those "who have more power than us" because in indigenous communities all should be equal. Current local events supported this interpretation. The recently instated president of the Nahualá Midwife Committee, Consuelo, was also just placed by Nahualá's mayor as the president of the city's Women's Rights Office. Of the 118 midwives in Nahualá, she is one of only a few who speak Spanish.

One physician, Dr. Rodríguez, commented on the scarcity of Spanish-speaking midwives: "This poses a problem in the rotation of midwife leadership because those that don't speak Spanish don't want to [be leaders] because they know that today or tomorrow or the next day they are going to have to leave Nahualá. And what are they going to do? They aren't going to understand anything that is said. . . . They aren't going to bring any information. The situation is that . . . they [the midwives] elect them [the Midwife Committee]. Generally they choose someone who speaks Spanish. . . . The Midwife Committee is elected by all the midwives." This confirms that although the other midwives seem to envy the power of their Spanish-speaking counterparts, monolingual midwives are reluctant to place themselves in positions of leadership due to the language barriers they would face. This translates into a very small portion of midwives who are politically empowered both inside and outside their community. The monolingual midwives retain their prestige and influence in Nahualá but are unable to move beyond their community.[4]

The envy midwives harbor has caused them to be individually empowered but competitive, judgmental, and divided as a group. Older midwives discriminate against those who have recently entered the profession. As one midwife described: "It would be good for us to organize . . . and communicate with the rest, but sadly, this situation hasn't worked out. But I wish it were like that, that we would help one another. . . . I would be the first to help. But sadly, the midwives who began much before us are the ones that look down on us."

Time on the job is not the only motive for envy among midwives. Speculation over whether or not a midwife is practicing because she was really called by God also causes divisions. One midwife said: "Among my fellow midwives, some don't like that I am doing this job. . . . They tell me that I got into this just because I wanted to, with different intentions than the others. They say that I got into this just so other people can see that I am like this [a midwife]. They practically don't talk to me and they don't like to see me at the trainings. Or, in other words, they envy the job I do."

Questioning a midwife's motives for entering the profession comes as a result of envy when midwives compete for social prestige. In this regard, we note the contrast between the traditional midwife, who is called by God by being given a sign or healing someone (K. Wilson 2007), and the state's mode of recruiting new midwives by nominating women with Spanish-speaking capability and training them in courses. The former method, by God's calling, makes the midwife's authority over other women—and deviation from a life of household duties and petty commerce—something she did not seek. It is God's will and therefore not to be envied. By contrast, state recruitment occurs as a matter of choice—to attend training as either an aspiring or practicing midwife. Moreover, a difference in language and education level and the consequent state nomination to midwife status places one woman in authority over others, both between midwives and between a midwife and her pregnant charges. In brief, state intervention and its attendant hierarchization of women engender envy and break down the traditional notion that one is called to the craft by the luck or gift of God.

NAHUALENSE RECOMMENDATIONS FOR MIDWIFE EMPOWERMENT

Nahualense midwives had a number of good ideas for enhancing their ability to deal with the issues that vexed them in their profession. They did not wish to change everything. For example, these midwives recognized state-sponsored training sessions as a positive influence on their practice (though Goldman and Glei [2000] report no significant behavioral changes). Not only did training increase their knowledge; the sessions also familiarized them with other midwives and local medical personnel and gave them a small stipend for their time, all of which they appreciated.

But, like most interventions, midwife training had more consequences than those originally intended. For example, if the Ministry of Health had not decided to officially recognize midwives and attempt to standardize their practices, midwives would not have had the impetus to become politically active. Of course, midwives have long recognized the benefits of political petitions to obtain such things as funding. Now, with the initiation of state-sponsored training, midwives became aware of the threat of imprisonment. This knowledge thrust them into the national medical-political system and has created a greater perceived need for political activism. Nahualense midwives suggest that the six main factors discussed above have impeded their activism: lack of formal education, not knowing Spanish, Ladino discrimination, absence of networks, corruption, and envy.[5]

To help overcome these impediments to the political empowerment they desire, Nahualense midwives offered several suggestions. They gave these solutions in the hope of overcoming their sense of disempowerment so they could maneuver the political system to obtain more training, funding, and legal protection in case of maternal death. However, in keeping with their sense of political disenfranchisement, most felt incapable of putting into effect their own proposed solutions. They instead assumed that educated youth, outside organizations, or we interviewers were in a better position to fulfill their requests for social change.

We, however, personally decline to offer our ideas for solutions, for we concur with Freire (1993:94), who objected to outsiders presuming they could propose resolutions that would work in a given local situation: "Many political and educational plans have failed because their authors designed them according to their own personal views of reality, never once taking into account (except as mere objects of their actions) the men-in-a-situation to whom their program was ostensibly directed." Based on Freire and other cultural critics, we conclude that it is of utmost importance that midwives—the women-in-this-situation—must be the authors and instigators of solutions.

Concerning their lack of formal education, midwives suggested that the government require that a deeper legal orientation to the issues of their craft be a part of the nationwide mandatory training. This would provide all midwives with a greater base of knowledge, allowing them to see the flaws inherent in midwifery legislation and to choose more specific areas of political activism.

Concerning the language barriers midwives face, informants offer two solutions. In the short term, they suggest using a translator to convey their political stances and requests to government officials. As a longer-term solution, they suggest that free Spanish classes be offered them. The Spanish classes would not only make it easier for them to be politically empowered but would also help them be of more assistance to those patients who need to give birth in a hospital, for then the midwife could act as a translator and cultural and institutional system broker. Funding would, of course, be essential for either of these proposed solutions to function. However none of my informants seemed to be sure whom, or how, they could ask for funding. They felt, however, that if the Nahualá Midwife Committee were to begin to involve all of the Nahualá midwives instead of just the few on the committee, together they could negotiate ways of obtaining such funding.

Unfortunately, none of my informants proposed a way to overcome the existence of envy. As an appropriate mode of political change, however, they did recognize the need to include all midwives within a committee, rather than exclude some. The midwives also felt that if the Nahualá Midwife Committee were to involve *all* the midwives, envy between them might decrease and a sense of group solidarity would, hopefully, take its place. This was the only solution midwives gave to solve the problem of internal strife and envy. Essentially, it was a plea to let the core indigenous cultural values of equality and a community council, rather than intrusive Ladino preferences for status hierarchy, stand as the operant code in relations between indigenous midwives.

Obviously, their solutions remain very tentative and dependent on the formation of a more cohesive group of midwives. Yet, the mere recognition of the barriers that exist, their self-reflective analysis of their place in the situation, and their proffering of possible solutions that could help them overcome those barriers put midwives on a path to greater political empowerment.

THINKING ABOUT NAHUALÁ'S MIDWIVES IN A DISCIPLINED WAY

Nahualense midwives' understanding of their marginalization and disempowerment fits well with Foucault's (1994) concept of "biopower"—the power inherent in valorizing biological and medical technologies as a form of human control and bodily discipline—in this case as a form of racialized public health. Guatemala spends very little on its social infrastructure, such as public health care (World Health Organization 2011).[6] By enlisting the aid of indigenous midwives as an antidote to tragically high infant and maternal death rates, the state regulates and controls midwives through training, which is further seen in the creation of the local midwife committee. Imposed here is a "rational and voluntary" form of conduct that Foucault (1988) would see as the operation of medicine on the social body—not simply the body of birthing mothers and their infants, but also the body of midwives and the shaping of their conduct relative to one another, as well as to the state. And if an infant or mother dies under her care, this model of social medicine renders the midwife legally vulnerable. Midwives are thus in a double bind that renders them and their patients biologically and legally at risk (see Hsu and Lincoln 2007:16). Rural poverty leads to working conditions that are difficult at best, yet midwives cannot lose a single patient. It would be hard to imagine the most skilled physician being able to live up to that demand. In sum, the governance of the medicalized, Maya social body underscores the "fatal coupling of power and difference" (Hsu and Lincoln 2007:30). Racism, poverty, and state intervention in the indigenous villages combine to ensure that midwives' impact and reach are restricted, their vulnerability is heightened, and their political voice is thwarted.

Notes

Fieldwork: Rebecca Edvalson: 2006, plus residence in Nahualá (including giving birth and raising a family) 2010–11 during J. Edvalson's dissertation research
John Edvalson: 2003, 2006, plus doctoral fieldwork in Nahualá 2010–11

1. See K. Wilson (2007) for a picture of midwifery in Nahualá in 1995, when the National Health Service had not yet implemented its controls and had only begun training sessions. See Jones's (2007) description of the national health care outreach.

2. This list of political objectives concords with Hinojosa's (2004) discussion of problems of midwifery in San Juan Comalapa, where he mentions limited education and illiteracy, oral-didactic lecture-delivered training with no hands-on component (in violation of the long-known Maya cultural propensity to learn by observing and doing rather than talking and asking questions (as detailed

by M. Nash [1967] in the thread mills of Cantel), and the need to buy one's own "modern" medical instruments and supplies.

3. This curious plural usage ("trainings") reflects the fact that midwives receive a series of separate mini-courses to acquire certification, rather than attend a continuous or integrated one-time program. Hinojosa (2004:640, 642, 643) uses the same plural translation for what midwives and health officials in Comalapa call *adiestramientos*.

4. The phenomenon described here reproduces the same language-based discrimination and privileging of educated youths that undermined the cofradía system, the gerontocratic judicial system, and the indigenous mayors. Among others, see Brintnall (1979), Falla (2001), and Watanabe (1992).

5. We leave to others the task of ascertaining why women generally do not fare well in securing positions of leadership in this or other societies. Here our intent is simply to describe the blockages as Nahualenses see them.

6. The World Health Organization (2011) notes that the total expenditure per capita on public health care in Guatemala is a scant US$337. For Mexico—which has a notoriously poor public health system—it is US$846. In the United States, by contrast, it is US$7,410.

CHAPTER 6

Gangs, Community Politics, and the Social Production of Space in Nahualá

John J. Edvalson, James H. McDonald, John P. Hawkins, and Walter Randolph Adams

In 2005, *Newsweek* declared the transnational MS-13 gang "the most dangerous gang in America, with a possible total of 700,000 members worldwide" (Campo-Flores 2005). *Foreign Affairs* described Central American gangs as committing mass murders, connecting themselves with Mexican drug cartels, and preying on immigrants at the Mexico-Guatemala border, killing and maiming any who had not paid gang-connected "coyotes" (Arana 2005:103). In summer 2010, the U.S. State Department determined Guatemala to be Central America's "drug-trafficking epicenter" (CNN 2010). Most recently, the Pentagon categorized Central America as the deadliest non-war zone in the world (Murine 2011). Brands (2010:v) notes ominously that "an unholy trinity of criminal elements—international drug traffickers, domestically based organized crime syndicates, and youth gangs—have dramatically expanded their operation since the 1990s, and are effectively waging a form of irregular warfare against government institutions."

Guatemalan Mayas may not be aware of U.S. perspectives on these matters, but they certainly know about gang violence in Guatemala City and throughout the country. The nation's newspapers—read daily by many citizens and most municipal policy-makers in the Maya town centers—provide an almost daily fare of lurid pictures and explicit articles portraying the murders and extortion schemes of *maras* and *pandillas*, as the gangs are called, and detail the tragic results in the lives of Guatemalans, rich and poor alike. It is little wonder that Maya communities feel threatened by the prospect of gang-related violence in their communities and take steps to address those concerns. This chapter explores how one community in the Western Highlands—Nahualá—confronted this threat.

Throughout my (Edvalson's) second season of fieldwork in 2004, residents in Nahualá were debating the problem of youth gangs and their impact on the community. The notorious gangs Mara Salvatrucha (MS-13) and Mara Dieciocho (Mara-18) had allegedly been making inroads by trying to connect with and recruit Nahualense youths. The gangs reportedly used as recruiters members who had migrated to the United States and returned to the nearby urban centers of Quetzaltenango (nicknamed Xela) and Guatemala City. These youths were rumored to have returned from their initiation into American urban gangs with the goal of recruiting resident youths to create local satellites for these larger transnational gang networks.

Elder community members' apprehensions about the existence of these gangs culminated on the evening of August 12, 2004. A vigilante mob was organized in response to a rumor that gang members from the nearby city of Quetzaltenango had been recruited to kill the uncle of a girl involved with one of the maras in Nahualá. This girl had been ordered by her relatives to remain in the family home, presumably to sever her relationship with young men from the gang. This allegedly provoked the local gang to invite its Xela counterpart to help "rescue" her from familial house arrest. While ferreting out the alleged gang members (most of whom, whether real or not, "escaped" to Xela), the local men appointed to this particular security committee apprehended two young men and a young woman, all allegedly from Quetzaltenango, together with their illegal handmade firearm.

A debate arose among the mob regarding what they should do with or to the youths in their custody. A number of people in the mob suggested they be lynched. According to my informants (and supported by recent newspaper reports), this practice had become characteristic of vigilante justice in the region.[1] However, events several years prior surrounding the lynching of suspected thieves, along with the contested legal fallout thereafter, led the mob to be more cautious (see Bybee, chapter 2).

During these deliberations, the local military police observed from a distance. They were careful not to incite the members of the community to more violence and appeared to understand that their presence was unwanted. The mob decided that instead of lynching the suspects, they would strip them of their clothing, pour water on them, and beat them with belts.[2] Afterward, the youths were released to the custody of the national police, who arrested and charged them with possession of an illegal firearm. Referring to the incident and the rising influence of gangs in the community, one man remarked: "It's [just] that the people there are tired of all this by now."

Afterward, many members of the community and the people who had participated in the mob that rounded up the three suspected gang members expressed ambivalence about how the national police and the Guatemalan legal system had handled this and other related situations. In informal interviews regarding the incident, all participants remarked that the youths would probably be released after a few days because their underage status would keep them from being prosecuted in Guatemala's justice system.

The initial ambivalence and unease about the gang situation in Nahualá and the perceived inability of the state to deal with it led to more-direct action by political leaders, culminating in a set of extralegal procedures to deal with maras and other delinquents. This arrangement was introduced by the mayor, his appointed municipal officials, and a group of distinguished town elders known as *principales*, a political unit consisting of older men who had served as neighborhood committee leaders and who in some cases had once been part of the now defunct *cofradía* system in Nahualá (see Brintnall 1979:98; Dracoulis, this volume, chapter 1; Grandin 2000:20–21; C. Larson, in review; Tax 1937:443; Watanabe 1992:109–12). This local justice system, as it has come to function in Nahualá, consists of procedures that have become the standard method for dealing with any issues associated with maras, theft, or violence in the community.

Gangs challenge community-held notions of respect and authority in Nahualá. Maya responses to maras in highland communities in Guatemala are symptomatic of a larger set of social, legal, and security problems that have become associated with the post–Peace Accords period in Guatemala (Burrell 2009; Little 2009). This paper describes, contextualizes, and interprets these local extralegal developments and their controversial nature with respect to Guatemalan penal law. It also considers how expressions of gang punishment relate to Maya conceptions of order, respect, and the governmentality of public spaces. I will also examine what people believed to be the causes of gang activity, how they chose to deal with their perception of the presence of gangs in their community, and the local rationale for responding as they did.

I argue that municipal leaders have sought to curtail gang activity primarily by reclaiming public physical spaces, especially the main plaza, parks, and cemeteries, and by asserting their authority over matters that, according to state standards, should fall within the jurisdiction of the national police and Guatemala's justice system. Gangs challenge community-held notions of correct behavior by congregating and painting graffiti in public spaces. The municipal order reestablishes its authority in the same places by punishing the perpetrators at the very sites of their tactical resistance—on the soccer fields and in the town plaza—thus "reconquering" the site and shaming gangs into submitting to communal notions of respect and accountability for crimes committed. Such actions reinforce the order of communities and enforce notions of authoritative control. Nahualense leaders accomplished this by reestablishing autonomous security committees to patrol streets at night and through displays of local political power and "traditional" authority within the community, rather than relying on the state for support.

Bybee (chapter 2) focuses specifically on how this local justice system came into play as a strategy to avoid mob lynching and state repercussions. The details of youth and intergenerational conflict are worked out by Call (chapter 7). This chapter, in contrast, discusses how elders interpret youth delinquency and gang behavior and how they used locally determined law to address illicit gang behavior. In addition, I describe gang activities in Nahualá and analyze the comments of former gang members.

GANGS IN NAHUALÁ

Nahualense gangs share some cross-cultural similarities with gangs in other places. Vigil's (1988) study of Chicano gangs in Los Angeles provides a basis for comparison. Yet I recognize the substantial differences in economy, mode of production, and ethnicity in the respective gang contexts. Unlike Vigil's depiction, gang members in Nahualá live in a rural agricultural area and are part of an indigenous community whose structure and social composition differ from Latino communities in Los Angeles in several ways. Nahualense subsistence strategies are radically different from those of urban Los Angeles; the majority of Nahualense males work in hand-hoe agriculture, preferably on their own plots, while some own small businesses in the town center, or run shops, weave, or engage in other crafts and sources of supplemental income in the hamlets.

Despite these differences, the causes of Nahualense youth gang initiation and activity share much in common with Vigil's study. Vigil (1988:1) argues that "the lives of street youths who comprise the barrio gang reflect multiple stresses and pressures, which result in a multiple marginality." One source of stress and marginality for both Nahualense and Angelino gang members derives from the pressures of disintegrating family status and the attractions of small-group sociality and care. Vigil (1988:2) describes East Los Angeles gangs as "made up largely of young males, from 13 to 25 years of age . . . [acting in] response to the pressures of street life and [serving] to give certain barrio youth a source of familial support, goals and directives, and sanctions and guides . . . spending their time in the usual cohort activities found in any neighborhood where adolescents and other youth congregate."

Compare Virgil's summary to the thoughts of one former Nahualense gang member: "We helped each other. . . . There were two other youths that I knew: The mom died from drinking. Their father died as well and the two children were left as orphans. There in the gang, they felt like we were a family because we were very united then. That is how it starts; many times I have noticed that the majority of the youths that become gang members do not have a father. They might have a mother, but she cannot do anything for them." Interviews with former and current members of Nahualá's gangs confirm this pattern of the gang as a substitute for perceived inadequate familial support.

As in Vigil's description of gangs in Los Angeles, many Nahualense gang members were orphaned sons and daughters of parents who had died of alcoholism or had abandoned them for migrant work, perhaps in Guatemala City or the United States. These orphans commonly drifted from one household to another of their extended family, passing on to another relative when they become too much of a nuisance. They typically spent the majority of their time "in the street," especially as they aged beyond childhood. Indeed, it is perhaps no coincidence that the alleged female gang member mentioned in the beginning of this chapter was an orphan living with her extended family.

In Nahualense belief, such family instability has consequences. A former mayor who witnessed the rise of maras in Nahualá argued that the phenomenon of youth involvement in gangs "comes largely as a result of familial disintegration," which, in his mind, leads to a propensity to violence against society. Thus, he explained, a youth who "from his childhood . . . does not receive affection from his mother or father" becomes "a person who does not feel remorse when he does damage to someone."

Unreliable family supervision or tumultuous family status was not the only source of marginalization that drew Nahualenses to gangs. For others, marginality derived from trying to mimic the symbols of modernity they saw on TV or had seen in the cities of Guatemala or as migrants to the United States. Adults identified many youths as gang members simply because—from an adult or parental perspective—they listened to the wrong kind of music and dressed the wrong way. They were marginalized by family and neighbors in a community with entrenched conservative social values—values enforced by fairly strict codes of behavior prescribed by the many Protestant and Charismatic Catholic congregations that prohibit drinking alcohol and listening to nonreligious music.

Nahualenses stereotyped gang members as being intoxicated much of the time, engaging in fights on the street, and stealing from members of the community. When asked about his activities, one former Nahualense gang member stated: "In the first place, [we look for opportunities to go] drinking, but before you drink you need to find money. To find money, some people work. But there are others that do not. So they go out and rob at night."[3] In fact, during the first phase of this research project, four local stores had been broken into and money and merchandise stolen, a crime not taken lightly in Nahualá. As a result, my host family and others I interviewed admonished me repeatedly not to go out at night because of the gang presence.

To Nahualenses, much of the change that needs to take place in their community involves the families of the gang members themselves and the morals they teach their children regarding their role in society. According to one teacher: "To speak of a youth who is a gang member, we say that there is now a lack of morals. Having morality is to have good attitudes, to have respect, to be obedient, do the things that are good, not only for just yourself but for all of society." In concert with this sentiment of gang members lacking feeling or morality, many Nahualenses described gang members in animalistic terms, as lacking natural human feelings and generally behaving in ways counter to the elders' ideal expectations for a Maya youth. In a public meeting related to the threat of gangs in the community, one Maya *principal* asked rhetorically, "Could it be that they are beasts, that they are animals? Could it be that they are in our homes? Could it be that they are our sons, even our daughters?" Here, intergenerational conflict between leaders in the older generation and youths in the rising generation manifested itself in a public forum. Gang members were described as "animals" and "beasts"; clearly they did not act in ways that human beings should in Nahualá. As with an animal, people should be careful with a gang member lest he "does damage" or attacks them, as the former mayor averred.

In interviews, Nahualense adults tended to categorize any behavior that did not conform to their ideals of respectful youth comportment as potentially placing that youth in the dangerous category of gang member. Being out late at night, spending too much time in the street with friends, hanging out and getting in fights in soccer fields, drinking, wearing dark clothing, and more, were all considered taboo. For Nahualá's older generation, correct youth behavior involved staying inside the boundaries of the family compound in the evening and night hours, carrying out chores and other household duties, and deferring to older Nahualenses, especially in public forms of behavior. As one teacher remarked about gang behavior: "In the Maya culture, we are always taught that if there is an old woman in the path and I come, as a youth, the other way, out of respect I should always step aside and give the old woman the right of way. This is part of our culture, but those that are in a gang now do not do that. When an old woman comes, they push her. 'Get out of the way and let us pass,' they say. So you can see, now they have no respect at all." Respect and submission to parental and civic authority, of course, are all-important Maya, humanizing values.

RESPECT FOR PLACE AND SPACE

From the beginnings of Mesoamerican ethnography, anthropologists have remarked on the importance of the municipio, the place and space where a Maya is born, through which she or he acquires identity. Through both direct and indirect observation, I saw that gang members spent a great deal of their time engaging in activities that violated Nahualense ideas about correct behavior in public spaces. Gangs would often "tag" or spray-paint graffiti on the walls of the market near the plaza, in the municipal park, and throughout the cemetery. Nor were local churches immune; many bore the tags of the MS-13 or -18. Graffiti often contained rough approximations to English profanity.

Some tags bore satanic references, such as a phrase painted prominently in the market: "We have seen the power of the devil." Interviews confirmed the supposed connections between gangs and satanic themes. Considering the religious conservatism of parents and other adults in the community, gang members likely adopted these powerful symbols in reaction to the religiosity of their parents. One informant, a male schoolteacher in his thirties, averred that gangs, as part of an initiation ritual, were rumored to visit cemeteries and on a dare dig up dead people's bones, grind them up, and place them in vials around their necks. In these rituals, gang members supposedly prayed to the devil for the strength to commit their crimes. While I was unable to substantiate these claims, the suspicion in 2006 that gang members had beaten to death four men who were passed out drunk on the street, stealing what little money they had, suggests the evil connections believed to inhere in them.

Regardless of the veracity of these claims, adult Nahualenses sensed an "out of placeness" of youth whom the adults believed to have ties to some of the most dangerous gangs in Central America. And while the dress and behavior of these local youths were not as extreme as that of gangs in the urban centers in Guatemala, their behavior was, for community elders and parents, a legitimate cause for concern. Gangs occupied public places in ways most adult citizens deemed highly problematic. These alternative uses of space became one of the main issues addressed by public officials in combating the problem.

For example, I would often see supposed gang members loitering around the park, soccer fields, or main plaza. Only occasionally did I observe them harassing someone or otherwise causing trouble. The reaction of leaders and citizens who found the loiterers' presence in these places unwanted resonated with many Nahualenses, especially if their presence interfered with prescribed uses of that space. On one occasion I saw a group of darkly dressed youths harass a female market vendor. Their behavior prompted another female vendor to comment, "there is no peace now, there is always fear." To invert Douglas's (1966) proposition a bit, fear is matter out of place.

Nahualense public officials responded in a manner they understood and thought harmonious with local cultural and historical conditions of the community. In short, they sought to control public space. In the following sections I will describe these extrajudicial means by which Nahualenses dealt with the gang presence in relation to the average Nahualense's communal sense of space and place.

CAUSES AND REMEDIES FOR THE GANG PROBLEM

Nahualenses shared significant understandings of the causes of gang participation, some of which are mentioned above in the qualitative ethnography. To get quantitative data, I asked one hundred survey participants in 2004 what they thought were the causes of and solutions for gang participation in the community. Fifty-six men and forty-four women responded, their average age twenty-eight and median age twenty-four. Three main categories emerged as descriptive labels for the motivation of youths who were joining Nahualá's gangs, along with four proposed solutions to the gang "problem."

1. **Familial disintegration.** Answers centered on the breakdown of the family unit or a lack of responsibility taken by parents in the upbringing of their sons and daughters (for example, parental alcoholism, orphaned status of gang member, or lack of attention by parents)
2. **Personal responsibility**. Answers placed blame on the individual gang member (for example, a lack of respect, laziness, bad nature, personal vices)
3. **Outside influences.** Answers focused blame on outside forces as a cause for gang affiliation (for example, friends, media, alcohol, unemployment)

Among those who answered the question regarding the causes of gangs in Nahualá, 30 percent pointed to familial disintegration as the main cause of gang behavior; 38 percent referred to issues dealing with personal responsibility; and 32 percent pointed to outside influences. These results were consistent with my qualitative observations about maras in Nahualá. While it would be extremely difficult to determine causal relationships, the consistency between these quantitative and qualitative data suggests shared local conceptions of the multifaceted causes of the gang problem in Nahualá, causes that perhaps apply in other parts of Central America.

As for remedies, Rodgers (1999:18) provides a useful general outline of the types of intervention programs that have been used to deter gang-related behavior in Latin America. His scheme provides a backdrop against which to compare the Nahualá case. Rodgers notes that there is little information on gang intervention programs in Latin America and adopts the United States as his model for proactive gang intervention. He outlines four types of interventions:

1. **Suppression:** programs that attempt to reduce youth gang activities through punitive means, usually involving police action
2. **Community organization:** projects that aim to change the context in which youth gangs operate by mobilizing and organizing gang-affected communities, thus reducing the scope for gang activities
3. **Social intervention:** projects that include outreach and counseling programs aimed at preventing youth gang delinquency and reducing gang membership through face-to-face contact with gang members
4. **Provision of opportunities:** programs that seek to redirect gang activities into more constructive pursuits, including job training, employment, and education programs

Using Rodgers's categories, I coded the open responses of the hundred Nahualenses surveyed. I had asked participants to propose a solution to the gang problem; they received no prompting or suggestion of categories on my part. As one would expect, Nahualense responses did not fit neatly into Rodgers's categories. Some responses overlapped with Rodgers's categories. Some did not fit culturally. However, by coding my informants' answers with Rodgers's categories, while accounting as best as I could for the cultural factors present in Nahualá, I was able to determine some parallels between Rodgers's model and proposed Nahualense solutions.

Regarding the question of solutions or responses to gangs, 25 percent mentioned some kind of suppressive measure. These included suggestions that the national and local government authorities intervene with a plan to limit and suppress gang activities by enforcing a set of rules or to remove gangs from public spaces. Of those who responded, only 7 percent mentioned getting the police or other national officials directly involved. By implication, many Nahualenses feel enforcement should be local.

Forty percent of participants favored community-based organizational solutions, which best matched Rodgers's second category. This large percentage includes both familial and religious-based solutions, which are an important component of Nahualense cultural life, perhaps reflecting the fairly strong social cohesion that still exists in this community.

Twenty-eight percent favored social intervention projects, resonant with Rodgers's third category. These included rehabilitative classes for gang members, recreational programs, and counseling services. A large number of respondents advocated rehabilitative programs involving sports or other athletic activities, which formed a popular pastime among youths.

Finally, only 7 percent favored programs to provide more opportunity. While this result seems counterintuitive, it may also reflect a bias in my coding, coupled with a lack of local experience with opportunity-providing programs. I included recreational activities as part of "Social intervention." One can easily argue that recreation should have been included under "Provision of opportunities."

I shared the initial results of the survey with the municipal government before it established any gang intervention. Whether the mayor and members of the security committees were influenced by any of my data, I cannot say. However, the solutions they arrived at roughly fit Rodgers's second category, community organization approaches to gang prevention. According to Rodgers (1999:19): "Community organization programs can take a number of forms. All, however, take as a basic premise that youth gang violence is at least partly a result of social disorganization and that if local-level social institutions or networks were created or strengthened within these communities, youth gangs would become less of a problem."

Two years later, in 2006, I had the opportunity to evaluate what the Nahualense community officials had implemented to reduce their gang problem. Nahualense officials did seek to strengthen local institutions, as Rodgers suggested, but they favored a combination of suppressive measures and community organization programs. This might have much to do with the relatively low cost of locally directed prevention programs (compared with the expense of hiring experts), the conservative nature of Nahualense officials, and the historical context of Nahualá. In the following section, I discuss those actions and analyze what they reveal about Nahualense attitudes regarding law and order as well as youth delinquency in the difficult context of twenty-first century Guatemala.

GANG SOLUTIONS, 2005–2006

Security problems and the reaction to them in Nahualá reflect the legacy of insecurity and violence that Mayas experienced during the civil war. The addition of street gangs as a new problematic category generated heated debate among Nahualenses and caused them to reflect on more generalized problems of insecurity that seem a part of living in Guatemala during the early twenty-first century.

Central American gang networks highlight the effects of poverty, transnational migration, and social disintegration endemic throughout Central America. Rodgers (2006, 2007), working in Nicaragua, is one of the few voices in anthropology to describe the rise of youth gangs in Central America after the civil wars of the 1980s (for an excellent exception, see Wolseth 2011). Of this period, Rodgers (2007:318) contends that "the most obvious reflection of this state disintegration is generally seen to be the dramatic explosion in criminal violence that has affected the country during the past decade and a half, which many interpret as signaling an inability of the state to impose order over society." In her article on gangs in the Mam-speaking Maya community of Todos Santos, Burrell (2009:98) refers to Sieder's suggestion that "in the post–Peace Accords period . . . the legal culture in indigenous communities throughout Guatemala consists of 'a hybrid mixture of local adaptation and practices and elements of universalist or national legal norms'" (Sieder 1998:107).

In her analysis of circumstances in Todos Santos, an indigenous municipio in many ways similar to Nahualá, Burrell (2009:98) further argues that "In a post-Accords 'irony of power,' unexpected alliances are forming in the name of suppressing community youth rebellion (maras) in Todos Santos. Former civil patrollers and guerrillas mobilize under the umbrella of community security, utilizing the older and once state-sanctioned, but now illegal form of *comité de seguridad* (civil patrol)."

Similarly, by regaining control over public spaces through the establishment of security committees approximately like those of Todos Santos, Nahualá officials have asserted their autonomy and political authority by using many of the same extralegal strategies used by the government during the civil war era to which Burrell alludes. Below I discuss the Nahualense efforts to make these actions "legal" within the authority of the municipal government. To set the stage for that discussion, however, I must first examine the historical context in which security committees operate in Nahualá and other municipalities, and the implications that their recent organization has for Maya communities.

Security Committees and Gangs

The current spate of indigenous security committees operating at the municipal level throughout Guatemala has special historical significance. In theory, each rural hamlet (larger *aldea* or smaller *caserío*) and each urban ward (*cantón* or *barrio*) is authorized by the mayoral commission to elect a committee of its respected citizens to deal with security issues. The committee organizes its adult male citizens on rotation, authorizing a small group each night to patrol the paths, roads, and streets within its own boundary. In practice, patrols might not function every night. But the patrol mechanism generally exists and can mobilize, especially during municipal fiestas or periods of alert when security committee members sense any reason for local concern.

The patrols are similar in form and function to the Patrullas de Autodefensa Civil (PACs) of the 1980s—that later became the Comités Voluntarios de Defensa Civil (CVDCs) that were active in the 1980s and early 1990s. These institutions played an integral role in the military's scorched-earth campaign directed against indigenous communities (see Green 1999:171–74; Hale 2006:67; Stoll 1993:6–7). The military roles of the PACs varied from one town to another, and in Nahualá their activities were fairly modest compared with the tragic violence between alleged leftist guerrillas and the Guatemalan military, primarily to the north and south of the municipality (see Green 1999; Manz 2004; Stoll 1993). Nahualenses kept levels of violence low by avoiding interaction with the government. They accepted military demands to organize and root out suspected guerrillas, but they did so on the condition that their PACs be governed by the community without military supervision. Furthermore, Nahualense officials did not allow its members to carry firearms, but only machetes and clubs. According to my consultants, the military did conduct raids in Nahualá during the civil war to search for suspected leftist guerrillas, but they did not set up a military base in the community.

During the civil war, after formal training took place, Nahualense men staffed security outposts throughout the municipio. These men patrolled the streets and rural paths at night, watching for guerrilla activity, whether intrusive or internal and "subversive." After the civil war abated, the military withdrew from the area, and peace talks between the guerrillas and the Guatemalan government began in the early 1990s. Security patrols became less frequent and the men assigned to them gradually abandoned their responsibilities. Over the next decade, no equivalent organization had been functioning in Nahualá until the gang issue inspired renewed attention to community security.

Since 2006, for Nahualense men, participation in the newly formed security committees is just one more civic duty. Its members do not seek this position nor are they paid for their efforts. Rather, security committee members are appointed by local leaders through frequent neighborhood and municipal-level meetings. From 2005 to 2008 these committees patrolled Nahualá's streets regularly at night, primarily as a way to deter gang activities. During my fieldwork I asked to accompany the men as they made their rounds but was declined because it would make both me and them more of a target and place their activities at greater risk. Through interviews with community members, I determined that the security committees consisted of small groups of men walking through the town's streets from about 9:00 P.M. to 4:00 A.M. If they found someone who looked suspicious or lacked pressing business justifying his or her presence, they asked the person to go home. Indeed, local cultural beliefs relating to evil spirits and tales of a malevolent being (*winche*) that has the ability to shift into animal form are enough to deter most residents from being outside at night. When the men on patrol found people engaged in illegal activity, those individuals were turned over to municipal authorities, though they often got a good beating in the process of capture. If they were found guilty (in a process described by Bybee, chapter 2), they were punished in the central plaza. By 2011, security committee patrols were not as regular as they once were, but they did occasionally patrol the streets. With the advent of cell phones, patrollers were (and still are in 2012) only a call or two away from mobilization by the mayor or the hamlet or canton security committee head if needed to settle a security issue.

Reclaiming Contested Town Space through Public Punishment

During the two months I spent in the community in 2006, a total of seven customary punishments were meted out on two thieves, three gang members, three girls, twenty to thirty of the town's drunks (in two separate episodes), and two other groups of women and men for fighting and kidnapping. Bybee (chapter 2) provides an excellent description of the frequency of public punishment and the private and public stages by which such punishment takes place. To this, we would like to add a few additional details. First, minor crimes are punished at the soccer fields, which also serve as a locale for public forums at the neighborhood level. As noted by Bybee, more severe criminal acts are dealt with at the municipal building, with public punishment taking place on its balcony facing crowds standing in the town's main plaza. Under the pressure of the public gaze, a microphone is held in front of each offender's face. As they kneel on rocks, the criminals can confess or otherwise explain their actions. If family members are found guilty by association (for example, if they knew of crimes committed), they, too, can be forced to kneel on rocks. The admonitions given the criminals during the punishment had a quasi-religious feel, partly due to frequent mentions of God and divine justice. Spectators would watch for hours as the crimes were explained, confessions were elicited, and lectures on the ills of delinquency and the power of repentance were imparted to the audience. Using the same spaces in which gangs had committed their crimes to enact the punishment had the effect of reclaiming Nahualense space for legitimate, collective, lawful use.

Goldstein's work in Bolivia suggests that the structure of the colonial city remains a significant source of political control and that "for all of the apparent chaos, disorder, and violence that today seem to characterize it, the Latin American city did not come to being without a tremendous amount of planning and forethought" (Goldstein 2004:6). Nahualá's layout also follows the classic layout of the Latin American city, and perhaps serves, as Goldstein (2004:6) suggests, to represent "the ideal of rationality, [and] of order reflected in the physical layout of the city."

According to Little's study of Antigua, the former capital of Guatemala, "the Central Plaza, or *ruk'u'x tinamït* (literally, 'the heart of the city'), is where commercial, ceremonial, and political power should be located" (Little 2008:271). In Nahualá, the central plaza is indeed surrounded by local symbols of political and religious authority. On the southern side sits the Catholic church, while on the western side sits the municipal building with its balcony overlooking the main plaza.

On the surface of the main plaza, the symbol of Nahualá, the *k'ot* (double-headed eagle) is laid out in a red tile formation. This same symbol is often woven into women's clothing and ceremonial fabrics. For Nahualenses, the eagle represents the ancient authority of the ancestors and legitimizes the current authority of the mayor and the principales who direct Nahualá's political affairs. According to one informant, schoolteachers in Nahualá remind their students of the symbolic value of the k'ot. It is said that one of the eagle's heads looks back to the past, reminding people of their traditions and to respect the elders who came before. The other head looks forward to remind everyone to plan for the future and to live a virtuous life by carefully avoiding mistakes, pride, and the various other shortcomings that tempt humans.

The use of this space as a location to punish gang members and other delinquents is significant and helps reestablish the social order that local people felt was threatened by the presence of gangs. For Low (2000:127), the effort of spatialization means "to locate—physically, historically, and conceptually—social relations and social practice in space." She argues that "the social production of space includes all those factors—social, economic, ideological, and technological—that result, or seek to result, in the physical creation of the material setting" (2000:127–28). When gangs violated Nahualense standards of order in their public spaces, municipal leaders used those same spaces to correct such dissonance. Despite the controversial nature of these public displays, the eventual decline in gang activity might be claimed as evidence of public punishment's efficacy.

There are deeper historical resonances. We note again the parallels with the marriage and other religious ceremonies. Here we call attention to the structural similarity between the social dramas presented on the mayor's balcony in front of the plaza today and the structure of sacred Passion plays presented on the second-floor balcony of many colonial churches and monasteries that also overlooked a central plaza. Perhaps the trend goes deeper still. Ancient Mayas held their political-religious dramas high on the sides of temples and public buildings, punishing wrongdoers and people who threatened the integrity of society there and on altars in the plaza, presumably enacted before an enthralled citizenry.

We return to a less speculative present. Despite the apparent success of public gang punishment, its extralegal nature caused concern among community members, especially those who saw it as a violation of human rights and worried about its indiscriminate use. In summer 2006, the municipal government of Nahualá sought approval from the Ministry of Governance for its new set of regulations. After months with no response from the national government, they decided to administer public punishment on the basis of the general consent of the municipal leaders.

As the administration of these punishments continued unsanctioned, I began to hear complaints from local people about the practice. Some of my consultants pointed out that the municipal government had no mechanism to thoroughly investigate the crimes, nor did security committee members participate in any formal law-enforcement training. Rather, my consultants suspected that many criminals were tried more as a result of rivalries and envy between families than on any actual evidence of wrongdoing.[4]

Despite the extralegal nature of these punishments, the codification of norms, the attempts to approve them locally and nationally, and their enactment in public as a visible communal event resulted in sufficient legitimacy as far as local officials were concerned. Thus, municipal leaders felt justified in continuing their implementation and supported by a legitimizing rationale: they had codified the customs, established limits for them, and defined the acceptable forms of punishment. They had sought approval at the national and local levels, thereby showing good-faith transparency, especially important as a buffer against criticism. Perhaps in such cases it is indeed better to ask forgiveness than to obtain permission, especially in Guatemala.

The provisions and rights laid out in the 1996 Peace Accords provided further support for Nahualense legal practice. The provisions in this document, commonly discussed in schools and at indigenous leadership conferences, provided a space for indigenous Guatemalans to reestablish community forms of justice that had been prohibited by the military regimes of Guatemala. Specifically, the tenuous legal basis for the legitimacy of Maya customary law as it is currently constituted originates in the Agreement on Identity and Rights of Indigenous Peoples in the 1996 Peace Accords (Section IV, E).

This agreement provided a significant space wherein people in Nahualá (and other indigenous municipios) have sought to operate their system of justice in accordance with the national legal system. However, this freedom provides a certain amount of ambiguity regarding its implementation. On the one hand, they must comply with national law. On the other, the provisions of the Peace Accords were externally imposed and failed formal ratification through a 1999 referendum, thus leaving them open to ongoing contestation and challenge (see introduction, this volume). A provision in the Guatemalan Constitution, however, does provide significant support for respect of indigenous culture.

As Nahualenses dealt with the problems associated with gangs in their community, community members openly debated notions of legality and morality. In addition to the administering of public punishment, many principales were in favor of enforcing curfews and destroying athletic fields that had attracted loiterers and delinquents. This sentiment was not held by many of the teachers in the community, who felt that in addition to punishing maras, the community needed to provide alternatives: recreational and educational resources for youth in the community. They felt it would be better to look at some of the larger concerns facing youth, including alcoholism and unemployment.

Soccer was seen as one of the few positive outlets for youth, which underscored its centrality as a form of delinquency prevention. One of my consultants, an active opponent of the principales, argued that soccer-playing youths were generally engaged in positive athletic activity and not in the types of negative behavior described by the town elders. A few Nahualenses who considered themselves progressive or modern thus critiqued the principales, arguing that their conservative, hard-line approach would only exacerbate the gang problem. They contended that youths needed professional counselors, development of educational opportunities, and more vocational training. Finally, they argued that the principales were blind to the "real" problems (for example, various cantina owners openly sold alcohol to minors—an issue of lax enforcement, from their perspective). Here, these "progressives" unknowingly replicated the recommendations of Rodgers (1999) regarding provision of opportunities.

One of the likely reasons soccer is targeted by the principales is that gang boundaries have long been associated with soccer team boundaries. Ironically, these principales would often use the same soccer field they wished to destroy to make public speeches about the problem, seeking to gain public support from other community members.

Despite the protests of the "progressives," the system established by the principales with the mayor's support is considerably less expensive than Western rehabilitative models of justice, while still meeting public demand. Social workers, vocational training schools, and recreation centers required funding that did not exist at the municipal level. What did exist was the willpower of the members of their political system to try and deal with gang activity punitively but in a way that simultaneously restored local offenders to the community. Nonlocal offenders, however, were much more likely to be summarily lynched, and if they survived, to be turned over to national authorities.

The solutions that Mayas have applied to their gang problem reflect some of the issues Foucault raises in his work analyzing systems of governmentality. The process through which Nahualá officials gained consent is relevant to Foucault, given the dramatic nature of the public punishment itself. Issues that concern "how to govern oneself, how to be governed, how to govern others, by whom the people will accept being governed, how to become the best possible governor" (Foucault 1991:131) are all relevant to the case of Nahualá insofar as they relate to methods where legitimacy of governance is established.

In Guatemala, various factions within the state compete for supremacy. The national government wishes simultaneously to control and to ignore its less powerful citizenry and their municipal legal systems. Other players include the employees who exist, in theory, to serve the state, and finally, the local-level actors who seek to use their agency within these imposed structures to obtain their goals as far as the state will allow.

For Foucault, this dynamic of state and individual contending with each other over goals matters greatly. According to Foucault, at one end of something like a continuum you have "the art of self-government connected with morality; the art of properly governing a family, which belongs to economy; and [at the other end,] the science of ruling the state, which concerns politics" (1991:134). To achieve these ends, Foucault argues that the state embeds the meaning and purpose of government with discourses that justify its existence as being for the common good of the people. However, what governments are really after is not necessarily related to the common good "but to an end which is 'convenient' for each of the things that are to be governed" (Foucault 1991:137).

This is accomplished by deploying certain tactics that involve protecting a myriad of interests simultaneously. The authority to do this lies in the sovereign power of the state and in the laws it creates that, over time, theoretically begin to change people's behavior. Thus, the power the state exercises is not merely destructive but creative as well, insofar as it embeds itself in the daily practice of its subjects and basically allows them to govern themselves according to a "disciplinary regime" they have established.

In the case of Nahualá, little in the way of central discipline has been established, and Indian communities are left on their own to work out systems of governance, for better or for worse. Recently, mayors and leaders have been finding out what works by attending indigenous culture and leadership conferences. From central government's perspective, little has been invested, and if local governance leads to problematic or embarrassing results, the Mayas can always be blamed for being backward and ignorant.

As Hale (2006:35) argues, "proponents of neoliberal governance reshape the terrain of political struggle to their advantage, not by denying indigenous rights, but by selective recognition of them." In essence, Hale argues that by reframing the relationship between state and society, neoliberal political arrangements have given lip service to certain "rights" while subversively denying Maya and other marginalized groups that which is truly essential to creating more equitable relations in the country. For Hale, equitable relations would involve restructuring the political economy to provide poor people more concrete opportunities for economic advancement, thus undermining the power-hold of Guatemala's richer class.

Thus, by superficially granting provisions of the Peace Accords—such as autonomy in enacting "traditional law" or resources for language and cultural awareness, while simultaneously deregulating and privatizing public services—national elites allow Mayas to feel that they have more legal and political autonomy than they actually do. In truth, Mayas in Nahualá and elsewhere have remained economically and politically marginal in Guatemala despite the rhetoric of democracy and equality.

To conclude, we assert that Mayas in Nahualá have been given both the freedom and the exigency to develop a set of "legal" procedures that actually do work to eliminate the presence of gangs in their community. This is happening despite these Mayas' relative powerlessness to significantly alter the larger political and economic conditions and problems in Guatemala, which Hale and others view as essential. The power of Peace Accords rhetoric and the ambivalence of national law provided Nahualense officials the opportunity to legitimate their claims to authority and their right to execute "law" as they saw fit. These "procedures," as Watanabe (1999:120) describes them, "entail the play of power in routinized, mutually accepted behavioral and institutional forms; yet unlike hegemony, [they] frame interactions across differences of power and privilege without an a priori idea who or what ultimately controls them or whose interests they ultimately serve."

Despite dissent from members of the Nahualense community who wanted to implement rehabilitative models for gang prevention, community punishment has become institutionalized. For the past five years, Nahualense political officials have been engaged in building and strengthening security committees and have established a system of punishment to apprehend and prosecute the perpetrators of petty crimes and other delinquent behavior. Nahuelenses are aware of the comparisons between this system and the previous, government-imposed system of civil patrols. Nahualense leaders maintain, however, that as long as security committee patrols are under local control, they will not be corrupted easily. In addition, by reestablishing local control of public spaces, Nahualense officials were able to provide a concrete set of legal methods that local people understood as effectively suppressing gang participation.

After seven years in Nahualá, I have had the opportunity to observe both the rise and fall of gang participation in the community. The actions of municipal leaders were legally ambiguous, yet informants unanimously assert that gang activity is no longer a problem. Indeed, most of the obvious signs—graffiti, youths congregating at night, and petty acts of crime and delinquency in the name of Mara Salvatrucha or Mara Dieciocho—have been markedly reduced. Nahualenses have, it seems, successfully recaptured their public space from disorder and fear. In so doing, they have preserved their identity through yet another severe trial.

No longer an isolated village of corn farmers, Nahualá is now active in the global economy. Consequently, the rise in gang activity in Nahualá is and will continue to be closely related to the presence of drug-trafficking cartels in Guatemala. While cartels dominate much of the country (*Prensa Libre* 2011), with relatively minor exceptions, the narco-economy has largely bypassed Nahualá, unlike Alta Verapaz and the Péten to the north, Zacapa to the east, and Huehuetenango to the west (Martínez-Amador 2011). It is not that the town is somehow miraculously immune, or that powerfully organized elders have somehow banded together to drive out its pernicious influence. Rather, Nahualá is not located along major transshipment routes. The wayward youths of Nahualá are thus less likely to be recruited as cartel foot soldiers (cf. Archibold and Cave 2011). Because they are largely responsible for their own security, Nahualenses are in a sense lucky. By virtue of their location, they are not now in the direct gaze of the cartels. If that were to change, so too would their situation relative to gangs and public security. They certainly could not count on the state for protection. A local teacher reflected on the larger security issues facing Guatemala and underscored the urgency and utter contingency of public security concerns for his beleaguered country: "The government can add more soldiers and more police, but if there is no plan, they cannot do anything. This is like a sickness; the sickness is now in the people. What it needs is to be really healed—to cure all of it—so that it does not return again. If [the government] only tries to sort of calm things down, it does not help anything. The government is very influential in this case, but as we are now, it is a little difficult. It's not that one is a pessimist, but this is the reality."

Notes

Fieldwork: 2003, 2004, 2006, 2010, 2011–12

1. The United Nations Mission of Inspection to Guatemala (Misión de las Naciones Unidas para Guatemala, MINUGUA) was tasked to keep track of the number and prevalence of lynchings in Guatemala. MINUGUA has defined the lynchings as incidents of physical violence perpetrated by great numbers of private citizens against one or various individuals accused of committing a "criminal" offense. The mob violence need not result in the death of the victim to be classed a lynching. MINUGUA documented 421 cases of lynching from 1996 to 2001 with 817 victims, of whom 215 died (Fernández García 2004:14, citing United Nations Mission of Inspection to Guatemala, "Lynching, a Persistent Scourge," *MINUGUA Inspection Report*, p. 7).

2. We are unable to ascertain whether we have here one incident of pouring water (Bybee's description) or two different incidents of the community dealing with perceived gang penetration in separate years, in roughly similar ways, indicating an emergent traditional punishment.

3. "En primer lugar, a tomar. Pero antes de tomar, necesitan conseguirle dinero. Para conseguir dinero, hay unos que trabajan, pero hay otros que no trabajan. Entonces, se dedican a robar de las noches."

4. Here one of the core problems of the war years reappears: the use of state or local mechanisms for private vengeance or gain.

CHAPTER 7

"There Is No Respect Now"
Youth Power in Nahualá

Tristan P. Call, John P. Hawkins,
James H. McDonald, and Walter Randolph Adams

> Youths [as represented by the Popol Vuh's Hero Twins] are active subjects with meaning and with outward projections of their lives. Their struggle is a cosmic battle. . . . We could never finish [this book] were we to consider all the changes triggered by the generations of youths, that, like waves, continue impacting the shape of the community, one after another. These changes do not take place just because they happen to the youths, but because youths are in interaction with their history (migration, resistance, refuge), with their geography (jungle, rich earth, neighboring border with Mexico), with institutions (education, church), with the community (people, authorities, powers), with politics (the State, political parties), and with occult influences (narco-traffic), etc.
>
> Ricardo Falla (2006)

One summer day in 2006, I wandered into a crowd that jammed one of Nahualá's soccer fields and clogged the nearby dirt paths in every direction. Speakers mounted a platform and addressed the crowd in K'iche' through a megaphone. As one speaker followed another, I edged closer to try to pick out recognizable words, drawing stares from the people nearest me. I backed away again when people started frowning and pointing at a fellow gringo student who had waded into the mass of people with a camera to take some close-up photos.

The gathering was prompted by recent local tragedy. When I sidled up to a Nahualense friend standing at the margins of the crowd, he explained with mixed amusement and alarm that three teenage girls from the neighborhood had run away to the coast and only two had come back. The two girls who had returned were being publicly indicted, in some communal fashion I had not begun to decipher, for the apparent kidnapping of their friend. Local leaders had brought freshly cut switches to whip the offenders, but the girls' families had come without bringing their daughters, refusing to submit their family members to the punishment.

Having studied K'iche' for two semesters, I tried to understand the speeches and managed to pick out a single snippet: an exasperated man indignantly declared that the "gang clothing" worn by these youths was undermining their parents' authority over them. Apparently the girls had worn jeans, makeup, and short (shoulder-length) hair, a departure from traditional Nahualense costume.

At dinner over the next few weeks, my host family discussed new rumors almost every night about why the girls should be punished: they had run away from home, or joined gangs, or fought with their schoolmates, or lied to their parents, or kidnapped their friend, or used drugs, or sold their friend into prostitution. The prostitution angle proved especially popular for the first few weeks. Inevitably, gossipers would point out that the girls had worn clothing "of a certain style." Only a few Nahualenses claimed that wearing improper clothing constituted the girls' main offense, but those who didn't still maintained that the clothing and haircuts were clues suggesting that the girls needed urgent correction.

All three girls (including the "kidnapped" one, when she returned unharmed a few days later) were eventually subjected to the "traditional Maya" form of punishment that emerged in Nahualá that summer. These public ceremonies, typically carried out in front of an audience, involve being forced to kneel on corn-sized gravel (*xukub'axik chwi ixim ab'aj*) for up to several hours (see Bybee, chapter 2).[1] Their professed aim was to "scare" (*kexej kib'*) youths out of delinquency. These girls' sentence was one of about a dozen high-profile acts of public punishment inflicted on groups of "delinquent" youths in the Nahualá area that summer.[2] With over a hundred individuals punished this way, the participation of members of the mayor's office and regional observers, and the newsworthy precedent of an indigenous municipality claiming its constitutionally recognized right to mete out "traditional justice," these events stirred up interest and debate both in the national press and in local circles.

These local forms of punishment occurred in the context of growing outrage toward violent crime and youth delinquency across Central America. In the perceived absence of national law enforcement, high-profile gangs like Mara Dieciocho (Mara-18) and Mara Salvatrucha have sparked community-based mobilization and vigilantism throughout the region (see, for example, Burrell 2009 for a parallel process in Todos Santos). Although violent crime is much more common in urban Guatemala than in more isolated rural areas, the constant news reports of gang assaults have profoundly affected the way people talk and think even in calmer places like Nahualá. Winton (2004:4) explains: "There are no reliable data on the number of gangs operating in Guatemala or, indeed, on the proportion of crime attributable to youth gangs. Yet this very ambiguity, when coupled with the high visibility of this type of organized violence, has allowed the profile of gangs to be raised to such an extent that there seems little need for the perceived severity of the problem to be verified by actual data." Nahualenses, of course, feel that they have ample "actual data" on what youths are doing wrong in town, everything from change in clothing styles to infrequent but jarringly brutal murders. Indeed, Guatemala's Mayas face significant problems, theorized, for example, in Benson and Fischer's (2009) analysis of "neoliberal violence" as ambiguous; a world of clandestine violence, political fragmentation, intentional deception, and the anomie of rapid social change.

Nahualenses, however, tended to attribute local delinquency to a fairly straightforward problem: the lack of respect and hard work among youths nowadays. While Nahualenses' specific descriptions of delinquency (clothing, activities, character flaws) often came across as scattered and contradictory, they compensated for any perceived ambiguity with the clarity of their prescriptions for correcting the behavior. To be sure, there were debates in the community over what the girls had done wrong, followed by debates over whether those misdeeds were punishable crimes, mixed in with the perennial problem of how to select an effective and legitimate punishment for them, complicated by discussions of various legal restrictions, police protocols, and human rights codes about the rights of youths and prohibition of corporal punishment. All of these issues combined to create a tricky, if not insoluble, legal problem. Town elders, however, neatly sidestepped the legal and moral complexities of the situation with prompt and concrete physical action. Forcing their youths to kneel on rocks demonstrated symbolic and physical control and connoted the return of parental rule.

Field Site and Research Program

When I arrived in Nahualá for a four-month research trip in 2006, my plan was to study how youth participated (or didn't) in the political mobilization leading up to municipal elections. During participant observation and interviews, though, the topic always seemed to drift toward more general issues of youth identity and intergenerational divisions—often circling around worries about gangs and delinquency, the disorienting array of new opportunities (like migration and formal education) that were becoming more accessible but still felt out of reach, *rok* and *reguetón* music culture, and of course how emerging alternative culture related to Nahualá's high-profile public punishment. I eventually embraced the study of youth identity, not as a digression but as a prerequisite to understanding youth politics. Perhaps, I reasoned, the conversations always strayed because my informants felt the need to correct some of my misplaced assumptions and priorities.

For Nahualense youth, elections do not feel more important or even necessarily more "political" than curfews, black T-shirts, and soccer tournaments. For town elders, most questions of governance are not as pressing as the general concern that the youths "have no respect." This paper is an effort to understand those priorities.

Questioning the "Generation Gap"

According to most ethnographies and guidebooks to Guatemala, the Spanish conquest divided Guatemala between *indígenas*, the Mayas; and *Ladinos,* the Spanish-speaking, mixed-ethnicity class that withholds economic and political power from indígenas. But during the twentieth century, especially after the construction of the Pan-American Highway through Nahualá, Nahualenses have mingled with Ladino society to the point where they crisscross what used to be considered standard markers and unambiguous dividing lines: Nahualenses migrate to and from or reside permanently in urban centers and foreign countries, rather than remain in indigenous villages; they adopt components of Western dress or assume it entirely rather than hold to styles deemed indigenous; they engage in state politics as youthful thirty- or forty-year-olds, or even as twenty-year-olds, rather than wait for age and service to earn them respect and political status in the local village; they preferentially speak Spanish or switch to it with fluidity rather than remain monolingual in an indigenous language; they attend services of any of the new religions, Protestant or Catholic, rather than consult the shamans of tradition; and they successfully play the game of capitalist accumulation rather than hold to intensive corn agriculture in what Annis (1978) has called "milpa logic."

These traits, formerly used to distinguish indígenas from Ladinos, now are rarely reliable ethnic markers. So young Nahualenses are reconsidering, but not rejecting, what it means to be indigenous. The starting point is that they know they are indígenas: they are children and grandchildren of indígenas; they are native Nahualenses and members of their neighborhoods. They claim a sense of ethnic similarity and shared history apart from simple shared geographic or class interests, and at the local level, they are connected by dense kinship networks. They feel the prejudice of Ladinos when they travel outside of the community. They all still eat handmade corn tortillas, even when the accompanying meal is chow mein. Understanding the foundations of indigenous identity for the Nahualense is an important starting point for exploring how the community's youth are caught between competing demands of conformity and change, and why the accusations leveled by elders that youth are "abandoning their culture" carries considerable moral force.[3]

But youths also say they want things not traditionally available to indígenas. During the high school seminars I sat in on, I listened to Nahualense students nervously confess their dreams of becoming nurses, accountants, doctors, lawyers, computer programmers, and teachers. No one said they wanted to be a farmer. Most would like to study or work abroad. When I asked about their favorite kinds of music, even shy teenagers would talk enthusiastically about Switchfoot, an American rock band, or Ricardo Arjona, a Guatemalan pop star of international renown.[4]

When it comes to education for higher-paying professions, most adult Nahualenses are happy to support nontraditional aspirations in their children, but Nahualense parents are increasingly baffled (along with others throughout the hemisphere) by a youth culture that is increasingly difficult for them to distinguish from gang culture. In an interview, one elder said: "[Gangs] also have other ways of being identified. Now there are groups that wear all black, T-shirts and black pants, so that's how you identify them—if they wear that kind of clothing, then they are gangs, boys and girls."

If so, more of the young men in Nahualá's town center are *mareros* (gang members) than not. Fully 30 percent of youths responding to our survey marked *rok* or *reguetón* as their favorite genre of music, styles that community leaders condemned almost universally as "gang music." In public meetings on gangs in Nahualá in 2005, much to the chagrin of the youths in the crowd, public officials named the *rokeros* (local youths whose black T-shirts, tight jeans, necklaces, and sass mark them as rock music fans) as one of the four or five main criminal gangs in town. In the aftermath of the meetings, one rokero told me that his friends "are afraid of going out now" because people will think they are in gangs and punish them. I saw his fears confirmed just a few weeks later: When a pickup truck full of youths returned to Nahualá after a rock concert in neighboring Ixtahuacán, some community members discovered that they had been drinking and were out after curfew. The rokeros were all *xe'ukub'axik*—punished by forcing them to kneel on rocks—except for the student anthropologist accompanying them. The confusing thing about this repression (for those rokeros and also for me at the time) was that no rokero would have thought to describe rokero networks as *maras* (gangs).

Despite their syncretism, unorthodox ambitions, and some deliberate rebellion, most youths suspected of being mareros still say they respect the traditions of their parents. The rock concert in Ixtahuacán exemplifies the point. It was a performance by a local Ixtahuaquense musical group, Kab'awil, and the concert they played was a hometown bash they threw in order to get footage for their new music video. Kab'awil (a K'iche' word meaning "double sight" or "looking both ways") is a band in the new Rok-Maya movement, a musical genre that bridges the musical old and new, incorporating electric guitar, drums, bass, traditional instruments like the marimba, and vocals in the local K'iche' language.[5] With songs like "Thank you, Grandfather, thank you, Father," their lyrics often extol the virtues of tradition in a modernizing world. In a twist that illustrates the muddled world from which Rok-Maya arose, Kab'awil's songs were played as prelude music over Nahualá's municipal PA system before public meetings in which the mayor proceeded to denounce rokeros as a criminal gang—whose main vice is that they listen to such music.

It has become the conventional wisdom that youths are "abandoning their culture." Adult Nahualenses say it. One of my fellow anthropology students wrote in 2004 that "young men no longer seek to be identified with things that are indigenous; rather they adopt Western dress, music and attitudes," creating a "culture gap." However, a literal "gap" overstates the distance between past and present, origin and innovation. The very idea of a "gap" ultimately de-emphasizes the agency of today's Nahualenses to construct their own identity from the ground on which they stand. The striking contrast of picturesque *huipil*-clad mothers alongside hair-spiked young men with Converse sneakers and earphones can tempt us to see them as one or the other, indigenous or not. But regardless of the wishes of their parents and municipal elders, Nahualense youths claim an ability to mix the new and the old. One rokero explained: "People who listen to the marimba [the traditionalists] criticize rock one hundred percent. On the other hand, the rokeros, they listen to the marimba as well."

Through their TV screens and the stories of their relatives in Los Angeles, these youths know a world beyond their municipal borders. But their lives are not changing simply because of "imported Western values." For example, Nahualense youths may want to buy land to begin building a family compound in their hometown. Land prices, however, have skyrocketed in recent years—fueled by population growth and also by an influx of remittances from the United States. So these youths struggle to save enough cash to buy land or construction materials. When they leave Nahualá to work for higher wages, they do not generally want to leave the community permanently and often indicated that they were "leaving in order to stay." Green's (2003) study on rural Maya youths and industrialization tells a parallel story of young women who work in the *maquilas* (tax-exempted export factories) of Chimaltenango to preserve their capacity to remain indigenous:

> Adolescent women used their wages to buy their traditional clothing, the woven blouse (*huipil*) and the wrap skirt (*corte*), an outfit that can cost upwards of US$500, depending on quality. These young women said that, because of the financial constraints within the family and the rising prices of thread and textiles, it was more difficult for their fathers to provide them with their traditional dress. Through factory work, they were able to garner resources to maintain an important symbolic expression of their indigenous identity, even if they were unable to weave for themselves. For these young women it was

> particularly important to be dressed "properly" (as an Indian) as they looked for a suitor. (Green 2003:65)

Most of the available routes to "success"—measured either by global icons of consumption or the purchase of traditional signs of indigenous identity, like expensive indigenous clothing or inflated milpa land—lure youths out of the home. Parents and other kin often support their children's education, work, and migration because they hope increased income will translate directly into increased investment in the home.

Still, the locus of youth activity is moving to the educational institute, the workplace, or a city of the United States known only by name and postcard-picture. Increasingly, as youths set their hearts on opportunities outside the home, they have internalized the idea that youths *should* be independent actors outside of their homes. Now that they are formally educated, and often bring greater financial resources to the family than their parents and grandparents, they are beginning to take pride in their youth power and expect some respect from others. Therein lies the irony embedded in the frequently heard phrase "there is no respect now." The question is and the contest concerns: who should respect whom, and how?

Noticing Youth Power

Having addressed some questions of generational identity, I return to the initial focus of this study: many youths feel that they are left out of their communities' decision-making processes, and they feel ignored and belittled by the older generation. In the frustrated words of the twenty-five-year-old leader of a Catholic youth group: "Someone died here in my *cantón* and we got together for the wake. Some youths were in charge of it, but other men came, some older men, and they asked us, 'Why are you making decisions, if you still can't reason?'[6] That's what they said. And how did the people who were in charge feel? They didn't want to continue anymore, because they had been discriminated against, I guess." Anecdotes like this one about youths feeling disempowered by the inertia of age-based social status (or by its active enforcement) are common in the literature on youths in Latin America as well as in Nahualá (see, for example, Cazali, Reyes, and Moscoso 1998; Green 2003; Vigil's 1988 analysis of "multiple marginality").

Likewise, whenever I asked about youth participation in the upcoming mayoral elections, I would receive a confused response such as, "Youths don't participate." In a focus group I conducted with high school students, one student reported that when he went to community meetings, people would always ask him, "Where are your parents?" instead of including him in the meeting, telling him that if his parents weren't present he shouldn't be there. Another student said that at the community meetings she had attended, if a young person ever gave his or her opinion, it was rejected. These responses highlighted the dominant discourse regarding youth, reinforcing the idea of youth as unprepared, apathetic, or excluded.[7]

Indeed, my interview transcripts overflow with stories about underappreciated youth—I think, because I identified with the youths of the town far more than I did with their parents throughout my summer of research. Hearing their stories evoked my own struggle against surveillance and control by parents and religious patriarchs during adolescence and college. Realizing the effect that my own personal history had on data collection, in this chapter I attempt to approach youth power through the experiences of both youths and older people, including those elders in Nahualá who view the challenge of their progeny's youth power with the same alarm that mine did in Alabama.

Brintnall investigated the breakdown of traditional politics in Aguacatán, another largely indigenous highland town in western Guatemala. He observed the emergence of "a new Aguacatán where Indian political power is increasingly shifting to younger men . . . and where more orthodox Christian beliefs and practices are displacing the old cult of the dead" (Brintnall 1979:2). In traditional Aguacatán, elders bequeathed agricultural land in periodic installments to their children. Because young men had no alternative to farming for a living, control of inheritance conferred immense power on the patriarchy. But with the mid-twentieth century coincidence of cash-cropping, micro-capital, and the availability of economic alternatives through education and migration, elders lost the material basis of their authority. Not only do Maya elders no longer have their traditional power base, they are often, as Green notes, "unemployed and unemployable" (2003:58), consigned to even lower rungs of Guatemala's neoliberal economic hierarchy than their children.

Brintnall is certainly right that changing environmental and demographic conditions have increased the income and mobility of young people, but the rise of youth power goes considerably beyond the undermining of the material components of traditional authority. For example, formal education, sponsored both by the Guatemalan state and by Nahualense parents, has tilted the power of knowledge from elders to youth. Formal education presents an almost irresistible trap to many Maya families because it simultaneously promises additional resources *for* the home and yet it alienates their children *from* the home. Elders who invest in educating their children—with the expectation of building up stability, capital, and prestige in the household that they head—are, at the same time, investing in their children's own power, an investment that often returns as a challenge to the elders' authority. One parent explained the financial incentive: "Now that our children have a chance to get a salary, we send our children to school. They used to say 'a woman that goes to school doesn't learn anything except laziness,' but they changed their minds when this girl graduated as a teacher and quickly got work and makes thousands of quetzales."

Another parent, however, expressed frustration at the arrogance that a little education brings: "The youths take advantage of their opportunity. Their parents don't have education, so they feel like they are more prepared than their parents, and sometimes the father lets himself be dominated by his son."

Unlike in the United States, where dropouts threaten the regnant culture of success and are likely to be stereotyped as gang members, Nahualenses often emphasize that most mareros are students. Elders complain that youths, freed from the traditional obligation of manual labor, hang out in the streets after school. Similarly, in her analysis of the "criminalization of generational conflict" in Todos Santos, Burrell (2009) argues that "gang activity" in rural towns, unlike in urban organized crime networks, is essentially a leisure activity that is only available to relatively well-off youths, and "gang members" tend to be relatively privileged youths from prominent families.

If youths did their hanging out in the disguise of acceptably Nahualense everyday dress, as defined by adults, perhaps there might be less "gang crisis" or constant discussion of "youth problems" in Nahualá. But, capitalizing on and visually illustrating the rapid buildup of youths' economic power, youth fashion has become open semiotic warfare. Black T-shirts (*rokero*) and baggy clothes (*cholo*) are of particular concern, as the elders of Nahualá make proclamations both explicit and implicit that people dressed "in a certain style" will be punished for their lack of respect and the many crimes this lack of respect breeds. And, as much as those youths nervously smile and dismiss the older generation's ignorance of guitar-pick necklaces and long hair, there is something insightful in the old guard's (over-)reactionary response.

Through their slang and clothes and music, youths are exercising their power, not only of direct confrontation, but of evasion. They are asserting the power to create a new language, unintelligible in the vocabulary of the old. Possibly the most significant and most overlooked element of youth power is this: the power of youths to *end you just by ignoring you*. Youths have the power to topple the world of their parents by choosing an alternative. Indeed, I had never felt the numbing, terrifying sting of having one's age, experience, and effort ignored until the summer of 2009, when I spent a couple of frustrating hours fruitlessly trying to get a few dozen teenage kids from a Boys and Girls Club in Salt Lake City to listen to me talk about organic urban farming. I stopped my presentation. No one noticed. I discovered how sad it feels to want so badly to pass on the urgency of knowledge, the ethics for right living, the passion I felt for something exciting and vitally important, yet wholly uninteresting to these youth. Then I realized: Youth power is control of the future. Youths have the power to ignore, to avoid, to drop out, to plug ears and hunker down, and as a result, they have the power to kill off every beautiful thing I care about, and everything I want to make possible in the world. Youths have the power to end my influence just by not listening to me. The problem, the difficulty, of generational transmission of culture is indeed universal.

This is why it is so desperately crucial to Nahualense elders to be able to *orientar* (orient, instruct, correctly direct) youth. What elders (in any culture) believe and do barely matters unless younger people can be recruited into the project. This is the power youths have—the power to outwait the elders—that makes it so urgent for elders to dominate and control youths and strip away their right to ignore; why elders have to seize youth's attention and obedience. Youth power is one power elders cannot gain access to other than by commandeering youths themselves.

In that Boys and Girls Club moment, I realized why, to Nahualense elders and parents (and parents everywhere), the battle over T-shirts, rock music, and respect was not some small conflict over curfews or even a big fight over political participation and shared decision-making processes, but a culture war—a battle of cosmic import to these elders—for losing it portends the end of identity as well as the end of the cultural and material world these elders understood, managed, and benefited from. In that club moment I learned to empathize with the elders of Nahualá; I realized—with distaste—that for the rest of my life, I, too, would feel the Nahualense elders' numbing, urgent terror concerning cultural transmission.

Disempowering Youth

This, then, brings us to the opposite of youth power. Simultaneous with the power young people command because they are engaged in a neoliberal field inaccessible to their elders—which gives them income, mobility, agency—is the imperative to *disempower* youth, to put them in their place, to dismantle or perhaps to co-opt their vitality and direct it back into traditional channels.[8]

To understand the methods Nahualenses began using to combat "delinquency," we need to pay attention to what they declared youths to be delinquent in. One former town mayor explained the etiology of Nahualá's gangs:

> Before, everyone used to work from morning until late, so boys didn't have the chance to go and walk around or hang out in the street. . . . My parents woke me up early. At five o'clock we would leave to gather firewood and we would get back at ten or eleven, and we would go again and get back at three or four in the afternoon. After that there was no chance to go out in the street. . . . Now we are ashamed to work: Picking up a hoe or a machete embarrasses us. So the youth doesn't work anymore, and he gets used to not working. From there, he begins to go out, because he doesn't have anything to do. He goes to the street and joins the gangs and the delinquents. . . .
>
> The boys got together and they've created their groups. They don't work in the house anymore and they don't obey their father or mother. They don't have respect at home or with their family. . . . They want to be the boss of the house even though they are young. And, little by little, they've formed

> groups, the maras. They have lots of groups, you know? And even girls join with them. . . . Laziness has entered into them, [and they say] "it's better not to work." And they just sleep a little during the day. Then they go to school, and at night they go out looking for trouble, to steal things.

This quote reveals a number of undercurrents common in Nahualense indigenous thought: the value of work, the threat of leisure, and the threat of these to deconstruct household and community authority. All of these Hawkins (1984) observed in other communities that much earlier had entered the path of globalized marketization.

In Nahualá, citizens' frustration with "youth trouble" reached a breaking point in July 2005. After the mayor and other officials called a meeting and addressed a crowd of over a thousand in the town plaza regarding their "gang problem," citizens initiated the creation of local "security committees."[9] These committees included members of stature—older people—from each administrative-geographical subdivision of Nahualá, following traditional lines of authority: religious leaders, household heads, former municipal officeholders, and elders, all taking on various attributes of the old system of principales. The committees were put in charge of maintaining the peace that they felt the police had failed to keep.[10] They were given considerable autonomy to act as a first-response neighborhood tribunal.[11]

Adults, as cantón and hamlet security committees, began patrolling the streets and paths, enforcing an eight o'clock curfew. After this hour, youths were prohibited from being out on the streets or trails unless they could prove they were on a legitimate—meaning sent by an adult—errand. The security committees gathered groups of youths, stripping them to the waist, inspecting them for tattoos, and subjecting those found to possess tattoos to *xe'ukub'axik,* kneeling on rocks. The security committees administered this "traditional" public punishment dozens of times.[12] Youths were no longer allowed to attend evening youth-group meetings, concerts were shut down, and youths were threatened with corporal punishment if they continued to wear rokero clothing.

Despite their apparent willingness to act boldly, most Nahualense adults shied away from confronting what they readily identified as the primary causes of delinquency: migration and education. They focused instead on controlling some of the most visible symptoms, like the nighttime activities and clothing. This non-confrontation should come as no surprise. Among the major influences that drive recent delinquency—which Nahualense elders mentioned again and again in interviews—are familial disintegration due to economic migration and lack of respect toward elders due to increased formal education. Yet these two influences have thoroughly infiltrated Nahualense lives because they promise substantial financial returns. Even as they feel their power slip away to teachers and textbooks, parents do not remove their children from school, because schooling is a direct investment in their children's earning power, a power that they and their families hope to rely on as they age. So youths find themselves in a bewildering paradox. They have the support of their parents, the state, and their teachers in practicing some independence, exploring their creative potential, and building their skills, knowledge, and confidence. At the same time, they wonder why they are denied a role in community rule and are not given a chance to champion their own interests.

Indeed, the effort to disempower youth has been so constant, broad, and far-reaching that some Nahualenses described it as a "war on youth" wherein young people are considered synonymous with delinquents and gang members. In a country whose people have not yet recovered from an ethnocidal civil war directed against "subversivos," such imagery connotes hidden, deep, powerful emotions regarding youth subversiveness. Sometimes the sense of war on youth is unconscious and implicit. Thus, a little after sundown one night, I was ending a visit with a family in the town center, and as I left their compound to return home, the mother called out to me, warning me that I should be very careful walking at night because it was Sunday and "there are lots of youths in town tonight." Sometimes it is direct and explicit: one town elder, in an interview, asserted that "nowadays it's very few [of the youth] who are respectful; it's possible that it's only 10 or 15 percent now; the majority are now involved in their gangs."

Just weeks after the public punishment of the three girls (for running away), the youth group Amigos en Acción (Friends in Action) met for an organizational meeting on the very soccer field where the punishment had taken place—a soccer field that, as the cantón's only accessible public recreational and political meeting place, had become a central symbolic battleground between old and young. Each of the dozen youths who showed up at the meeting introduced him- or herself and spoke for a moment about the plight of youth. One teenage boy, speaking gravely and passionately, captured the general mood: "I want to prove to the adults that youths aren't just bad."

Unfortunately, the strategy to disempower and marginalize youth is, at best, only a partial solution to a problem, from the elders' perspective. Youths must be re-empowered and drawn into the system, rather than disempowered and marginalized. NGOs try to do this by involving them in development and activity programs conducted under the international banner of protecting youth rights. Elders need to find a way to reenfranchise youth that recognizes and values the youth experience while also encouraging acceptance of traditional norms.

RE-EMPOWERING YOUTH

As youths' earning power and mobility increase and as they shoulder the difficult role of cultural innovation, NGO activists have sensed a gap between youth's importance (high) and their formal power (low) and are taking up that same project articulated by the teenager on the soccer field who wanted to show that "youths aren't just bad." Dozens of NGOs, publications, and government programs have sprung up to advocate for youths or help them organize.[13] Tellingly, these projects are usually thought of as *capacitación* (training), rather than (as I have argued) an effort to re-empower youth and reverse traditional elders' attempts to dismantle youth power. Empowerment discourse—and the funding for it—is being deployed as if youths were simply "unempowered" or "underprivileged" or "vulnerable" populations that need a little help. This discourse is willfully silent about the ongoing battle over youth power as a matter of generational and therefore cultural succession and about the many people who feel that youths should have less power and know their place. This silence on the part of activists and scholars may stem from a wish to avoid seeming anti-indigenous or anti-traditional; they don't want to alienate elders and they want to maintain a myth that "indigenous rights," "human rights," "equality," "democracy," and the specific rights of youth to autonomy are all consistent elements of a single politically progressive program.

The position that youths preexist as underprivileged and unprepared and simply need to be carefully included to achieve "participation" has been surprisingly common even from scholars who are close students of the background power relationships that set the stage for formal politics. In an article about "fault lines" in participatory democracy in Peru, Markowitz (2001:13) illustrates how even explicit attempts by NGOs to include minority voices in regional decision-making falter because, "for representatives of some of the more physically remote communities, speaking in front of a large group, filled with professionals and political authorities, is intimidating." Markowitz is certainly right, but she fails to note that that such intimidation is almost always part of an active and intentional program carried out by members of the traditional hierarchy, a program that attempts to manage women as a political underclass (the focus of Markowitz's study) much as it attempts to subordinate and discipline youths in Nahualá. Markowitz cites Abers's concept of "inequality problems," and the latter specifically notes that "disadvantaged groups . . . often do not have the self-confidence to voice their opinions in public spaces, even if they do have the time and money to attend" civic meetings (Abers 2000:9). But again, while perhaps accurately diagnosing the problem of low self-confidence, citing "inequality problems" remains oddly agnostic about the etiology of those problems. Approaches that value "participation" usually fail to consider that when "disadvantaged groups" are loath to speak, they may still be participating; that is, silence can be a deliberate form of participation (one of submission or evasion), whether it is willfully chosen or due to fear or lack of skill.

Theorizing "Mobilization"

Both activists and scholars see youth as a component of their own political projects. Activists, would-be agents of change, see youth as one part of their strategy for development, a view that improves their chances for funding and fuels their hope for success. Scholars, such as Falla (2006), take a more complex view. But, activist or academic, most analyses deploy different understandings of economy, identity, and historical progress from any that Nahualense youths and their parents would recognize.

For example, one FLACSO (Latin American School of Social Sciences) study mixes Marxist and liberal democratic paradigms of social progress, asserting that Guatemalan youths are "to a certain point, demobilized, without a revolutionary project or radical change, and who privilege their own personal interests" (Cazali, Reyes, and Moscoso 1998:13). There seems to be no question, for these authors, what mobilization would look like: public, concerted political engagement, with youths making speeches, organizing marches, forming independent organizations, and otherwise challenging vested powers. In the absence of what they expected, they write off youths as "demobilized."

But these definitions ignore the possibility that youths could be quite well mobilized but acting within traditions that explicitly suppress revolutionary projects and radical change. Moreover, youths might actively suppress alternative ways of knowing, understanding, and valuing their worlds in order to maintain key traditions and hegemonies.

Key among those alternatives is youths' political interests and sense of power in a world dominated by elders who control traditional forms of authority. One adds to this mix of Nahualense youth and elder interests the goals of a variety of NGO and activist groups that seek to mobilize youth toward multiple ends. Presumably, these NGO and activist approaches to political mobilization have been shaped by the practical experience of jockeying for moral authority in contemporary political discourse and by the challenges of NGO financing. With the slow evolution of funding priorities and political values in an ostensibly democratic world, NGOs and activist scholars have considerable incentive to claim that youth participation is an outcome that only they can provide. In order to get and keep funding, organizations take roll and count heads at their gatherings to certify their effectiveness.

But "participation" defined as "mobilization" rewards the scholars and NGOs for missing the point: participation does not always mean attendance. In many cases, it can mean the exact opposite: a participant who skips the meeting, stays in the shadows, doesn't vote. But NGO and activist organizers are not likely to view *not* doing something (like not walking around at night after curfew in Nahualá, when some youth groups have their meetings) as participation. They can't be counted for sponsorship purposes, and they can't be leveraged easily into the rhetoric of a rising mobilization against authority.

How youths respond to organizational efforts may vary considerably depending on their perception of the organizer's motives and the risk involved with openly challenging dominant forms of authority. Indeed, there are often competing forms of organizational efforts that may find themselves in conflict. We seek to show that in Nahualá, the apparent "demobilization" of youths that Cazali and others lament is actually an effort by local elders to remobilize youth power. In the context of competing attempts to control youth, elders are as active as their NGO and activist counterparts, though their goal is quite different—to reintroduce a system of age-based respect and authority.

For Nahualense youth, at least, ostensible "lack of participation" may be a misreading. Their "passivity" could also be understood as an active attempt to show respect in a cultural realm marked by distrust of outsiders, careful management of public versus domestic space, and reactionary responses to rapid cultural change. Nahualense youths may feel that they *are* doing their best when anxious about public speaking, because confidence would connote that they knew as much as an older person. On the other hand, there is a danger to projecting too much of this submission as intentional. As illustrated through the use of corporal punishment, the hegemony of age may be instilled through coercion, and intentional submission cannot be separated from the tutelage of physical domination.

The Nahualense youths' experience of feeling intimidated makes sense given the forces arrayed to keep them in their place. These forces are intentional, broadly approved, and understood as a proactive response by indigenous authorities to real threats. Perhaps NGOs and applied researchers are being willfully silent about the intricacies of "participation." That is, when their mandate to foster and protect traditional indigenous rights clashes with their mandate to empower youths, development professionals' funding depends on a simplified understanding of oppression and empowerment.[14]

Beyond the NGOs that foster young people's participation and education, youths have other allies. While the elders attempt to control youth through a newly invented "customary law" materialized through "traditional punishment," the allies of youth independence have marshaled legal discourses of human rights and discrimination to challenge the punishment. Advocacy organizations have buttressed youth power by characterizing generational control as a crime, complete with a victim (youth) and a perpetrator (mayor, parents, and the like). Campaigns addressing "youth discrimination" flow from earlier efforts to combat gender and racial injustice. This is a clever designation that lends "youth equality" the full force of the democratic imperative and human rights discourse, creating a claim to power out of youth disempowerment. The tactic puts advocates of the traditional order on the defensive by threatening to protect children from traditional practices that are now called child labor, domestic abuse, corporal punishment, and forced marriage. Replacing traditional youth roles with "enlightened" alternatives, like individual freedom and autonomous organizations, further encourages the independent power of youths that their parents find so troubling.

When NGOs fund youth groups, they compete with parents for their children's loyalty. One of the primary ways that Nahualense parents explain the relationship between parents and children is through the idiom of reciprocal material investment: parents provide breast milk, clothing, shelter, food, and education; youths are obligated to return respect, obedience, and work, and especially, to take care of their parents in old age. Usually the competition between parents and NGOs for youth allegiance remains implicit, but sometimes that competition flares into direct confrontation. For example, when a now well-established local Evangelical Christian kindergarten was first starting up its *padrino* (sponsorship) program, in which European adults would fund aid and supplies to "needy" children in Nahualá, many parents protested and removed their children from the program. A longtime staff member of the kindergarten explained that parents were worried their responsibilities would be bypassed and then replaced by well-to-do foreigners, eventually leading to complete transfer of the child from the local family to the foreign, through adoption. Such is the power of belief in required reciprocity, when culturally amplified.

The ability of NGOs to partially usurp traditional parental roles became clear when I spent three days participating with an NGO-organized human-rights youth group of students recruited from local schools. Elías, a thirty-year-old youth organizer for the NGO, led a group of about twenty Nahualense youths (between ages seventeen and twenty-five) in three days of constant, all-expenses-paid community activism. The weekend began with an evening gathering at a local eatery, where the group drafted a survey on gender discrimination and the rights of youths while they enjoyed the first of six complimentary meals supplied by the NGO. The next day at dawn, after receiving (free) official T-shirts and name tags, they hopped into vans Elías had hired and embarked on an all-day excursion to various outlying hamlets so that the youths could administer a survey to local residents. The third day, again meeting at dawn, their weekend culminated in an all-day human rights festival in the municipal park at the center of the Sunday market, complete with local youths dancing to American pop music, clowns brought in by the NGO, copious decorations, and bingo.

Elías explained the disempowerment that youths face: "Youths experience a lot of discrimination. . . . They participate very little, from the educational centers, to the COCODEs [community development councils], NGOs, youth groups, it's very little. The older people depend on them, but the adults make their own plans and they don't even ask [the youth] what they want, yes or no. [Adults] just use them [youth] like tools." Elías elaborated on the negative consequence of such limited avenues for youth participation in community decision-making or independent social life:

> If the youths don't participate, all the energy that should be directed into good activities will be directed into bad things. For example, forming gangs, forming groups to satisfy this need for activity. Because one is already a leader, a good leader at the core, but when he sees that he can't participate in good things, he goes to bad things and becomes a leader anyway, but a leader of evil. All of his energy, all of his leadership, all of his intelligence, all of his participation falls into something bad, in order to create his own space, in order to release his anger. If he was given the opportunity to participate, maybe [gangs] wouldn't exist anymore, because his energies would be consumed in good activities, appropriate activities.

On the surface, Elías had the same objective as Nahualá's security committees: combating delinquency and gang involvement. But after days of financial and organizational support, another message to youths was also clear: "your community does not understand you, it does not appreciate you as it should, and we do." In this sense, NGO-sponsored youth groups were a threat to traditional life just as gangs were—and enough Nahualense parents thought so that local youth groups constantly complained that they were treated like gangs, with their parents banning participation in such groups on that basis. Indeed, during the human rights festival, the NGO supplied the youths with paint to produce a mural. Their mural, however, was later removed in a gang-related anti-graffiti cleanup of the town center instigated by municipal leaders.

It seems only fair to note that youth power may also have found new allies in the proliferation of social scientists, journalists, development consultants, and political activists who scrutinize youths to produce an array of new publications, policy priorities, and project evaluations. The attentive gaze of professional researchers has capitalized on (and perhaps helped create) "modernization" fetishes that add extra intrigue to studying "new, Westernized generations" of one ethnicity or another. And, compounding these other incentives, many researchers find they relate best to these Internet- and language-savvy youngsters in an otherwise foreign culture. Youths often become convenient key informants and culture-brokering employees, as they have for centuries, to the ministers of change—be they Catholic, Protestant, state, or global missionaries.

Thus youth-focused research and NGO projects leave youth groups open to criticism alongside criminal gangs because NGOs and gangs—and their researchers—are engaged in essentially similar activities: the overthrow of an age-based system of local authority that places youths securely below their elders. Nahualense elders may not care which age group I focus on in a paper published in English, read only by foreigners. But presenting papers in Spanish on youths and the politics of their control at the fieldwork scene might provoke greater interest and perhaps even a direct confrontation with established power.[15]

NEGOTIATING ETHICAL COMMITMENT THROUGH FIELDWORK

Despite a desire for moral clarity, I have found myself consistently unable to judge between the interests of youths and older people in Nahualá. I began in sympathy with youth, initially channeling my own experience as a frustrated Mormon boy who continued poking tiny holes in the fabric of his own conservative society. On reflection, I took a different tack, that of trying to appreciate the hopes and dreams of those rokeros' parents as well as those of the youth. In doing so, I found myself drawn to exceptionally evocative understandings of episodes that I had previously seen merely as obstacles to research—such as when a former mayor tried to shut down the youth group I was studying.

Interviews with town elders suggested that they found youth clothing and music fads directly and inherently threatening. One teacher said flatly, in the aftermath of a town punishment, "if mareros really wanted to change their lives, they have to change their clothes first." And yet, at town and school gatherings, youths are ubiquitously dressed in otherwise scandalous costume, performing to foreign hip-hop, displaying lascivious dance moves, apparently celebrating international gang subculture, and embracing the symbols that elders vocally condemn as antisocial and irredeemably polluting.

Developing a framework of "youth power" and a more complicated view of mobilization, subordination, and cultural transmission suggested an explanation for contradictory data: ultimately, elders are not as concerned with the symbols themselves as by what they represent: independent, autonomous youth power, a rebellion against parental authority. Once elders can contain or recapture the (perhaps inevitable) independent vitality and power of youth and deploy it for their own purposes, even the most alien symbols of youth power become tame, acceptable, and perhaps, in a Marxian sense, even productive.

Yearly school celebrations vividly enshrine this taming co-optation of rebellious symbols. There, under the direction of their elders, teenage boys and girls sport otherwise-objectionable shorts (on girls) and cholo clothing (on boys), staging a presentation choreographed to heavily profanity-laced English-language rap music in front of a panel of judges composed of teachers and respected municipal leaders. This eminently pragmatic arrangement mirrors ways that all power structures contain, co-opt, or redeploy otherwise threatening movements and symbols, just as Mayas have adopted Spanish language and state-sponsored education for their own purposes, and just as the conquistador-descended Guatemalan state has contained and captured indigenous Maya symbols for its own use.

Finally, I have concluded that the process of taking both youths' and parents' complaints seriously, as legitimate grievances deserving of detailed analysis in the style of Turner's (1972[1957]) social drama or Van Velsen's (1969) extended case method, will likely facilitate appropriate social change better than a superficial, polemical account decrying "discrimination against youth." Attending in detail to the explanations of the powerful is one necessary piece of an ethnography of micropolitics, revealing the "specificities of the relations of oppression" (Crehan 2002:6), and as such constitutes a powerful tool for strategists of universal emancipation. For example, Bobrow-Strain's (2007) ethnography of Ladino landowners in Chiapas in the aftermath of the 1994 Zapatista uprising admirably demonstrates the power of this approach, for his work portrays the perspective of the elite "bad guys" at the same time that it shows deep commitment to the liberation of the oppressed.

I don't mean to suggest that Nahualense elders or their rebellious youths are the equivalent of Chiapas *terratenientes* (large landowners). My experience in Nahualá leads to a more nuanced view of oppression, in which both youths and adults practice varying forms of physical and non-physical violence on each other as they attempt to negotiate a tolerable equilibrium. In taking this view, I feel I have made a tentative peace with myself and others by constructing a politically committed but ethical ethnography that transcends the immediate urge toward simple moral judgments.

Notes

Fieldwork: 2005, 2006, 2009, 2010

1. See figs. 2.1 and 2.2. This "traditional punishment" was still in use as of July 2010.

2. The multiple accounts and slightly variant perspectives on events in this volume, a product of having multiple anthropologists in the community at once living with different families and using different networks, simply reflect the contested and ambiguous reality of human interpretation in social life.

3. Burrell (2009) speaks to identity transformation and culture change in gangs in Todos Santos, while Hale (2006) reveals the complexities of Guatemala's ethnic transition from relatively clear ethnic boundaries with Ladinos in superior position, to relatively unclear ethnicities no longer bifurcated and with Ladinos no longer so clearly privileged.

4. My findings regarding aspirations of upward mobility and professional careers may be one effect of the fact that my research was skewed toward Nahualá's more urban municipal center and its student population, and thus toward Nahualá's middle-class youth.

5. More precisely, Kab'awil can be parsed [*Kab'*=two], [*aw*=second person singular before vowels], [*il*=to see], meaning, literally "you see two [ways/things]." In a freer translation, "you [better] look both ways" alternates ambiguously with "you see two things" or "double images." Given the plethora of K'iche' idioms regarding being two-faced or two-hearted as indicators of deception, duplicity, and hypocrisy, the ultimate psychological meaning is, "what you see is not what you get" or "what you see is not reality"; it parallels the Spanish idiom *Ojo*, meaning "Watch out: hidden deception/danger present."

6. In K'iche', na'oj, to reason or perceive correctly, is a core concept, and comes on late in life through experience and age. See Watanabe's (1992:81–84) discussion of the cultural meanings of *naab'l*, the cognate word in Mam, in which wisdom or sensibility likewise derives from experience later in life. His analysis would make complete sense to these K'iche' elders.

7. Of course, there were currents against the dominant trend. For example, I knew of several students who actively campaigned for their favorite candidate, and several classmates of those in the focus group actively served as electoral observers. But most informants focused on the marginality of youth and tend to deemphasize some compelling counter-narratives, narratives that have increasingly commanded my attention as I reflect on the salience of youth power in Nahualá.

8. One is reminded of Henry's argument in *Culture against Man* (1963) that the object of education is to make children docile with regard to alternate cultural paradigms.

9. Several scholars offer a variety of interpretations of postwar indigenous village security committees, patrols, and their behavior. Burrell (2009), for example, describes their status in Todos Santos. Fox Tree and Gómez (2007) detail their history in Nahualá. Carlsen (1997) lays out their use in Santiago Atitlán.

10. For an alternative reading of the "absence of police authority," exploring the potentially liberating consequences of the absence of coercive state authority and de facto community autonomy in peripheral parts of the world nation-system, see Graeber's analysis of a "provisional autonomous zone" in Madagascar (2007). While Nahualenses are highly unlikely to describe police inaction as a good thing, they are also loath to hand over coercive power to the police when they do arrive on the scene. Indeed, Nahualenses and residents of neighboring communities regularly discuss ejecting national police from the area entirely.

11. Suppressing youth power also empowers local officials. Most fundamentally, barring youth from equal political participation stratifies the population into two political classes, divided along age lines, justifying and requiring overseers to monitor and manage the activities of the political underclass. Youth's lack of involvement means that power is shared between fewer people, giving elders even more influence. Finally, containing and controlling youth power gives politicians a powerful issue to springboard their own rise to power. Both nationally and locally, politicians regularly include promises of law and order—*mano dura* (iron fist)—targeting youth as gangs and rowdy delinquents. An anti-youth-power platform is an asset to many politicians in gaining power vis-à-vis other politicians.

12. For a fuller explanation of the circumstances surrounding the controversial administration of "Maya justice" in Nahualá during the summer of 2006, see Bybee, this volume, chapter 2. "Traditional" is in quotes here because, as Bybee demonstrates, kneeling on rocks or bottle caps is a new form of punishment, called "traditional" because that label protects it under the provisions of the Peace Accords.

13. Examples of such youth mobilization and empowerment programs active in Nahualá in 2006 include the youth program of CALDH (Center for Human Rights Legal Action); the youth movement Paz Joven (Youth Peace), supported by the Human Rights Office (COPREDEH) of Guatemalan president Berger's administration; youth training sponsored by CODEIN, a local NGO; independent neighborhood groups like Amigos en Acción, and religious youth groups.

14. On NGOs noticing primarily what it is in their institutional interest to notice, see Mosse (2005:14–15, 21–46).

15. In 2007, I spent a month presenting my research to youth, teachers, and parents in Nahualá. The details of my reception and their responses to my ideas are the basis of another paper.

Conclusion

Fear, Control, and Power in an Unpredictable World

James H. McDonald and John P. Hawkins

> Threat is as ubiquitous as the wind, and its source as imperceptible. It just shows up. It breaks out. It irrupts without warning, coming from any direction, following any path through the increasingly complex and interconnected world. The longer it has been that a threat has not materialized, the greater the prospects must be that it will. . . . Absence makes the threat loom larger.
>
> Brian Massumi (2009)

Guatemala is full of accidents. Here we mean the unpredictable, the uncivil, and the violent. Guatemalans live in a post-conflict world where the once relatively focused political and ethnic violence has morphed into ever-escalating, generalized social violence (cf. Stoll 2009).[1] The problem becomes one of how people—both those in formal government positions of authority and those outside of them—come to know and understand a world of endemic, perpetual, hurtful accidents. Playing on Foucault, we suggest that the contingent, unpredictable violence that constitutes a major dimension of lived experience in Guatemala be termed "accidentality," in recognition of the multiple competing forces of violent governance and associated trauma that can befall anyone (though clearly the elite are far more buffered from this experience than are common people).

Arias and Goldstein (2010) take this idea further in their provocative argument that throughout Latin America, democratic government and violence are intimately intertwined. The Western idealized model of democracies as stable, economically dynamic, and supportive of individual prosperity does not hold for much of Latin America. Indeed, they contend that violent democracies, rather than merely a dysfunction or aberration, are commonplace. Violence is, in fact, central to those democracies' very survival. They paint a picture of an ebb-and-flow of "violent pluralism" among competing forms of governance (e.g., national governments, militaries, paramilitaries, street gangs, organized crime, cartels) (Arias and Goldstein 2010:5). As the relationships and stakes shift within and between these groups, violence erupts or subsides. In Arias and Goldstein's (2010) assessment of violent democracies, the distinction between functional versus failed state dissolves and becomes meaningless—a Western idealized myth more than a global reality.

While their analysis is a powerful one and reminds us that democratic government is not a panacea, they do not address the problem of violent pluralism from the perspective of the people who must endure it. If ordinary citizens are taken as the unit of measure, then violent democracies such as Guatemala have failed them miserably (e.g., security, health care, education, economic well-being, and political enfranchisement and ethical behavior). Take the following vignette as a starting point in the exploration of endemic "accidentality"—in this case a civil-military response to imminent, indiscriminate threat.

On the north side of the central plaza in the oldest part of Guatemala City stands the presidential palace. The plaza, the palace, the metropolitan cathedral, and all the surroundings appear run-down. Although the physical infrastructure of old-town "Zone 1" Guatemala is decaying, the area still buzzes with human activity—people going to and from the large market; workers of every stripe heading to jobs or tasks; street performers juggling, miming, and playing instruments. One even sees the occasional tourist. Despite the crowd and the bustle, Zone 1 is also a dangerous place. This poor neighborhood holds the potential of petty crime—theft, mugging, and the like—for the unwary and those who have not adequately veiled any signifiers of their wealth.

I (McDonald) first arrived in the central plaza on a late afternoon in July 2007. Stepping out of my taxi, I saw all attention turned toward the center of the plaza. There a large crowd of onlookers, heavily armed police clothed in black military-style uniforms, and camera crews from the local news stations all focused on a group of fifteen to twenty people seated on the ground, handcuffed (fig. C.1).

Who were they? People in the crowd offered up answers: One thought they were Nicaraguan migrant workers without papers. Another suggested they must be gang members (*maras*) from El Salvador. Someone else

Fig. C.1. Alleged *mara* (gang) of bus bandits detained by police in Guatemala City's central plaza. Photograph by James H. McDonald, 2007.

said they were Hondurans heading for the United States who had the misfortune of getting caught far short of their goal. A cameraman said that they were neither migrants nor maras; rather, a local gang that made its living robbing people traveling on city buses. The police hustled the dour-looking group into a van that drove off, and the crowd dispersed. How an entire gang of petty robbers could be apprehended together was unclear if not improbable.

Nevertheless, the capture was good media fare, ready-made for evening television and morning newspaper consumption. Regardless of who the detainees were and the nature of the crimes actually committed, the intended message was clear: the state was in control and acting against the agents and forces of "accidents."

What should we make of such "accidents?" From the perspective of Foucault's notion of "governmentality," state government seeks to harness, manage, administer, and regulate the thought and action of its citizens so that they become disciplined in the art of self-governance (cf. Ellison 2009; Gordon 1991). Governmentality, according to Foucault, operates in the service of neoliberal economics. Neoliberal economics valorizes individual autonomy, personal accountability and responsibility, individual choice, economic rights (as consumer *and* producer), and, ultimately, human freedom (cf. Ellison 2009). Stephen Collier (2009: 96, see also Ellison 2009) observes that governmentality centers on thinking about the nature of the practice of government: "it is a political rationality that shapes the possibility for thinking and acting in certain ways."

It would be a mistake, however, to conclude that Foucault understood this process to be a top-down, mechanistic affair where governments leave their indelible imprint on their citizenry. Rather, for Foucault, governmentality is an open and dynamic process that emerges and is practiced both inside and outside of formal governmental institutions. Governmentality, in fact, is best thought of as an effect of the actions of its multiple, hierarchically organized agents. In part, those agents fill various levels of state government, and their ideas, objectives, agendas, practices, and technologies may be variably aligned, misaligned, or even opposed in stark contradiction. As we have seen in these chapters, actors may even operate against their own political sensibilities because of the nature of the situational fields of power and force that form their contingent arenas of play (Gledhill 1999:242).

But governmentality also operates outside of those formal operations of government. Governmentality, thus, is also inextricably associated with non-governmental agents (from rank-and-file citizens to CEOs) whose actions influence and are influenced by formal government. It is therefore critical to ask how these informal agents embody governmental logics; deploy governmental logics in partial, imperfect, and sometimes unintended ways; and themselves shape and contribute to governmental ideas and practices. In a dialectical loop, governments certainly practice upon others, but these others also practice upon governments.

The chapters in this volume speak largely to the end of the governance spectrum that spans responses to the unpredictability and threat that characterize contemporary Guatemala. One need only glance at the daily newspapers to see that threat "shows up," "breaks out," and irrupts without warning" (cf. Massumi 2009:160). So much unpredictability, threat, and violence exist in the lives of rich and poor Guatemalans alike: a president nearly toppled by a staged kidnapping/murder; real murders and kidnappings of state governors, candidates for office, and mothers and children who happen to be in the way of someone else's nefarious business; women in abusive domestic relationships; the intimidation and disappearance of ordinary citizens. All of these suggest a failed, impotent, compromised government and a failure of governmentality in the lives of citizens to ameliorate accidents and risk.

There is another reading, however: that in Guatemala, governmentality consists in the ordinary citizen accepting violence, threat, risk, and accident as the essence of life. In this reading, the nature of governmentality in Guatemala is that citizens absorb, internalize, accommodate, and expect risk. Expected accidentality is governmentality. Indeed, the essays in this book underscore the tenuous nature of life for these impoverished Mayas living on the margins in a largely neoliberal world. Theirs is a life of visceral, physical, and immediate risk.

Massumi (2009:175) extends this argument beyond the immediate, visceral effects of risk and suggests that we also consider the more abstract risk of neoliberal markets. Markets are incubators of risk because neoliberalism opens them to global competition so complex that hazard becomes both endemic and unknowable. Mayas serve as a source of cheap labor on plantations and in factories that feed into those neoliberal global markets, while a business decision in a faraway place can close the very factory that keeps Maya families fed, all to recapture a few pennies of salary difference between countries. Increasingly impoverished, many rural Mayas cannot afford fertilizer for their *milpa* (rain-fed maize plots) and, consequently, have lower yields with which to sustain their families for at least part of the year. As the marginal utility of their milpa deteriorates, many sell out altogether. Thus, while the source of decline and insecurity may be relatively amorphous, rural Mayas know that they stand in a highly disadvantaged position in this economic scheme. There is little to buffer the poor, and especially Mayas in Guatemala, from this perpetual state of danger.

Massumi (2009:187) notes that living under the ubiquitous and conditioning pressure of risk and danger forces people to adapt and extracts a high personal and collective cost. The constant threat creates a population that is on continual alert and poised to assert "preemptive power" (Massumi 2009:174). In the case of lynching and other exaggerated responses to threat, we see the dark force of preemptive power taking its shape out of fear, a need to impose social control, and the moral force of neoliberal notions of the individual that leaves marginal people autonomous and accountable but bereft of resources (fig. C.2).

Fig. C.2. Gang tags above graves in the *camposanto* (cemetery) of Nahualá. Here teens challenge the holy ground of the community, its custodial territory, its elders, and its respect for the dead. They contest the old and affirm their fearlessness of a "brave new world" in a feared but culturally central place. Photograph by James H. McDonald, 2010.

Given that in Guatemala, "threat is as ubiquitous as the wind, and its source as imperceptible" (Massumi 2009:160), it is a short leap to argue that Guatemalans, and poor Mayas particularly, suffer from a form of collective post-traumatic stress disorder (PTSD). Though clinical practitioners commonly locate PTSD in the individual (see, e.g., McDonald 1997a), anthropologists have indirectly found PTSD culturally encoded through such institutionalized expressions as the ghost dance, cargo and Hauka cults, and other forms of millenarian movements. These movements seek a return to a nostalgic, traditional world through appropriate ritual intended to expunge the world of colonial agents of change and cultural chaos. That is, these movements are a political-religious response to colonization, radical culture change, and a resulting cultural system of meaning and practice which has collapsed.

In this case, there is no "post" to fifty years of continuous social and personal trauma. Guatemalans have found themselves mired in chronic sociocultural stress as their country has gone from the largely directed political and anti-Indian violence of the civil war (1960–96) to the more generalized and therefore less predictable social violence of the postwar period.[2] In general, those who can, avoid back roads for fear of banditry. The few intrepid joggers stick to populated streets and daylight hours to elude being mugged or raped. Laptops and other valuables get stowed discreetly in generic backpacks to deter robbery. People without other options use intercity buses, but they do so with a twinge of fear; they universally try to avoid nighttime travel on the ubiquitous chicken buses that traverse Guatemala, but they do so if they must. Only the poor and the desperate use the urban buses in Guatemala City, for these have become pawns in the gang turf-wars that have made using urban public buses increasingly hazardous and, in numerous cases, lethal. As a taxi driver noted, "you try to appear as plain as possible to not attract attention." He explained, "In a country as corrupt as Guatemala, you do not know who to trust. So you do not trust anyone."

Speaking about Guatemala and his own experience as a torture victim in Chile, Ariel Dorfman (cited in McDonald 1997a:135) notes how acts of torture against individuals create a culturally shared resonating chamber of fear and mistrust—a pervasive cultural dis-ease. As in Chile, Guatemalans experienced torture and its reverberations of fear and distrust, amply documented in various sources (Comisión para el Esclarecimiento Histórico 1999; Proyecto Interdiocesano Recuperación de la Memoria Histórica 1998). Speaking of such trauma, both Sabin et al. (2003) and Putnam et al. (2009) note the high frequency of clinical PTSD among Guatemalans, in part the residuals of war, but also the expression of more recent fear and the experience of generalized social violence and endemic threat.[3] For example, Sabin et al. (2003) found that among Guatemalan refugees still located in Mexico twenty years after fleeing the civil war, 11.8 percent suffered from PTSD, which the authors considered significantly higher than expected (the U.S. average, for example, is estimated to be 7.8 percent). Putnam et al. (2009) also discovered disturbingly high levels of PTSD—36 percent—in Guatemalan human rights aid workers.

In his study of PTSD in postwar Peru and Colombia, Elsass (2001) argues persuasively that repeated, long-term traumatic experiences can become embedded as a deep cultural understanding of the world. He contends that PTSD must be considered in cross-cultural context. Elsass argues that the particular social and cultural organization of a society impacts the way PTSD is collectively embodied and expressed. The case of Peru is germane in this regard and closely approximates Guatemala, for in Peru, as in Guatemala, "local communities consist of collective, functional units, [and] people do not react with conventional posttraumatic stress disorder symptoms, nor feel that traumatic memories should be treated with crisis intervention" (Elsass 2001:306). He suggests that to intervene most successfully in a Peruvian-like community-oriented context, one must strengthen the institutions within local communities.

As the chapters in this volume show, however, Guatemalan communities have been weakened significantly, and in a variety of ways, during the civil war and postwar eras. Prolonged civil war followed by economic erosion that resulted from demographically induced economic pressure coupled with neoliberal economic policies and a gutted tourist economy have left traditional forms of political-religious authority undermined and communities in disarray. Manz (2004) poignantly details the crushing of community and the distrustful individualism that emerges from war-torn submission to military rule. The loss of trust is very much at the center of peoples' experiences and day-to-day reality.

Other forces have likewise nurtured individualism. National political reforms have forced the mayor and advisory council to be chosen by democratic election. Elections marginalize traditional authority. Worse, they introduce national party politics (rather than a focus on local issues) into the mayoral process and inject money-induced corruption into the villages. An ever-changing socio-religious landscape has restructured age-graded hierarchies, which has given younger community members opportunities and spaces to seriously challenge the authority of parents and elders. In sum, we see substantially weakened communities that have been largely abandoned by state government.

Under these circumstances, it should be of little surprise that defensive regimes of preemptive power and hyperreaction have sprung up and operate in rural Guatemala as adaptations and coping mechanisms to confront and control threat. This observation aligns well with Hawkins and Adams's volume (in review) on religious expression in Guatemala's Western Highlands. Hawkins finds that new forms of Evangelical Protestantism and Catholicism are increasingly pervasive and far more dramatic, expressive, and sense-accosting than anything seen in the past. Evangelical rituals are long, arduous affairs that may now include speaking in tongues and hyper-amplified music, oratory, and bodily movement. Pentecostal liturgy (both Catholic and Protestant) presents a visual, auditory, kinetic, and ideological spectacle. Hawkins, however, pursues a critical reading of religious spectacle in Guatemala: Pentecostalism "exposes and manifests" a wrenching response to the trauma induced by a collapsing system of meaning and practice, with no known or likely avenues of escape or success except through individual asceticism.

Hawkins (in Hawkins and Adams, in review) points out that such forms of religious spectacle may be thought of as ways to express both the pain of systemic cultural collapse and the lack of an orienting social and moral compass in a world untethered. Mayas are now subjected to a new neoliberal order that has eroded the old guideposts of community hierarchy, authority, control, and stability. Thus, as Elsass (2001:310) observes, hyperreaction to trauma can be found not just in the excessive consumption of alcohol, prescription tranquilizers, and illegal narcotics. Hyperreaction can also be found in a pentecostalized, charismatic spirituality that delivers a message about unholy times caused by ungodly, violent acts that can be cleansed only by enduring personal pain, adhering closely to God's word, and accepting God's will.

In a country commonly thought of as Catholic, Hawkins estimates that between 70 and 92 percent of the population has converted to some form of pentecostal faith, whether Evangelical Protestant or Charismatic Catholic. Such numbers confirm the sweeping ideological and structural changes that Guatemala has experienced since the mid-1970s, when mainstream Catholicism was the order of the day. This transformation, of course, coincides with civil war and its aftermath of pervasive social violence.

Charismatic and ecstatic religion can be thought of as another form of preemptive power that Mayas draw upon in a system where, absent the state, governmentality must be generated in civil society. As with secular forms of sociopolitical control that we have seen in lynchings and other materialized acts, clearly, bodies and thought are disciplined through these ceremonies. But beyond the physical, these religious trends exert preemptive power by trying to gain spiritual control of salvation and the afterlife, by disciplining the body through alcohol avoidance and sexual refocus, and by domesticating men to a family orientation

(Brusco 1995). Thus, in the realm of the spirit and the realm of the political we see parallel but related hyperreactive self-defense and community-defense processes at work.

Both political and religious hyperreactions or preemptive stances of power in the face of continuous threat, chaos, and unpredictability resonate with Foucault's notion of governmentality. Governmentality is an agency-based concept in which government is best thought of as a highly mutable, dynamic suite of actors, fields of performance, actions, and ideas. What we perceive as government is, in essence, epiphenomenal of that constellation of activities. At the national level in Guatemala, formal government elements combine with non-government elements—Ladino elites and organized crime—to form a highly interpenetrated governmental regime. It is prudent to ask: under such conditions, who is in control—the government or its shadow? Levels of corruption render a murky landscape in which mistrust is rampant and control through the rule of law is highly compromised.[4]

As Gledhill (1999:203) notes, in poor countries, global neoliberal economics tends to divert power to the "shadow state" tied to informal markets. Indeed, it could be argued that neoliberalism champions informal markets over their formal counterparts because informal markets are largely unregulated. The Guatemalan situation where "elements of the state government are themselves emerging as a form of cartel in their own right," described in this volume's introduction, is an example of a complex shadow-state in which government and non-government actors merge ambiguously. Gledhill would undoubtedly agree that rogue government officials undertaking illegal activities should not be considered an idle act of corruption (that is, a few bad apples to be rooted out, thus restoring the normative order of law). Rather, Gledhill would likely argue that there exists a systematic "second political economy" that is aggressively and often violently entrepreneurial, a hidden polity that has the potential to accumulate massive wealth and power.

As leaders implement neoliberal policies and downsize governments, the potential for private enterprise to take on governmental roles increases, further blurring the distinction between public and private (Gledhill 1999:204). In the case of Guatemala, an already small, weak government with a limited tax base has, de facto, limited reach and therefore limited ability to protect anyone. Given this lack of protection, one sees the rise of private security firms that one can contract, the creation of covert private armies tied to elites and paid but not for hire, and the elaboration of competing forms of governance in the form of cartels, organized crime, and street gangs, all of which continue to employ various forms of terrorism. Gangs on the one hand and private armies on the other, each defending and extorting from both legitimate and illegal commercial interests, vie as para-states within the failing state. Thus, Guatemala has always had a strong private sector looming behind—and some would say controlling the puppet strings of—its government. These private-sector forces are referred to in Guatemala as its "occult powers": the power behind the politicians; those who animate the law by acting as intermediaries to bring cases forward by virtue of their networks and connections; those who manipulate government policy to benefit their own private ends.[5] Therefore, threat, fear, and terrorism—both implicit and explicit—are not things of the past, of the war period, but forms of governmentality actively and competitively used in present-day Guatemala by state, para-state, and quite a few non-state actors.

The political class, on its part, historically has converted state resources into private wealth (cf. Gledhill 1999:209). The land-grab economics of colonial Spanish and recent Ladino relations with Indians has been described by Hawkins (1984), Martínez Peláez (1970), and McCreery (1994), among many others. Today, the neoliberal global economy offers a new opportunity, a new opening for legal and illicit economic actions, a new way to grab wealth. The Mayas—always on the margins—remain poor, marginalized, and underrepresented. In this scheme, they constitute an exploitable labor class (when work is available) that is cheap to reproduce and considerably immobilized by municipal affiliation and "milpa logic" orientation that tends to maintain their attachment to increasingly smaller parcels of land (Annis 1987). Mayas, relatively stuck and vulnerable, submit to the Guatemalan arts of governance and do their best to reinvent what they can of a locally workable culture and either subvert, or integrate with, what they cannot adapt.

Our essays suggest that the governance of the Guatemalan social body has significantly broken down. Maya towns and hamlets have been largely abandoned by the central government.[6] A "new kind of war" or a permanent "low-intensity conflict" has replaced the politics of the civil war. The resultant processes have, on the whole, further marginalized and impoverished the Maya masses.

At the same time, external transnational forces have reshaped internal community political dynamics and processes. The 1985 revision of the constitution, for example, created a set of guidelines intent upon increasing democratization but which also served to undermine traditional forms of authority. The United Nations and other sources of international pressure—including the conferral of the Nobel Prize on an obscure Indian woman—pushed the nation toward the 1996 Peace Accords and their countervailing emphasis on ethnic cultural preservation and valorization. Governmentality is neither individual, nor local, nor national, nor transnational, but a complex mix of these.

These powerful outside political-legal forces together have opened up politics to those who can afford it and undermined traditional political-religious hierarchies of community-affirmed authority. One strand among these forces, the Peace Accords, has opened a window of opportunity that seems to authorize Maya communities to use or create "traditional culture" to govern themselves judicially. While the results vary, on the whole, the outcome seems favorable for Indians (see Dracoulis, Bybee, and Dabb, this volume). Nevertheless, those tandem processes have led to intergenerational culture change and conflict as youth identity and representation are culturally transformed and youths acquire increasing economic power (J. Edvalson and Call, this volume). Locally focused Indians and state-focused (or individually focused) outsiders contest and negotiate the management of communally held natural resources. Living on a fixed land base in communities stressed by serious demographic pressure and in an environment where government intervention tries to change the rules and orientations from community to state, Mayas contest, negotiate, abrogate, and reconstruct the old verities of common property, the local institutions of natural resource management, the processes of judicial and communal respect, and the nature of gender and birthing.

As Marx said, all is in flux. As a result, in this zero-sum game, land is grabbed and boundaries get challenged and breached. Yet, with no helpful presence, mediation, or intervention from state government, violence erupts (Dabb, J. Edvalson, and Call, this volume). In a related vein, Brown (this volume) argues that when the state does intervene in a program of supposed "decentralization" of governance, important decision-making about local resources becomes highly centralized—with destructive community outcomes. "Decentralization" thus is little more than a deceitful trope and set of practices for new forms of centralization. In effect, "decentralization" is government newspeak.

Likewise, the case of the highland Maya midwives highlights the unconstructive intervention of the state. The success and pervasiveness of local midwifery, combined with state efforts to introduce its version of health standards (Adams and Hawkins 2007a, 2007b; R. Edvalson, this volume; Hawkins and Adams 2007; K. Wilson 2007), have brought midwives under the gaze of government authorities and made them visible and accountable in new ways that are likely to either reduce their participation in midwifery or drive their activities underground.

This suite of ethnographic explorations into contemporary Maya communities underscores the dystopian world being imposed on the Maya population. In response, these Mayas attempt, however imperfectly, to understand, respond to, and cope with the economic restructuring that accompanies Guatemala's embrace of neoliberal prescriptions for economic management. While we document two examples of largely unsuccessful state intervention (Brown and R. Edvalson, this volume), the overall sense drawn from these essays is one of abandonment by the state.

In closing, we return to Gledhill's (1999:242) concerns regarding twenty-first century governmentality: "The politics of the new millennium will be different from those of the start of the twentieth century. This is not simply a matter of what states do, and the claims they are prepared to recognize from different elements of civil society, but how citizens imagine the state and the nation." If Guatemala's current president, Álvaro Colom, is to succeed as a social reformer, he must develop alternatives to a full-blown commitment to participation in the global market. But such deviance is highly unlikely, given strong external pressures from the World Bank and powerful states, such as the United States, to conform to neoliberal policies that facilitate economic globalization. Thus, the Central American Free Trade Agreement (CAFTA) is not likely to be rescinded or revised any time soon. To succeed as a reformer, Colom must provide some level of resource reciprocity back to poor communities that desperately need support. Such redistributive justice would not play well with the "occult powers" of today, either in Guatemala or in the United States, any more than it did in the days before U.S. interests clandestinely overthrew the democratic social-reformist government of Árbenz in 1954. Moreover, even without the external threat, Guatemala could hardly execute redistributive justice unilaterally because it lacks the resources needed to maintain even the most basic services.

Finally, the task of quelling the rampant violence that engulfs Guatemala challenges Colom and all Guatemalans. That brutality is now being transformed from widespread social violence to attacks against the state, in what is being officially labeled as "acts of terror" by the president and other high government officials (Lara et al. 2010a) and is commonly spoken of as Guatemala's "narco-violence." Indeed, we see a lethal "Mexicanization of violence," to include attacks on police and alarming numbers of murders throughout the country—sixty murders, in one case, over a single weekend (Alvarado 2010). By "Mexicanization of violence" we mean the growing presence in Guatemala of Mexican cartels that have terrorized parts of Guatemala and gained effective control of whole departments, most recently resulting in President Colom's declaration of a state of siege (*estado de sitio*) in the northern department of Alta Verapaz because of the pervasive presence and intimidating violence of the Mexican Zetas cartel (*Prensa Libre* 2010a). Mexican cartels are also actively recruiting poor Guatemalans into their ranks (Archibold and Cave 2011; Hawley 2010). Guatemalan crime groups, state-sponsored and otherwise, are responding in kind to the violent invasion. Eighty-four percent of the shipments of cocaine that enter the United States pass through Central America, a sharp increase from 44 percent in 2008 (Archibold and Cave 2011). The objective of the Mexican cartels is to control lucrative drug corridors that link Colombia to Mexico and the United States, leading the U.S. State Department to declare Guatemala as the Central American epicenter for drug trafficking, with more than 40 percent of the country under the control of cartels (*Prensa Libre* 2010c).[7]

We suspect that the task of quelling this violence can only occur with widespread economic investment in the form of jobs and the creation of social welfare infrastructure. As we completed the manuscript of this book in 2010, we predicted that a failure to reduce violence would lead to a political opening for the likes of opposition candidate General Otto Pérez Molina and his carceral vision of governance. His election win in 2011 portends a recycled chapter of political violence in an already terribly damaged country. To paraphrase Massumi (2009), the threat of social violence is as ubiquitous as the wind in Guatemala. But the relative absence of political violence for nearly thirty years, in a Guatemala struggling to democratize and deal with ethnic incomprehension, makes the threat of an irruption of political violence loom larger. Unfortunately, reviving political violence to cauterize Guatemala's endemic accidentality would treat the traumatized Maya with more trauma.

Notes

1. In an article proclaiming the discomforting news of a government cutback on police and security institutions, *Prensa Libre* reported that between January 1 and July 13, 2010, the murders of 2,445 Guatemalans occurred. Looking at overall crime, 43 percent was orchestrated by organized criminals and narco-traffickers, another 20 percent was attributed to gangs, and 7 percent derived from general delinquency. Five urban bus attacks occurred in Guatemala City in the week of July 12, 2010, which included an assault with grenades, and 19 police officers were killed along with 5 prison guards (Ismatul and Díaz 2010). For another example, we use data on extortions. In January 2010, Guatemalan police reported receiving an average 20 calls per day. In July 2010, that number had risen dramatically to 60 or 70 calls per day. Sixty percent of those extortion efforts were orchestrated from inside Guatemala's notoriously corrupt and brutal prison system. The other 40 percent were perpetrated by local gangs (*pandillas, maras*) or private individuals, to include friends and family of the victims (Orantes 2010). Not surprisingly under these conditions, in the first half of 2010, almost 94 percent of business owners felt that the security climate had deteriorated, 78 percent had experienced some act of crime or violence, 41 percent felt the leading problem was extortion, and 97 percent felt that the national government would do little or nothing to solve the security problem (Valdez and Alvarado 2010).

2. Newspapers provide anecdotal proxies for levels of tension and personal insecurity. In July 2010, in the wake of a lethal urban bus bombing in the capital, along with a rise in murders, one Guatemalan newspaper boldly proclaimed: "*Violencia provoca psicosis en la capital*—Violence Provokes Psychosis in the Capital" (*El Periódico*, July 16, 2010). Another blasted: "*¡Basta ya! La población está indefensa ante la delincuencia*—Enough Now! The People are Defenseless against Delinquency" (*Nuestro Diario,* July 16, 2010). Of these highly unsettling events, Interior Minister Carlos Menocal stated, "They [organized criminals] want to create a psychosis of terror . . . a psychology of fear" (Molina 2010). In an act of impressive frankness, President Colom openly called the summer 2010 wave of violence "terrorist acts" (Lara et al. 2010a).

3. Metz, Mariano, and López (2010:23) also make an argument for widespread PTSD in eastern Guatemala among Ladinos and Ch'orti' Mayas alike, both of whom were victimized during the civil war. They note that PTSD-like symptoms are identified by a number of anthropologists—Thomas Csordas, Nancy Scheper-Hughes, and Philippe Bourgois—working with populations experiencing long-term existential trauma.

4. Regarding the collapse of public security, Replogle (2005) reports, for example, on the rise of paramilitaries in Guatemala as a response to gang-related lawlessness and the impotence of the police in response. Private security guards outnumber police three-to-one. She links the sharp 40 percent increase in murders from 2001 to 2004 with this paramilitary activity, which some Guatemalan officials ominously label as a form of "social cleansing," including, in some cases, signs of torture prior to death. This could also be the product of conflict between gangs. Regardless, it is another marker of the instability and unpredictability that envelop Guatemala. As another piece of anecdotal evidence, we have been repeatedly told never to trust the police under any circumstances, for it is impossible to know their intentions. In general, police are cast as predatory, while robbers are cast as merely parasitic.

5. See Little (2009). Note that in Spanish, the concept of "occult" refers to that which is hidden, not that which is mystical.

6. It is important to provide a qualifier to this statement because there are certainly instances when the state government makes its presence known in these highland communities. As Brown (chapter 4) and R. Edvalson (chapter 5) argue, when the state government does penetrate and vie for control in indigenous communities, dysfunctional outcomes ensue. For example, under the rubric of "decentralization," as Brown demonstrates, the government simply reconstitutes centralized administration in new ways.

7. Note the absence of named bylines on *Prensa Libre* stories (2010a, 2010b, and 2010c) related to narco-violence or narco-control, an indication of escalating danger to those who report—which also follows the Mexican press's experience.

References

Abers, Rebecca. 2000. *Inventing Local Democracy*. Boulder, Colo.: Lynne Rienner.

Acuña, Claudia. 2010. Tribunal emite condena en el caso Rosenberg. *Prensa Libre* (Guatemala City). July 16.

Adams, Richard N., and Santiago Bastos. 2003. *Las relaciones étnicas en Guatemala, 1944–2000*. Antigua, Guatemala: Centro de Investigaciones Regionales de Mesoamérica.

Adams, Walter Randolph, and John P. Hawkins, eds. 2007a. *Health Care in Maya Guatemala: Confronting Medical Pluralism in a Developing Country*. Norman: University of Oklahoma Press.

———. 2007b. Introduction: The Continuing Disjunction between Traditional and Western Medical Beliefs and Practices in Guatemala. In *Health Care in Maya Guatemala*, edited by Walter Randolph Adams and John P. Hawkins, 3–23. Norman: University of Oklahoma Press.

Administración Miguel Tzep Rosario. n.d., ca. 2000. Historia. Nahualá: Administración Miguel Tzep Rosario, 2000–2004. "Políticas" flyer in possession of Curtis Dabb.

Agrawal, Arun. 2001. The Regulatory Community: Decentralization and the Environment in the Van Panchayats (Forest Councils) of Kumaon, India. *Mountain Research and Development* 21(3): 208–11.

———. 2005. *Environmentality: Technologies of Government and the Making of Subjects*. Durham, N.C.: Duke University Press.

Ajpacajá Tum, Florentino Pedro. 2001. *Tz'onob'al Tziij [Betrothal Words]: Discurso Ceremonial K'ichee'*. Guatemala: Cholsamaj.

Al Jazeera. 2010a. Guatemala Arrests Former President. January 29.

———. 2010b. Guatemala's Anti-Drug Tsar Arrested. March 4.

Alvarado, Hugo. 2010. Se registraron 60 muertes el fin de semana. *Prensa Libre* (Guatemala City). July 16.

Anderson, E. N., Aurora Dzib Zihum de Cen, Félix Medina Tzuc, and Pastor Valdez Chale. 2005. *Political Ecology in a Yucatec Maya Community.* Tucson: University of Arizona Press.

Annis, Sheldon. 1987. *God and Production in a Guatemalan Town*. Austin: University of Texas Press.

Arana, Ana. 2005. How the Street Gangs Took Central America. *Foreign Affairs* 84(3): 98–110.

Araneda, Kelly C. 2005. "The Commitment": Transformations of Courtship and Marriage in Santa Catarina Ixtahuacán. In *Roads to Change in Maya Guatemala*, edited by John P. Hawkins and Walter Randolph Adams, 99–123. Norman: University of Oklahoma Press.

Arce, Roberto, and Norman Long. 1993. Bridging Two Worlds: An Ethnography of Bureaucrat-Peasant Relations in West Mexico. In *An Anthropological Critique of Development*, edited by Mark Hobarth, 179–208. London: Routledge.

Archdiocese of Guatemala. 1999. *Guatemala, Never Again! Recovery of Historical Memory Project: The Official Report of the Human Rights Office*. Ossining, N.Y.: Orbis.

Archibold, Randal C., and Damien Cave. 2011. Drug Wars Push Deeper into Central America. *New York Times*. March 23.

Arias, Enrique Desmond, and Daniel M. Goldstein. 2010. Violent Pluralism: Understanding the New Democracies of Latin America. In *Violent Democracies in Latin America*, edited by Enrique Desmond Arias and Daniel M. Goldstein, 1–34. Durham, N.C.: Duke University Press.

Asociación CODEIN (Asociación Comunitaria de Desarrollo Integral de Nahualá). 2008. *Reconstrucción de la memoria histórica del municipio de Nahualá y sistematización de principios y valores*. Guatemala: Asociación Comunitaria de Desarrollo Integral de Nahualá.

Bailey, F. G. 1988. *Humbuggery and Manipulation: The Art of Leadership*. Ithaca, N.Y.: Cornell University Press.

———. 2001[1969]. *Stratagems and Spoils: A Social Anthropology of Politics*. Boulder, Colo.: Westview.

Barrios, Lina. 2001. *Tras las huellas del poder local: La alcaldía indígena en Guatemala del siglo XVI al siglo XX.* Guatemala City: Universidad Rafael Landívar, Instituto de Investigaciones Económicas y Sociales.

BBC News. 2010. Guatemala Attorney General Sacked. June 11.

Benson, Peter. 2004. Nothing to See Hear. *Anthropological Quarterly* 77(3): 435–67.

Benson, Peter, and Edward Fischer. 2009. Neoliberal Violence: Social Suffering in Guatemala's Postwar Era. In *Mayas in Postwar Guatemala: Harvest of Violence Revisited*, edited by Walter E. Little and Timothy J. Smith, 151–66. Tuscaloosa: University of Alabama Press.

Benson, Peter, Edward F. Fischer, and Kedron Thomas. 2008. Resocializing Suffering: Neoliberalism, Accusation, and the Sociopolitical Context of Guatemala's New Violence. *Latin American Perspectives* 35(5): 38–58.

Berkes, Fikret, Johan Colding, and Carl Folke. 2000. Rediscovery of Traditional Ecological Knowledge as Adaptive Management. *Ecological Applications* 10(5): 1251–62.

Berkes, Fikret, and Carl Folke. 1998. Linking Social and Ecological Systems for Resilience and Sustainability. In *Linking Social and Ecological Systems*, edited by Fikret Berkes and Carl Folke, 1–26. New York: Cambridge University Press.

Bernard, H. Russell. 2011. *Research Methods in Anthropology*. 5th ed. Lanham, Md.: AltaMira.

Binford, Leigh. 1985. Political Conflict and Land Tenure in the Mexican Isthmus of Tehuantepec. *Journal of Latin American Studies* 17(1):179–200.

Bird, Richard M., and Francois Vaillancourt. 1998. Fiscal Decentralization in Developing Countries: An Overview. In *Fiscal Decentralization in Developing Countries*, edited by Richard M. Bird and Francois Vaillancourt, 1–48. New York: Cambridge University Press.

Blas, Ana Lucía. 2006. Promueven justicia indígena: Defensoría Maya busca el reconocimiento de normas y principios. *Prensa Libre* (Guatemala City). August 20.

Blaser, Jürgen, Christian Küchli, Carol J. Pierce Colfer, and Doris Capistrano. 2005. Introduction to *The Politics of Decentralization: Forests, Power and People*, edited by Carol J. Pierce and Doris Capistrano, 1–11. London: EarthScan.

Bobrow-Strain, Aaron. 2007. *Intimate Enemies*. Durham, N.C.: Duke University Press.

Bocaletti, Elizabeth de, Renata Schumacher, Elena Hurtado, Patricia Bailey, Jorge Matute, Jean McDermott, Judith Moore, Henry Kalter, and René Salgado. 1999. *Perinatal Mortality in Guatemala*. Available at http://pdf.usaid.gov/pdf_docs/PNACJ798.pdf.

Bourdieu, Pierre, and Löic J. D. Wacquant. 1992. *An Invitation to Reflexive Sociology*. Chicago: Chicago University Press.

Brands, Hal. 2010. *Crime, Violence, and the Crisis in Guatemala: A Case Study in the Erosion of the State*. Washington, D.C.: Strategic Studies Institute.

Brintnall, Douglas E. 1979. *Revolt against the Dead: The Modernization of a Maya Community in the Highlands of Guatemala*. New York: Gordon and Breach.

Brown, Linda A., and Kitty F. Emery. 2008. Negotiations with the Animate Forest: Hunting Shrines in the Guatemalan Highlands. *Journal of Archeological Method and Theory* 15(4): 300–37.

Brusco, Elizabeth E. 1995. *The Reformation of Machismo: Evangelical Conversion and Gender in Colombia*. Austin: University of Texas Press.

Burrell, Jennifer L. 2009. Intergenerational Conflict in the Postwar Era. In *Mayas in Postwar Guatemala*, edited by Walter E. Little and Timothy J. Smith, 96–109. Tuscaloosa: University of Alabama Press.

———. 2010. In and Out of Rights: Security, Migration, and Human Rights Talk in Postwar Guatemala. *Journal of Latin American and Caribbean Anthropology* 15(1): 90–115.

Cambranes, J. C. 1992. *500 Años de lucha por la tierra: Estudios sobre propiedad rural y reforma agraria en Guatemala*. Vol. 2. Guatemala City: Facultad Latinoamericana de Ciencias Sociales.

Campo-Flores, Arian. 2005. The Most Dangerous Gang in America. *Newsweek*. March 28.

Cancian, Frank. 1965. *Economics and Prestige in a Maya Community: The Religious Cargo System in Zinacantán*. Stanford, Calif.: Stanford University Press.

Cardona Caravantes, Karla J. 2002. *Arqueología, etnohistoria y conflictos de tierra en la región sur del lago de Atitlán*. Guatemala City: Universidad del Valle de Guatemala.

Carey, David, Jr. 2001. *Our Elders Teach Us: Maya-Kaqchikel Historical Perspectives, Xkib'ij Kan Qate' Qatata'*. Tuscaloosa: University of Alabama Press.

———. 2004. Maya Perspectives on the 1999 Referendum in Guatemala: Ethnic Equality Rejected? *Latin American Perspectives* 31(6): 69–95.

———. 2006. *Engendering Maya History: Kaqchikel Women as Agents and Conduits of the Past, 1875–1970*. New York: Routledge.

Carlsen, Robert. 1997. *The War for the Heart and Soul of a Highland Maya Town*. Austin: University of Texas Press.

Carmack, Robert M. 1988. *Harvest of Violence*. Norman: University of Oklahoma Press.

———. 1995. *Rebels of Highland Guatemala: The Quiche-Mayas of Momostenango*. Norman: University of Oklahoma Press.

———. 2009. Conclusions to *Mayas in Postwar Guatemala*, edited by Walter E. Little and Timothy J. Smith, 181–94. Tuscaloosa: University of Alabama Press.

Castillo, Aida. 2002. National Law and Indigenous Customary Law: The Struggle for Justice of Indigenous Women in Chiapas. In *Gender, Justice Development and Rights*, edited by Maxine Molyneux and Shahra Razavi, 384–413. New York: Oxford University Press.

Castillo, Rubén. 2007. General Pérez Molina promete seguridad con "mano dura." *Nación* (San José, Costa Rica). September 7.

Cazali, Lilian de, Virgilio Reyes, and Victor J. Moscoso. 1998. *Perspectivas de los jóvenes sobre la democracia en Guatemala: Reporte de investigación*. Guatemala City: FLACSO.

Certeau, Michel de. 1984. *The Practice of Everyday Life.* Berkeley: University of California Press.

Chance, John K., and William B. Taylor. 1985. Cofradías and Cargos: An Historical Perspective on the Mesoamerican Civil-Religious Hierarchy. *American Ethnologist* 12(1): 1–26.

CNN. 2010. Top Guatemalan Officers Arrested. CNN World. March 4.

Collier, George A., and Elizabeth Lowery Quaratiello. 1994. *Basta! Land and the Zapatista Rebellion in Chiapas*. Oakland, Calif.: Food First Books.

Collier, Stephen J. 2009. Topologies of Power: Foucault's Analysis of Political Government beyond Governmentality. *Theory, Culture, and Society* 26(6): 78–108.

Comisión para el Esclarecimiento Histórico (CEH). 1999. *Guatemala, memoria del silencio*. 12 vols. Oficina de Servicios para Proyectos de las Naciones Unidas. Guatemala City: F&G Editores.

Congreso de la República de Guatemala. 1996. Decreto número 101-96: Ley Forestal.

Craven, Christa. 2007a. Laboring On: Birth in Transition in the United States. *Contemporary Sociology: A Journal of Reviews* 36(6): 585–87.

———. 2007b. A "Consumer's Right" to Choose a Midwife: Shifting Meanings for Reproductive Rights under Neoliberalism. *American Anthropologist* 109(4): 701–12.

Crehan, Kate. 2002. *Gramsci, Culture and Anthropology*. London: Pluto.

Day, Richard J. F. 2005. *Gramsci is Dead: Anarchist Currents in the Newest Social Movements*. London: Pluto.

DeWalt, Billie R. 1975. Changes in the Cargo Systems of Mesoamerica. *Anthropological Quarterly* 48(2): 87–105.

DeWalt, Billie R., Martha W. Rees, and Arthur D. Murphy. 1994. *The End of Agrarian Reform in Mexico: Past Lessons, Future Prospects*. San Diego: Center for U.S.-Mexico Studies, University of California, San Diego.

Dewees, Peter A. 1995. Trees and Farm Boundaries: Farm Forestry, Land Tenure and Reform in Kenya. *Africa: Journal of the International African Institute* 65(2): 217–35.

Diamond, Larry. 1999. *Developing Democracy: Toward Consolidation.* Baltimore, Md.: Johns Hopkins University Press.

Diario de Centro América. 1985. Constitución Política de la República de Guatemala. June 3. Available at www.glin.gov/view.action?glinID=64380.

Douglas, Mary. 1966. *Purity and Danger: An Analysis of the Concepts of Pollution and Taboo.* London: Routledge and K. Paul.

Durrenberger, E. Paul, and Gisli Palsson. 1987. Ownership at Sea: Fishing Territories and Access to Sea Resources. *American Anthropologist* 14(3): 508–22.

The Economist. 2010. Kamikaze Mission: The UN's Prosecutor Resigns, Taking an Enemy with Him. June 17.

Elías, Sivel, and Hannah Wittman. 2005. State Forest and Community: Decentralization of Forest Administration in Guatemala. In *The Politics of Decentralization: Forests, Power and People*, edited by Carol J. Pierce and Doris Capistrano, 282–95. London: EarthScan.

Ellison, James. 2009. Governmentality and the Family: Neoliberal Choices and Emergent Kin Relations in Southern Ethiopia. *American Anthropologist* 111(1): 81–92.

Elsass, Peter. 2001. Individual and Collective Traumatic Memories: A Qualitative Study of Post Traumatic Stress Disorder Symptoms in Two Latin American Localities. *Transcultural Psychiatry* 38(3): 306–16.

Falla, Ricardo. 2001. *Quiché Rebelde: Religious Conversion, Politics, and Ethnic Identity in Guatemala.* Austin: University of Texas Press.

———. 2006. *Juventud de una comunidad maya: Ixcán, Guatemala.* Guatemala City: Instituto AVANCSO, Editorial Universitaria, Universidad de San Carlos de Guatemala.

Falleti, Tulia G. 1999. New Fiscal Federalism and the Political Dynamics of Decentralization in Latin America. Paper presented at the conference "International Institutions, Global Processes, Domestic Consequences," Duke University, Durham, N.C., April 9–11.

FAO (Food and Agriculture Organization of the United Nations). 1999. Annotated Bibliography Forest Cover Change: Guatemala. Forest Resource Assessment Program Working Paper 13. Rome: FAO.

———. 2005. *Status of Tropical Forest Management 2005.* Rome: FAO.

Feiser, Ezra. 2010. Guatemala Becomes a Model for Crime Investigation. *Christian Science Monitor.* May 12.

Ferguson, James, and Akhil Gupta. 2002. Spatialized States: Toward an Ethnography of Neoliberal Governmentality. *American Ethnologist* 29(4): 981–1002.

Fernández García, María Cristina. 2004. *Lynching in Guatemala: Legacy of War and Impunity*. Cambridge, Mass.: Weatherhead Center for International Affairs, Harvard University. Available at www.wcifa.harvard.edu/fellows/papers/2003–04/fernandez.pdf.

Ferroukhi, Lyès, ed. 2003. *Municipal Forest Management in Latin America*. San José, Costa Rica: CIFOR (Center for International Forestry Research) and IDRC (International Development Research Centre).

Fischer, Edward. 2001. *Cultural Logics and Global Economics: Mayan Identity in Thought and Practice.* Austin: University of Texas Press.

FLACSO (Facultad Latinoamericana de Ciencias Sociales). 2001. *Informe de estudio de línea base CARE.* Proyecto MIBOSQUE. Guatemala City: Facultad Latinoamericana de Ciencias Sociales.

Foley, William A. 1997. *Anthropological Linguistics: An Introduction.* Malden, Mass.: Blackwell.

Foucault, Michel.1977. *Discipline and Punish: The Birth of the Prison.* New York: Vintage Books.

———. 1986. Of Other Spaces. *Diacritics* 16(1): 22–27.

———. 1988. *The Care of the Self.* Vol. 3 of *The History of Sexuality*. New York: Vintage Books.

———. 1991. Governmentality. In *The Foucault Effect: Studies in Governmentality, with Two Lectures by and an Interview with Michel Foucault*, edited by Graham Burchell, Colin Gordon, and Peter Miller, 87–104. Chicago: University of Chicago Press.

———. 1994. *The Birth of the Clinic: An Archaeology of Medical Perception.* New York: Vintage Books.

Fox Tree, Erich, and Julia Gómez Imatá. 2007. *Junamaam Ib'*: Solidaridad y defensa colectiva en Nahualá durante la violencia guatemalteca. *Mesoamérica* 28(49): 59–81.

Franklin, Jonathan. 2010. The Truth About Guatemala's YouTube Murder. *The Guardian.* January 13.

Freire, Paulo. 1993. *Pedagogy of the Oppressed.* New York: Continuum.

Fridell, Gavin. 2007. *Fair Trade Coffee: The Prospects and Pitfalls of Market-Driven Social Justice*. Toronto: University of Toronto Press.

FUNCEDE (Fundación Centroamericana de Desarrollo). 1995. *Municipalidad de Nahualá: Diagnóstico del Municipio de Nahualá, Departamento de Sololá, Guatemala, Centro América.* Guatemala City: FUNCEDE / Konrad Adenauer Stiftung / Embajada Real de los Países Bajos.

Gibson, Clark C., Margaret A. McKean, and Elinor Ostrom, eds. 2000. *People and Forests: Communities, Institutions, and Governance,* Cambridge, Mass.: MIT Press.

Gledhill, John. 1999. Official Masks and Shadow Powers: Towards an Anthropology of the Dark Side of the State. *Urban Anthropology* 28(3–4): 199–251.

Glovin, David, and Andrew M. Harris. 2010. Ex-Guatemalan Leader Alfonso Portillo is Arrested. *Bloomberg Businessweek.* June 20.

Godoy, Angelina Snodgrass. 2002. Lynchings and the Democratization of Terror in Postwar Guatemala: Implications for Human Rights. *Human Rights Quarterly* 24(3): 640–61.

———. 2004. When "Justice" is Criminal: Lynchings in Contemporary Latin America. *Theory and Society* 33(6): 621–51.

Goffman, Erving. 1967. *Interaction Ritual.* Chicago: Aldine.

Goldín, Liliana R. 1999. *Identities on the Move: Transnational Processes in North America and the Caribbean Basin.* Albany, N.Y.: Institute for Mesoamerican Studies.

Goldín, Liliana R., and Brenda Rosenbaum. 1993. Culture and History: Subregional Variation among the Maya. *Comparative Studies in Society and History* 35(1): 110–32.

Goldman, Noreen, and Dana A. Glei. 2000. Evaluation of Midwifery Care: A Case Study of Rural Guatemala. Chapel Hill: Carolina Population Center, University of North Carolina. Available at http://pdf.usaid.gov/pdf_docs/PNACM169.pdf.

Goldstein, Daniel M. 2004. *The Spectacular City: Violence and Performance in Urban Bolivia.* Durham, N.C.: Duke University Press.

Gordon, Colin. 1991. Governmental Relations: An Introduction. In *The Foucault Effect: Studies in Governmentality, with Two Lectures by and an Interview with Michel Foucault*, edited by Graham Burchell, Colin Gordon, and Peter Miller, 1–51. Chicago: University of Chicago Press.

Graeber, David. 2007. *Possibilities: Essays on Hierarchy, Rebellion, and Desire.* Oakland, Calif.: AK Press.

Grandin, Greg. 2000. *Blood of Guatemala: A History of Race and Nation.* Durham, N.C.: Duke University Press.

Green, Linda. 1999. *Fear as a Way of Life: Mayan Widows in Rural Guatemala.* New York: Columbia University Press.

———. 2003. Notes on Maya Youth and Rural Industrialization in Guatemala. *Critique of Anthropology* 23(1): 51–73.

Greenpeace Central America. 1997. *Los Bosques de Totonicapán.* Washington, D.C.: Greenpeace.

Gutiérrez, Marta Estela, and Paul Hans Kobrak. 2001. *Los linchamientos: Pos conflicto y violencia colectiva en Huehuetenango, Guatemala*. Huehuetenango, Guatemala: Centro de Estudios y Documentación de la Frontera Occidental de Guatemala.

Hale, Charles R. 2002. Does Multiculturalism Menace? Governance, Cultural Rights and the Politics of Identity in Guatemala. *Journal of Latin American Studies* 34:485–524.

———. 2006. *Más que un Indio (More than an Indian): Racial Ambivalence and Neoliberal Multiculturalism in Guatemala*. Santa Fe, N.M.: School of American Research.

Hammill, Matthew. 2007. *Growth, Poverty, and Inequality in Central America*. Mexico City: United Nations Economic Commission on Latin America and the Caribbean.

Handy, Jim. 1990. The Corporate Community, Campesino Organizations, and Agrarian Reform: 1950–1954. In *Guatemalan Indians and the State: 1540–1988*, edited by Carol A. Smith, 163–82. Austin: University of Texas Press.

———. 2004. Chicken Thieves, Witches, and Judges: Vigilante Justice and Customary Law in Guatemala. *Journal of Latin American Studies* 36(3): 533–61.

Hardin, Garrett. 1968. Tragedy of the Commons. *Science* 162(3859): 1243–48.

Hart, Thomas. 2008. *The Ancient Spirituality of the Modern Maya*. Albuquerque: University of New Mexico Press.

Hawkins, John P. 1984. *Inverse Images: The Meaning of Culture, Ethnicity, and Family in Postcolonial Guatemala*. Albuquerque: University of New Mexico Press.

Hawkins, John P., and Walter Randolph Adams, eds. 2005. *Roads to Change in Maya Guatemala: A Field School Approach to Understanding the K'iche'*. Norman: University of Oklahoma Press.

Hawkins, John P., and Walter Randolph Adams. 2007. Good Medicine: Steps Toward a Maya-Accessible Health Care System. In *Health Care in Maya Guatemala*, edited by Walter Randolph Adams and John P. Hawkins, 215–35. Norman: University of Oklahoma Press.

Hawkins, John P., and Walter Randolph Adams, eds. In preparation. *"A Place for the Future": The Politics of Hurricane Disaster Resettlement in Maya Guatemala*.

Hawkins, John P., and Walter Randolph Adams, eds. In review. *The Religious Transformation of Maya Guatemala*.

Hawley, Chris. 2010. Cartels Recruit Guatemalans in Mexico Drug War. *Arizona Republic*. June 2.

Hendrix, Steven. 2000. Guatemalan "Justice Centers": The Centerpiece for Advancing Transparency, Efficiency, Due Process, and Access to Justice. *American University International Law Review* 15(4): 813–49.

———. 2002. Lessons from Guatemala: Renewing U.S. Foreign Policy on the Rule of Law. *Harvard International Review* 23(4): 14–18.

Henry, Jules. 1963. *Culture against Man*. New York: Random House.

Hinojosa, Servando. 2004. Authorizing Tradition: Vectors of Contention in Highland Maya Midwifery. *Social Science and Medicine* 59(3): 637–51.

Hobsbawm, Eric. 1983. Introduction: Inventing Traditions. In *The Invention of Tradition*, edited by Eric Hobsbawm and Terence Ranger, 1–14. New York: Cambridge University Press.

Holland, Dorothy, William Lacicotte, Debra Skinner, and Carole Cain. 1998. *Identity and Agency in Cultural Worlds*. Cambridge, Mass.: Harvard University Press.

Hostnig, Rainer. 1997a. *Esta tierra es nuestra: Compendio de fuentes históricas sobre denuncias, medidas y remedidas, composiciones, titulaciones, usurpaciones, desmembraciones, litigios, transacciones y remates de tierra (Años 1555–1952)*. Área Mam de Quetzaltenango, vol. 1. Municipios de Cabricán, Cajolá, Concepción Chiquirichapa, Huitán y San Martín Sacatepéquez. Quetzaltenango, Guatemala: Centro de Capacitación e Investigación Campesina.

———. 1997b. *Esta tierra es nuestra: Compendio de fuentes históricas sobre denuncias, medidas y remedidas, composiciones, titulaciones, usurpaciones, desmembraciones, litigios, transacciones y remates de tierra (Años 1555–1952)*. Área Mam de Quetzaltenango, vol. 2. Municipios de Ostuncalco, Palestina de los Altos, San Miguel Sigüilá, San Carlos Sija y Sibilia. Quetzaltenango, Guatemala: Centro de Capacitación e Investigación Campesina.

———. 1998. *Esta tierra es nuestra: Compendio de fuentes históricas sobre denuncias, medidas y remedidas, composiciones, titulaciones, usurpaciones, desmembraciones, litigios, transacciones y remates de tierra (Años 1555–1952)*. Departamento de Totonicapán, vol. 2. Municipio de San Miguel Totonicapán. Quetzaltenango, Guatemala: Centro de Capacitación e Investigación Campesina.

Hsu, Hsuan L., and Martha Lincoln. 2007. Biopower, *Bodies . . . the Exhibition*, and the Spectacle of Public Health. *Discourse* 29(1): 15–34.

Hudson, Andrew, and Alexandra W. Taylor. 2010. The International Commission against Impunity in Guatemala: A New Model for International Criminal Justice Mechanisms. *Journal of International Criminal Justice* 8:53–74.

Hunter, Billie. 2004. Conflicting Ideologies as a Source of Emotion Work in Midwifery. *Midwifery* 20(3): 261–72.

Hyde, Abbey, and Bernadette Roche-Reid. 2004. Midwifery Practice and the Crisis of Modernity: Implications for the Role of the Midwife. *Social Science and Medicine* 58(12): 2613–23.

Inda, Jonathan Xavier. 2005. *Anthropologies of Modernity: Foucault, Governmentality, and Life Politics*. Hoboken, N.J.: Wiley-Blackwell.

Instituto Nacional de Estadística. 2003. *Características de la población y de los locales de habitación censados*. [Drawn from Censos Nacionales XI de Población y VI de Habitación 2002.] Guatemala City: República de Guatemala, Instituto Nacional de Estadística.

Ismatul, Óscar, and Leonel Díaz Zeceña. 2010. Reducen fondos a seguridad. *Prensa Libre* (Guatemala City). July 21.

Jardine, Spencer J. In preparation. Myth, Relocation, and Identity in Nueva Santa Catarina Ixtahuacán. In *"A Place for the Future,"* edited by John P. Hawkins and Walter Randolph Adams.

Jones, Michael Duncan. 2007. "The Solution is Prevention": The National Rural Health Care System in Nahualá. In *Health Care in Maya Guatemala*, edited by Walter Randolph Adams and John P. Hawkins, 86–99. Norman: University of Oklahoma Press.

Katz, Elizabeth G. 2000. Social Capital and Natural Capital: A Comparative Analysis of Land Tenure and Natural Resource Management in Guatemala. *Land Economics* 76(1): 114–32.

Keen, Benjamin. 1971. *The Aztec Image in Western Thought*. New Brunswick, N.J.: Rutgers University Press.

Krishtofovich, Vyacheslav. 1997. *A Friend of the Deceased*. Film.

Kristof, Nicholas D. 2011. Our Fantasy Nation? *New York Times.* July 4.

La Farge, Oliver. 1947. *Santa Eulalia: The Religion of A Cuchumatán Indian Town*. Chicago: University of Chicago Press.

Lara, J., C. Orantes, S. Valdez, and C. Bonillo. 2010. Demandan combatir las acciones de terror. *Prensa Libre* (Guatemala City). July 20.

Lara, J., S. Valdez, and G. Contreras. 2010. Criminales desfían a la policía. *Prensa Libre* (Guatemala City). July 16.

Larson, Anne M. 2005. Democratic Decentralization in the Forestry Sector: Lessons Learned from Africa, Asia, and Latin America. In *The Politics of Decentralization: Forests, Power and People*, edited by Carol J. Pierce and Doris Capistrano, 32–62. London: EarthScan.

———. 2008. Indigenous Peoples, Representation and Citizenship in Guatemalan Forestry. *Conservation and Society* 6(1): 35–48.

Larson, Anne M., and Jesse C. Ribot. 2004. Democratic Decentralization through a Natural Resource Lens: Countering Central Resistance, Fostering Local Demand. *European Journal of Development Research* 16(1): 1–22.

Larson, Clay. In review. The Religious Cargos and Fiestas of Santa Catarina Ixtahuacán and Their Decline. In *The Religious Transformation of Maya Guatemala*, edited by John P. Hawkins and Walter Randolph Adams.

Lefebvre, Henri. 1974. *The Production of Space*. Translated by D. Nicholson-Smith. Oxford, UK: Blackwell.

Lemos, Maria Carmen, and Arun Agrawal. 2006. Environmental Governance. *Annual Review of Environmental Resources* 31:297–325.

Lesorogol, Carolyn K. 2008. *Contesting the Commons: Privatizing Pastoral Lands in Kenya*. Ann Arbor: University of Michigan Press.

Little, Walter E. 2008. Maya Handicraft Vendors, Crime, and the Social Re-Construction of Market Spaces in a Tourism Town. In *Economies and the Transformation of Landscape*, edited by Lisa Cliggett and Christopher A. Pool, 167–290. Lanham, Md.: AltaMira.

———. 2009. Introduction: Revisiting the Harvest of Fear in Postwar Guatemala. In *Mayas in Postwar Guatemala*, edited by Walter E. Little and Timothy J. Smith, 1–15. Tuscaloosa: University of Alabama Press.

Loening, Ludger, and Michael Markussen. 2003. *Pobreza, deforestación, y pérdida de la biodiversidad en Guatemala*. Discussion Paper 91. Goettingen, Germany: Ibero-American Institute for Economic Research.

Low, Setha.1996. The Anthropology of Cities: Imagining and Theorizing the City. *Annual Review of Anthropology* 25:383–409.

———. 2000. *On the Plaza: The Politics of Public Space and Culture.* Austin: University of Texas Press.

Malik, Waleed H. 2005. *Guatemala: The Role of Judicial Modernization in Post Conflict Reconstruction and Social Reconciliation*. World Bank: Social Development Notes.

Malkin, Elisabeth. 2010. Two Top Guatemalan Police Officials Are Arrested on Drug Charges. *New York Times.* March 2.

Manz, Beatriz. 2004. *Paradise in Ashes: A Guatemalan Journey of Courage, Terror, and Hope*. Berkeley: University of California Press.

Markowitz, Lisa. 2001. NGOs, Local Government, and Agrarian Civil Society: A Case of Evolving Collaboration from Southern Peru. *Culture and Agriculture* 23(1): 8–18.

Martínez-Amador, David. 2011. Crimen organizado. May 22. *Prensa Libre* (Guatemala City).

Martínez Peláez, Severo. 1970. *La patria del criollo: Ensayo de interpretación de la realidad colonial guatemalteca.* Guatemala City: Editorial Universitaria.

Massumi, Brian. 2009. National Enterprise Emergency: Steps toward an Ecology of Powers. *Theory, Culture, and Society* 26(6): 153–85.

Matheson, Craig. 1987. Weber and the Classification of Forms of Legitimacy. *British Journal of Sociology* 38(2): 199–215.

Maupin, Jonathan Nathaniel. 2008. Remaking the Guatemalan Midwife: Health Care Reform and Midwifery Training Programs in Highland Guatemala. *Medical Anthropology* 27(4): 353–82.

———. 2009. "Fruit of the Accords": Health Care Reform and Civil Participation in Highland Guatemala. *Social Science and Medicine* 68(8): 1456–63.

McAllister, Carlota. 2005. Rural Markets, Revolutionary Souls, and Rebellious Women in Cold War Guatemala. Working Paper Series. Toronto: Centre for Research on Latin America and the Caribbean, York University.

McCreery, David. 1994. Rural Guatemala, 1760–1940. Palo Alto, Calif.: Stanford University Press.

McDonald, James H. 1994. NAFTA and Basic Food Production: Dependency and Marginalization on Both Sides of the US/Mexico Border. *Research in Economic Anthropology* 15:129–43.

———. 1997a Film as Testimonial Literature. *American Anthropologist* 99(1): 135–43.

———. 1997b. Privatizing the Private Family Farmer: NAFTA and the Transformation of the Mexican Dairy Sector. *Human Organization* 56(3): 321–32.

———. 1999. The Neoliberal Project and Governmentality in Rural Mexico: Emergent Farmer Organization in the Michoacán Highlands. *Human Organization* 58(3): 274–84.

———. 2003. An Exploration in the Veiling of Power: The Politics of Development in Rural West Mexico. *Mexican Studies/Estudios Mexicanos* 19(1): 161–85.

———. 2009. The Cultural Effects of the Narcoeconomy in Rural Mexico. *Journal of International and Global Studies* 1(1): 1–29.

Mendelson, E. Michael. 1965. *Los escándalos de Maximón: Un estudio sobre la religión y la visión del mundo en Santiago Atitlán.* Seminario de Integración Social Guatemalteca Publicación 19. Guatemala City: Tipografía Nacional.

Mendoza, Carlos A. 2004. Collective Violence in Post-Conflict Guatemala: Understanding Lynch Mobs. Paper presented at the Latin American Studies Association meeting, Las Vegas, Nev., October 7–9. Available at www.nd.edu/~cmendoza1/datos/collectiveviolence1asa2006.pdf.

———. 2006. Structural Causes and Diffusion Processes of Collective Violence: Understanding Lynch Mobs in Post-Conflict Guatemala. Paper presented at the Latin American Studies Association meeting, San Juan, Puerto Rico, March 15–18. Available at www.nd.edu/~cmendoza1/datos/collectiveviolence1asa2006.pdf.

Merry, Sally Engle. 2001. Spatial Governmentality and the New Urban Social Order: Controlling Gender Violence through Law. *American Anthropologist* 103(1): 16–29.

Metz, Brent, Lorenzo Mariano, and Julián López García. 2010. The Violence after "La Violencia" in the Ch'orti' Region of Eastern Guatemala. *Journal of Latin American and Caribbean Studies* 15(1): 16–41.

Miller, Kassandra Lynne. 2004. Evaluating the Design and Management of Community-Based Ecotourism Projects in Guatemala. Master's thesis, University of Montana.

MINUGUA (Misión de Verificación de las Naciones Unidas en Guatemala). 2000. *Los linchamientos: Un flagelo contra la dignidad humana*. Guatemala City: Misión de Verificación de las Naciones Unidas en Guatemala.

———. 2002. *Los linchamientos: Un flagelo que persiste*. Misión de Verificación de las Naciones Unidas en Guatemala.

———. 2004. Registros de casos de linchamientos 1996–2002. Misión de Verificación de las Naciones Unidas en Guatemala. CD-ROM.

Molina, Carlos. 2010. "Es una psicosis," afirma Carlos Menocal. *Nuestro Diario* (Guatemala City). July 16.

Montejo, Victor. 2005. *Maya Intellectual Renaissance: Identity, Representation, and Leadership*. Austin: University of Texas Press.

Montero, Alfred P., and David J. Samuels. 2004. The Political Determinants of Decentralization in Latin America: Causes and Consequences. In *Decentralization and Democracy in Latin America*, edited by Alfred P. Montero and David J. Samuels, 3–32. Notre Dame, Ind.: University of Notre Dame Press.

Moore, Sally F. 1985. *Social Facts and Fabrications: "Customary" Law on Kilimanjaro 1880–1980*. Cambridge, Mass.: Harvard University Press.

Morales, Nery, and Fredy Rodas. 2006. Se salvan de ser linchados en Sololá. *Prensa Libre* (Guatemala City). August 13.

Morgan, Jesse. 2005. Standing at the Crossroads: Culture Change in Nahualá as Seen Through the Eyes of Javier, a Maya Elder. In *Roads to Change in Maya Guatemala*, edited by John P. Hawkins and Walter Randolph Adams, 61–96. Norman: University of Oklahoma Press.

Mosse, David. 2005. *Cultivating Development: An Ethnography of Aid Policy and Practice*. London: Pluto.

MotherCare. 1996. *Guía para facilitadores de comadronas: Contenidos técnicos para comadronas*. Guatemala City and Arlington, Va.: Ministerio de Salud Pública y Asistencia Social, Proyecto de Salud Materna-Perinatal, USAID y MotherCare / John Snow.

———. 1999. MotherCare/Guatemala. *MotherCare Matters* 8(2): 3–7, 11.

MSNBC. 2010. Guatemala Arrests Highlight Drug Corruption. MSNBC.com. March 3.

Murine, Anna. 2011. Pentagon: Central America "Deadliest" Non-War Zone in the World. *Christian Science Monitor*. April 11.

Nash, June C. 1968. The Passion Play in Maya Indian Communities. *Comparative Studies in Society and History* 10(3): 318–27.

Nash, Manning. 1967. *Machine Age Maya: The Industrialization of a Guatemalan Community*. Chicago: University of Chicago Press.

Nayap-Pot, Dalila C. 1997. The Social Role of Maya Women. In *Crosscurrents in Indigenous Spirituality*, edited by Guillermo Cook, 101–12. Leiden, Netherlands: E. J. Brill.

Naylor, Robert A. 1967. Guatemala: Indian Attitudes toward Land Tenure. *Journal of Inter-American Studies* 9(4): 619–39.

Nelson, Diane M. 2010. *Reckoning: The Ends of War in Guatemala*. Durham, N.C.: Duke University Press.

Nolan, Riall. 2002. *Development Anthropology: Encounters with the Real World*. Boulder, Colo.: Westview.

Nutini, Hugo G., and Barry L. Isaac. 2009. *Social Stratification in Central Mexico, 1500–2000*. Austin: University of Texas Press.

Nuttall, Christy Roser. In preparation. The Genesis of Exodus: The Relocation of Santa Catarina Ixtahuacán. In *"A Place for the Future,"* edited by John P. Hawkins and Walter Randolph Adams.

Oakes, Maud. 1951. *The Two Crosses of Todos Santos*. Princeton, N.J.: Princeton University Press.

Oates, Wallace E. 1993. Fiscal Decentralization and Economic Development. *National Tax Journal* 46(2): 237–43.

Oficina Forestal Municipal. 2006. Estadísticas, Santa Catarina Ixtahuacán, Guatemala.

Orantes, Coralia. 2010. Aumentan denuncias por casos de extorción. *Prensa Libre* (Guatemala City). July 16.

Orantes, Coralia, and Olga López. 2010. Embajadora ve violencia sin precedente en el país. *Prensa Libre* (Guatemala City). July 20.

Otzoy, Antonio. 1997. Traditional Values and Christian Ethics: A Maya Protestant Spirituality. In *Crosscurrents in Indigenous Spirituality*, edited by Guillermo Cook, 261–69. Leiden, Netherlands: E. J. Brill.

Paul, Lois, and Benjamin D. Paul. 1975. The Maya Midwife as Sacred Specialist: A Guatemalan Case. *American Ethnologist* 2(4): 707–26.

Peace Accords. 1996. Guatemala. Available at www.incore.ulst.ac.uk/services/cds/agreements/pdf/guat12.pdf.

Peña Nieto, Enrique. 2012. Mexico's Next Chapter. *New York Times*. July 3.

Perera, Victor. 1991. Guatemala Guards Its Rain Forests. *Nation* (July 8): 54–56.

———. 1995. *Unfinished Conquest: The Guatemalan Tragedy*. Berkeley: University of California Press.

Pieper, Jim. 2002. *Guatemala's Folk Saints: Maximon/San Simon, Rey Pascual, Judas, Lucifer, and Others*. Los Angeles, Calif.: Pieper and Associates.

Pitarch, Pedro, Shannon Speed, and Xochitl Leyva Solano. 2008. *Human Rights in the Maya Region: Global Politics, Cultural Contentions, and Moral Engagements*. Durham, N.C.: Duke University Press.

Polger, Steven. 1960. Biculturation of Musquakie Teenage Boys. *American Anthropologist* 62(2): 217–35.

Posey, Darrell A. 1985. Indigenous Management of Tropical Forest Ecosystems: The Case of the Kayapo Indians of the Brazilian Amazon. *Agroforestry Systems* 3:139–58.

Prensa Libre (Guatemala City). 2010a. Cobaneros aprueban estado de sitio en Alta Verapaz. December 19.

———. 2010b. Colom advierte que actos de barbarie no cesarán. July 14.

———. 2010c. Un 40% del territorio guatemalteco está controlado por carteles. August 23.

———. 2011. Wikileaks revela declaraciones de ex comisionado Castresana. February 16.

Proyecto Interdiocesano Recuperación de la Memoria Histórica (Guatemala), 1998. *Guatemala, nunca más: Informe*. 4 vols. Guatemala City: Oficina de Derechos Humanos del Arzobispado de Guatemala (ODHAG).

Putnam, Katharine M., Cindy Townsend, Jeanette Lantz, Rebecca Roberts, Autumn Gallegos, Amy Potts, Cynthia B. Ericksson, and David W. Fry. 2009. Reports of Community Violence Exposure, Traumatic Loss, Posttraumatic Stress Disorder, and Complicated Grief among Guatemala Aid Workers. *Traumatology* 15(3): 40–47.

Rabinow, Paul. 1992. Artificiality and Enlightenment: From Sociobiology to Biosociality. In *Incorporations*, edited by Jonathan Crary and Sanford Kwinter, 234–52. New York: Zone Books.

Radcliffe-Brown, A. R. 1967[1950]. Introduction to *African Systems of Kinship and Marriage*, edited by A. R. Radcliffe-Brown and Daryll Forde, 1–85. London: Oxford University Press for the International African Institute.

Replogle, Jill. 2005. In Guatemala, A Rise in Vigilante Justice. *Christian Science Monitor.* October 6.

———. 2008. Mexico Exports Its Drug War to Guatemala. *Time.* December 12.

———. 2009. In Guatemala, a Village that Cocaine Built. *Time.* April 16.

Ribot, Jesse C., Arun Argawal, and Anne M. Larson. 2006. Recentralizing while Decentralizing: How National Governments Reappropriate Forest Resources. *World Development* 34(11): 1864–86.

Richards, Michael. 1997. Common Property Resource Institutions and Forest Management in Latin America. *Development and Change* 28:95–117.

Rodgers, Dennis. 1999. Youth Gangs and Violence in Latin America and the Caribbean: A Literature Survey. World Bank Latin American and Caribbean Sustainable Development Working Paper no. 4. Urban Peace Program Series. Washington, D.C.: World Bank.

———. 2006. The State as a Gang: Conceptualizing the Governmentality of Violence in Contemporary Nicaragua. *Critique of Anthropology* 26(3): 315–30.

———. 2007. Joining the Gang and Becoming a *Broder*: The Violence of Ethnography in Contemporary Nicaragua. *Bulletin of Latin American Research* 27(4): 444–61.

———. 2009. Slum Wars of the 21st Century: *Mano Dura* and the New Urban Geography of Conflict in Central America. *Development and Change* 40(5): 949–76.

Roseberry, William. 1996. Hegemony, Power, and the Language of Contention. In *The Politics of Difference: Ethnic Premises in a World of Power*, edited by Edwin N. Wilmsen and Patrick McAllister, 71–84. Chicago: University of Chicago Press.

Rosenberg, Mica. 2007. Violence Haunts Guatemala Elections. *Time.* November 3.

Rouse, Roger. 1995. Questions of Identity: Personhood and Collectivity in Transnational Migration to the United States. *Critique of Anthropology* 15(4): 351–80.

Sabin, M., B. López Cardoso, L. Nackerud, R. Kaiser, and L. Varese. 2003. Factors Associated with Poor Mental Health among Guatemalan Refugees Living in Mexico 20 Years After Civil War Conflict. *JAMA: Journal of the American Medical Association* 290:635–42.

Schieber, Barbara. 2010a. Carlos Castresana, UN Commissioner against Impunity in Guatemala Resigns. *Guatemala Times.* June 8.

———. 2010b. Shake Up in Guatemala after UN Commissioner Castresana Resigns. *Guatemala Times.* June 11.

Scott, David. 1999. *Refashioning Futures: Critique after Postcoloniality*. Princeton, N.J.: Princeton University Press.

Scott, James C. 1998. *Seeing Like a State: How Certain Schemes to Improve the Human Condition Have Failed.* New Haven, Conn.: Yale University Press.

Scott, Winston, John P. Hawkins, and Walter Randolph Adams. In review. "Come Now!": K'iche' Maya Traditional Shamanic Ceremony and Cosmology in a Rural Hamlet of Santa Catarina Ixtahuacán. In *The Religious Transformation of Maya Guatemala*, edited by John P. Hawkins and Walter Randolph Adams.

Seijo, Lorena. 2006. Derecho maya: Sistema de justicia paralelo. *Prensa Libre* (Guatemala City). May 28. Available at www.presalibre.com/noticias/Derecho-Maya-sistema-justicia-paratelo_0_128987587.html.

Seminario Permanente sobre el Rol de los Partidos Políticos [21st]. 2005. *El sistema de partidos políticos de Guatemala a 20 años de la Ley Electoral y de partidos políticos*. Guatemala City: Asociación de Investigación y Estudios Sociales.

Sieder, Rachel, ed. 1998 *Guatemala after the Peace Accords.* London: Institute for Latin American Studies.

Smith, Carol A. 1990. Introduction: Social Relations in Guatemala over Time and Space. In *Guatemalan Indians and the State: 1540–1988*, edited by Carol A. Smith, 1–30. Austin: University of Texas Press.

Smith, Timothy J. 2009. Democracy Is Dissent: Political Confrontation and Indigenous Mobilization in Sololá. In *Mayas in Postwar Guatemala*, edited by Walter E. Little and Timothy J. Smith, 16–29. Tuscaloosa: University of Alabama Press.

Smith, Timothy J., and Thomas A. Offit. 2010. Confronting Violence in Postwar Guatemala: An Introduction. *Journal of Latin American and Caribbean Anthropology* 15(1): 1–15.

Smith, Waldemar R. 1977. *The Fiesta System and Economic Change*. New York: Columbia University Press.

Spergel, Irving A. 1998. Youth Gangs: Continuity and Change. *Crime and Justice* 12(1): 171–275.

Steger, Manfred B. 2003. *Globalization: A Very Short Introduction*. New York: Oxford University Press.

Stoll, David. 1993. *Between Two Armies in the Ixil Towns of Guatemala*. New York: Columbia University Press.

———. 2009. Harvest of Conviction: Solidarity in Guatemalan Scholarship, 1988–2008. In *Mayas in Postwar Guatemala*, edited by Walter E. Little and Timothy J. Smith, 167–80. Tuscaloosa: University of Alabama Press.

Tacconi, Luca. 2007. Decentralization, Forests and Livelihoods: Theory and Narrative. *Global Environmental Change* 17(3–4): 338–48.

Tarn, Nathaniel, and Martin Prechtel. 1997. *Scandals in the House of Birds: Shamans and Priests on Lake Atitlan*. New York: Marsilio.

Tax, Sol. 1937. The Municipios of the Midwestern Highlands of Guatemala. *American Anthropologist* 39:423–44.

Tedlock, Dennis. 1993. Torture in the Archives: Mayans Meet Europeans. *American Anthropologist* 95(1): 139–52.

———, trans. 1996. *Popol Vuh: The Mayan Book of the Dawn of Life*. New York: Touchstone.

Tiu López, Romero, and Pedro García Hierro. 2002. *Los bosques comunales de Totonicapán: Historia, situación jurídica y derechos indígenas*. Guatemala City: FLACSO / MINUGUA / CONTIERRA.

Torres-Rivas, Edelberto. 2003. Introducción: Linchar en democracia. In *Linchamientos: ¿Barbarie o justicia popular?* edited by Carlos M. Vilas, Carlos Mendoza, and Edelberto Torres-Rivas, 13–30. Guatemala City: Facultad Latinoamericana de Ciencias Sociales (FLACSO) / Proyecto Cultura de Paz de UNESCO.

Turner, Victor W. 1972[1957]. *Schism and Continuity in an African Society : A Study of Ndembu Village Life*. Manchester, UK: Manchester University Press.

United Nations. 2009. *Human Development Report*. New York: United Nations.

United Nations Development Programme. 2008. *Country Programme Document 2005–2008. Guatemala*. New York: United Nations.

Uphoff, Norman. 1989. Distinguishing Power, Authority and Legitimacy: Taking Max Weber at His Word by Using Resources-Exchange Analysis. *Polity* 22(2): 295–322.

U.S. Department of State. 2010. *Background Note: Guatemala*. Washington, D.C.: U.S. Department of State.

Utting, Peter. 1993. *Trees, People, Power*. London: EarthScan.

Valdez, S., and H. Alvarado. 2010. La criminalidad se ensaña contra comercios. *Prensa Libre* (Guatemala City). July 22.

Valladares, León A. 1957. *El hombre y el maíz: Etnografía y etnopsicología en Colotenango*. 2nd ed. Mexico City: Costa-Amic.

———. 1993. *Culto al maíz en Guatemala*. 2nd ed. Guatemala City: Oscar de León Palacios.

Van Velsen, J. 1967. The Extended-Case Method and Situational Analysis. In *The Craft of Social Anthropology*, edited by A. L. Epstein, 129–52. New Brunswick, N.J.: Transaction.

Veblen, Thomas T. 1978. Forest Preservation in the Western Highlands of Guatemala. *Geographical Review* 68(4): 417–34.

Vigil, James Diego. 1988. *Barrio Gangs: Street Life and Identity in Southern California*. Austin: University of Texas Press.

Vogt, Evon Z. 1969. *Zinacantán: A Maya Community in the Highlands of Chiapas*. Cambridge, Mass.: Harvard University Press.

Von Tempsky, G. F. 1858. *Mitla: A Narrative of Incidents and Personal Adventures on a Journey in Mexico, Guatemala, and Salvador in the Years 1853 to 1855*. London: Longman, Brown, Green, Longmans, and Roberts.

Wagley, Charles. 1941. *Economics of a Guatemalan Village*. Menasha, Wisc.: American Anthropological Association.

———. 1949. *Social and Religious Life in a Guatemalan Village*. Menasha, Wisc.: American Anthropological Association.

Wagner, Roy. 1981. *The Invention of Culture*. Revised and expanded ed. Chicago: University of Chicago Press.

Warren, Kay B. 1978. *The Symbolism of Subordination: Indian Identity in a Guatemalan Town*. Austin: University of Texas Press.

———. 2003. Voting Against Indigenous Rights in Guatemala: Lessons from the 1999 Referendum. In *Indigenous Movements, Self-Representation, and the State in Latin America*, edited by Kay B. Warren and Jean E. Jackson, 149–80. Austin: University of Texas Press.

Watanabe, John M. 1992. *Maya Saints and Souls in a Changing World*. Austin: University of Texas Press.

———. 1995. Unimagining the Maya: Anthropologists, Others, and the Inescapable Hubris of Authorship. *Bulletin of Latin American Research* 14(1): 25–45.

Weber, Max. 1958. The Three Types of Legitimate Rule. *Berkeley Publications in Society and Institutions* 4(1): 1–11.

Willis, Eliza, Christopher da C. B. Garman, and Stephan Haggard. 1999. The Politics of Decentralization in Latin America. *Latin American Research Review* 34(1): 7–56.

Wilmsen, Edwin N. 1989. *We Are Here: Politics of Aboriginal Land Tenure*. Los Angeles: University of California Press.

Wilson, Kevara Ellsworth. 2007. "Your Destiny Is to Care for Pregnant Women": Midwives and Childbirth in Nahualá. In *Health Care in Maya Guatemala*, edited by Walter Randolph Adams and John P. Hawkins, 125–47. Norman: University of Oklahoma Press.

Wilson, Richard. 1997. Anchored Communities: Sources of Pan-Maya Identity in the Maya-Q'eqchi'. In *Crosscurrents in Indigenous Spirituality*, edited by Guillermo Cook, 113–36. Leiden, Netherlands: E. J. Brill. Originally published as Anchored Communities: Identity and History of the Maya Q'eqchi'. *Journal of the Royal Anthropological Institute* 28, no. 1 (March 1993): 121–38.

Winton, Ailsa. 2004. Young People's Views on How to Tackle Gang Violence in "Post-Conflict" Guatemala. *Environment and Urbanization* 16(2): 83–99.

Wittman, Hannah, and Charles Geisler. 2005. Negotiating Locality: Decentralization and Communal Forest Management in the Guatemala Highlands. *Human Organization* 64(1): 62–74.

Wittman, Hannah, and Laura Saldivar-Tanaka. 2006. The Agrarian Question in Guatemala. In *Promised Land: Competing Visions of Agrarian Reform*, edited by Peter Rosset, Raj Patel, and Michael Courville, 23–39. Oakland, Calif.: Food First Books.

Wolseth, Jon. 2011. *Jesus and the Gang: Youth Violence and Christianity in Urban Honduras*. Tucson: University of Arizona Press.

World Bank. 2004. *Inequality in Latin America*. New York: World Bank.

———. 2006. Facts on Forests. Available at http://siteresources.worldbank.org/ESSDNETWORK/NewsAndEvents/20546068/WBFactsonForests.pdf.

World Health Organization. 2011. Countries—Guatemala. Available at www.who.int/countries/gtm/en/.

Wuqub' Iq'. 1997. Christian and Mayan Spirituality: A Dialogue. In *Crosscurrents in Indigenous Spirituality*, edited by Guillermo Cook, 241–60. Leiden, Netherlands: E. J. Brill.

Contributors

Walter Randolph Adams

Walter Randolph Adams received his PhD from Michigan State University in 1988 and held a postdoctorate fellowship from Brown University in 1994. His dissertation explores the intersections of evolutionary ecology and community evolution. That interest undergirds his participation in and co-directorship with John Hawkins of Brigham Young University's long-term field school in, and comparison of, Nahualá and Santa Catarina Ixtahuacán. The field school has spawned this volume and two additional published volumes: *Roads to Change in Maya Guatemala: A Field School Approach to Understanding the K'iche'* (Hawkins and Adams 2005) and *Health Care in Maya Guatemala: Confronting Medical Pluralism in a Developing Country* (Adams and Hawkins 2007). Adams has lived in Guatemala since 2001.

Jason M. Brown

At the time of his field study in 2006, Jason Brown was completing his bachelor's degree, majoring in anthropology with a minor in international development at BYU. In part because of this fieldwork, Brown decided to pursue advanced studies in the social sciences and philosophy of forests. He completed a master's degrees in both forestry and theology at Yale University. During summer 2012, he worked as a technician for the U.S. Forest Service, and he currently teaches religion and ethics at Utah Valley University and Salt Lake Community College.

ERIC RUIZ BYBEE

After participating in the 2006 Brigham Young University field school, Eric Bybee graduated in from BYU in 2007 with bachelor's degrees in humanities and Latin American studies. Following graduation, he entered Teach for America and taught for four years at an under-resourced public middle school in New York City. During this time, Bybee earned a master's degree from Pace University. He is currently pursuing a doctorate in cultural studies in education at the University of Texas at Austin.

TRISTAN P. CALL

Tristan Call's Nahualá experience began with the 2005 BYU field school, in which he focused on kinship and adoption. He did this as an eighteen-year-old freshman physics major, which he recognizes was a considerable gamble for the field school organizers. The experience, however, channeled him unexpectedly into anthropology and Central American human rights work. He returned to the field school in 2006, working on the topic in this volume. After graduating from BYU in 2008, he worked at an urban forest farm in Salt Lake City, an experience that dramatically shaped his later research interests in Guatemala. He is now a doctoral candidate in anthropology at Vanderbilt University, focusing on agroecology, labor, and social movements in Guatemala and the southern United States.

CURTIS W. DABB

Curtis Dabb graduated with a BA in anthropology from BYU in 2008. He works in the field of human resources with ConAgra Foods, where he oversees several corporate agricultural businesses with a diverse employee population, an estimated 95 percent of which is of Latin American descent. He is concurrently working toward an MBA at Washington State University. In his professional career, the principles and techniques developed during the field study are directly applied to business strategy in an environment where understanding how to approach conflict is key. Whether analyzing disputes over land access and fuzzy boundaries or investigating about discrimination and other business-related topics, the principles for understanding and analyzing conflict are similar.

Donald Y. Dracoulis

Immediately after participating in the 2006 field school in Guatemala, Donald Dracoulis graduated from BYU with a double major in political science and anthropology. He enrolled in Cornell University's master's program in health care policy and administration. In 2008 he was awarded a one-year postgraduate fellowship in hospital administration at the University of Illinois Medical Center in Chicago. He accepted his current position at Catholic Healthcare West implementing "Transformational Care" at its hospitals and health clinics in California, Nevada, and Arizona. He works with physicians and employees to redesign current health care processes to reduce medical errors, diminish waste, and improve the overall system for patients and employees.

John J. Edvalson

John Edvalson graduated from BYU in anthropology in 2004 and is one of a handful of students from the field school who continue to conduct ethnographic research in Guatemala. Over the past five years, he has been studying anthropology at the State University of New York at Albany, where his dissertation project focuses on teachers and community politics in Nahualá. Specifically, he is exploring how teacher-led school activities are informed by Maya political movements.

Rebecca A. Edvalson

Prior to traveling to Guatemala in 2006, Rebecca Edvalson spent two summers in Guadalajara, Mexico, volunteering in orphanages. In fall 2005 she taught literacy and studied gender-related issues in a rural village in Guanajuato, Mexico. She has accompanied her husband, John Edvalson, and their three children to Nahualá while he completes fieldwork for his dissertation. She currently works as a certified lactation counselor and has practiced as such for over two years. Her research with midwives in Nahualá has inspired her to become a professional midwife, a career she hopes to pursue in the near future.

JOHN P. HAWKINS

John Hawkins received his PhD from the University of Chicago in 1978. After doctoral fieldwork in Guatemala (January 1973–July 1974), he began teaching at Brigham Young University. In 1995, he began directing (with Walter Adams) the BYU field school in Nahualá and Santa Catarina Ixtahuacán, closing it in 2006. Hawkins has written *Inverse Images: The Meaning of Culture, Ethnicity, and Family in Postcolonial Guatemala* (1984) and coauthored and co-edited (with Walter Adams) two volumes on Nahualá and Santa Catarina: *Roads to Change in Maya Guatemala: A Field School Approach to Understanding the K'iche'* (Hawkins and Adams 2005) and *Health Care in Maya Guatemala: Confronting Medical Pluralism in a Developing Country* (Adams and Hawkins 2007).

JAMES H. MCDONALD

James McDonald holds a 1991 PhD from Arizona State University and is professor of anthropology and dean of the College of Humanities and Social Sciences at Southern Utah University. Before that, he was a longtime faculty member and administrator at the University of Texas at San Antonio. He is an applied cultural anthropologist whose major research interests include rural development, political culture, and security dynamics in Mexico and Guatemala. He has published over thirty articles and authored *The Applied Anthropology Reader* (2002). He served as senior editor of the American Anthropological Association journal *Culture and Agriculture* from 1998 to 2007.

INDEX

Page references followed by an "f" or "t" indicate figures or tables.

CPSIA information can be obtained
at www.ICGtesting.com
Printed in the USA
LVHW030100021221
705068LV00001B/125